Storytelling and Mythmaking

Storytelling and Mythmaking

IMAGES FROM FILM AND LITERATURE

FRANK McCONNELL

New York   Oxford
OXFORD UNIVERSITY PRESS
1979

Copyright © 1979 by Oxford University Press, Inc.

Library of Congress Cataloging in Publication Data

McConnell, Frank D 1942–
Storytelling and mythmaking: images from film and literature.

Bibliography: p.
Includes index.
1. Moving-pictures and literature.
2. Moving-pictures—Plots, themes, etc.   I. Title.
PN1995.3.M26   791.43'7   78-27538   ISBN 0-19-502572-5

Acknowledgment is made to the following persons and firms for allowing the use of material from their writings, songs, and publications:

Doubleday & Company and William Heinemann, Ltd.: from Homer, *The Odyssey,* translated by Robert Fitzgerald. Copyright © 1961 by Robert Fitzgerald.

The New American Library: from *The Satires of Juvenal: A New Translation with an Introduction by Hubert Creekmore.* Copyright © 1963 by Hubert Creekmore.

From *The Essential Rousseau,* translated by Lowell Bair. Copyright © 1974 by Lowell Bair.

W. W. Norton & Company: from *Beowulf,* translated by E. Talbott Donaldson (1966). From *Sir Gawain and the Green Knight,* translated by Marie Borroff (1967).

Penguin books Ltd.: from Virgil, *The Aeneid,* translated by W. F. Jackson Knight (Penguin Classics, revised edition, 1958). © 1956 by G. R. Wilson Knight.

From *The Quest of the Holy Grail,* translated by P. M. Matarasso (Penguin Classics, 1964. © 1969 by P. M. Matarasso.

Paul Simon: from "Mrs. Robinson." Copyright © 1968. Reprinted by permission.

The University of Chicago Press and Richmond Lattimore: from Homer, *The Iliad,* translated by Richmond Lattimore. Copyright 1951 by The University of Chicago Press.

The University of Michigan Press: from *The Song of Roland,* translated by C. K. Scott-Moncrieff (1959).

All photographs are from the Museum of Modern Art/Film Stills Archive.

Printed in the United States of America

For Carolyn, Christopher,
and Kathryn McConnell

Acknowledgments

This book was begun under a grant from the Northwestern University Office of Research and Sponsored Programs, and I thank Charles H. Gold, its director, for his encouragement and good will.

The main job of writing was done during my year's stay at the Woodrow Wilson International Center for Scholars in Washington, D.C. I cannot sufficiently express my gratitude to, or enthusiasm for, that institution. The exhilarating intellectual atmosphere, the cordiality, and the very real charity of the Wilson Center staff and fellows make my year there one of my best memories. Among the staff of the Center, I must particularly thank James Billington, Fran Hunter, Lois O'Neill, George Packard, Frank Sayre, Fred Starr, and George Seay for kindness and friendship; and among the fellows in my year, Sara Castro-Klaren, Marcus Cunliffe, Sukehiro Hirakawa, Norton Long, Berneice Madison, Gregory Massell, Herbert Spiro, Gloria Steinem, and M. S. Venkataramani—fondly remembered all, who contributed, in one way or another, to whatever is of merit here.

Leo Braudy, Kathryn Hume, Bruce Kawin, James Monaco, and Michael Silverman all read the manuscript and made useful, sometimes crucial suggestions. John Wright of Oxford University Press was infallible in his support, a fine editor and a valued friend. And the three people to whom the book is dedicated are those to whom my debt—for this and much else—is not only largest but happiest.

Evanston, Ill.   F.M.
April 1979

Contents

Storytelling and Mythmaking

I

Introduction

This book is about film and literature as kinds of story-telling. It argues that stories matter, and matter deeply, because they are the best way to save our lives.

You are the hero of your own life-story. The kind of story you want to tell yourself about yourself has a lot to do with the kind of person you are, and can become. You can listen to (or read in books or watch in films) stories about other people. But that is only because you know, at some basic level, that you are—or could be—the hero of those stories too. You are Ahab in *Moby Dick,* you are Michael Corleone or Kay Corleone in *The Godfather,* you are Rick or Ilsa in *Casablanca,* Jim in *Lord Jim,* or the Tramp in *City Lights.* And out of these make-believe selves, all of them versions of your own self-in-the-making, you learn, if you are lucky and canny enough, to invent a better you than you could have before the story was told.

After more than a century of handbooks on the subject, that is still the best version of "self-help" our civilization has invented. After almost twenty-five hundred years of literary criticism, it is the best reason anyone has thought of for taking stories seriously.

We can think or talk about stories in terms of their formal qualities, their narrative styles, their sociological and cultural sources and implications. We can talk about their technique or about the pure aesthetic delight of enjoying them. But at the end of that discussion we come back, in one way or another, to the fundamental perception that stories teach us—and teach us in ways, at levels nothing else does. *All* storytelling is didactic: anyone who has ever told the tale of Goldilocks and the Three Bears to a three-year-old, and then had to explain what it was all really about, and why everything happened the way it did, knows this, at least implicitly. Horace said that poetry (by which he understood, mainly, narrative poetry) should be both *dulce* and *utile,* "sweet" and "useful" or "escapist" and "instructive." But we find stories *dulce just because* they are *utile.* Even at the most unredeemed level of "escapist" entertainment, cheap novels or trash films, the didactic force of storytelling is still present and important. What kind of world does a person want to escape *to?* If reality is so intolerable, what is the daydream you would choose? The answer to that question is much the same as the answer to the question: what would you *like* to be told about the world you live in?

For four thousand years the most efficient way of preserving and repeating stories was the written word. For almost the last hundred years there has been another, competitive way of telling the tales that can save our lives, and that is the film. These two methods of storytelling—technologies, really, of preserving stories—are not antithetical, nor are they mutually interchangeable. A film can do things that a written narrative can't, and *vice versa.* There exists, in fact, a voluminous literature, by both film and literary critics, demonstrating this not very interesting point. Film and literature matter for us in their relationships, since both of them repeat, reincarnate, and recapitulate the elementary forms of story itself.

Are there such elementary forms? The last century of an-

thropology, comparative religion, literary criticism, and eth-
nology argues that there are, and that they can be cata-
logued. Literature and film may differ in their ways of
realizing these basic forms or "archetypes": but the archetypes still are there, and are undeniable. As a general formula for the distinction between film and literary narrative,
I suggest the following:

> WRITING, beginning with a technology at once highly
> associative and highly personal, strives toward the fulfill-
> ment of its own projected reality in an ideally objective,
> depersonalized world, while
> FILM, beginning with a technology at once highly ob-
> jective and highly depersonalized, strives toward the ful-
> fillment of its own projected reality in an ideally associa-
> tive, personal world.

Literary narrative, that is, always begins with the perception of the individual, the suffering, passionate, isolated consciousness, in reaction against the outer universes of both
society and unthinking, inhuman physical reality. This is
true even of the earliest narratives we have, for we know
more of the consciousness of the Babylonian hero Gilgamesh or of Achilles than we will ever know of the consciousness of Charles Foster Kane in *Citizen Kane* or Michael Corleone in *The Godfather*. In written narrative, we
begin with the consciousness of the hero and have to construct out of that consciousness the social and physical
world the hero inhabits. But in film the situation is, essentially and significantly, reversed. Film can show us *only* objects, *only* things, only, indeed, people as things. Our activity in watching a filmed narrative is to infer, to construct the
selfhood of the hero who might inhabit the objective world
film so overwhelmingly gives us. We know more, that is,
about the surrounding universe of a Charles Foster Kane or
a Michael Corleone than we will ever know about that of a
Gilgamesh or an Achilles. This is why so many "explana-

tions" of *Gilgamesh* and the *Iliad* tend toward archaeology and cultural history, and so many explanations of *Citizen Kane* and *The Godfather* tend toward psycholoanalysis: criticism in each case tries to make up what is missing, but what is creatively missing, in the technology of the story as told.

I emphasize this special complementarity because it describes not only the formal relationship between film and writing, but also the content of the stories both film and writing have to tell. That content is the subject of the rest of this book. As any number of anthropologists, from Durkheim to Lévi-Strauss, have argued, the major theme of all the stories of a civilization, the basic plot of all the tales of a culture, is its own etiology: how culture (*any* culture) came to be the way it is. We can generalize from this and say that the universal content of all stories is the emergence of the hero (whatever kind of hero he may be) within the idea of the City (whatever kind of City he inhabits). Storytelling, that is, is always the story of the individual in some sort of relationship to his social, political, or cultural environment. He can found that environment, he can civilize it, he can find it confusing, or he can hate it: but the basic terms of story are, like the basic terms of any human being's relationship to his world, always in one of these four versions: or in a fifth version, where the person passes into a new, mystical, "foolish," or visionary relationship to the people around him. That is what I meant by observing that stories are important because they are a way of saving your soul. Depending on the kind of story you find yourself in, you have a certain responsibility, a certain relationship, both to yourself and to the people around you. You are always a hero: but in different worlds of story you can be different *kinds* of hero.

This is to say that film and literature matter as much as they do because they are versions of mythmaking. "Myth," in this sense, is of course not to be taken as meaning "lie," "fairy tale," "superstition," or any of the other terms for which it is often substituted. It is, rather, to be taken in its original sense, the sense of the Greek *muthos*, "word," "story," or "tale."

That these tales can be correlated, that the stories told around the world can be collated into a single, complicated but uniform structure, is the discovery of a great number of scholars, anthropologists, and critics of our century. But no one, perhaps, has described their variants and vagrancies as completely as has Northrop Frye in his *Anatomy of Criticism* (1957). Frye makes the point that all stories can be examined not only in terms of their individual, stylistic, literary qualities, but also in terms of the overarching, determinative *myths* that they reincarnate. This is what "archetypal criticism" is all about, however many or various may be its later manifestations. At one degree of distance from the work of art, says Frye, what we see is not the individual articulation, the specific brushstroke on the canvas, but the shape in its most generalized and most permanent form: a version of one of four or five permanent mythologies of which humans are capable. And these general shapes, these archetypes, are in their way the fundamental modes through which we perceive the specificity of the individual work, even though we may not always recognize them as such. "The structural principles of literature," Frye observes, "are as closely related to mythology and comparative religion as those of painting are to geometry." The archetypes, in other words, do not predetermine the stories we tell ourselves, but they do predetermine the limits within which those stories can be filled out.

What, then, is the point of looking at narrative in terms of its archetypes? Simply this, that in this way we can begin to approach some kind of sense of what may lie beyond or behind story itself, what elementary forms of hoping or desiring or needing may motivate the myths we make up to satisfy our hunger. Frye identifies four basic kinds of myth, each of which relates both to an elemental human experience and to a basic response to experience: the Myth of Spring, or Comedy; the Myth of Summer, or Romance; the Myth of Autumn, or Tragedy; and the Myth of Winter, or Satire. The four seasons of the year, that eternal cycle whose endless recapitulations we live out, and whose rhythms are imprinted in our genetic material, are the basis of the stories we tell ourselves about our very triumph over that aboriginal bondage to nature. Of spring we make a celebration of marriage and new life; of summer a celebration of infinite potentiality, godlike ease and comfort; of autumn we make an image of our own sense of our mortality, with all its attendant melancholy; and of winter an image of death itself that at once separates us from the rest of the animals and mocks our self-congratulation at that difference.

Frye plots the succession of stories, the evolution of one myth from its precedent, carefully. Indeed, for him all four versions of myth are parts of a single monomyth, a single great story that we can paraphrase as the quest of man for his own salvation, the race's search for permanence and meaning amid the cycling of the years and eons. And I doubt that I could have written this book if I had not encountered Frye's work. With his general ideas of the importance of the archetypes for the individual manifestations of story, and with his conception of a great cycle of stories— which is not historical, but which does describe our own idea of how history ought to proceed—I am in complete agreement. And though the four (or five) phases of storytelling I shall describe here are not exactly the phases of Frye's system, I think that that variance is more a matter of focus than of field. We are both looking at the same thing, but I tend to look for something different from him.

Frye's description of the cycle of storytelling, based as it is upon the succession of the seasons, is a temporal one. But of course at any time in your life, you are fully aware of all the possible seasons, all the possible phases, of your existence: the mythologies, in other words, are all present (at least in potentiality) at any given point in time. The seasonal cycle, then, is really not the fullest description we can obtain of the cycles of storytelling. There ought to be another way of describing those cycles, so as to indicate not only their successive quality but also their simultaneity, the way in which—however temporal they may seem—they are always all present in the mind as *potential* forms of human life, *potential* levels of social organization. Such a description exists, and forms, indeed, the basic structure of this book.

Jean-Jacques Rousseau, in Book II, Chapter XII of *The Social Contract*, distinguishes among four types of laws, four types of relations between the individual and the state. These four types, he says, all follow from or derive from the aboriginal unnameable "relation of the whole to the whole, or of the sovereign to the state, and this relation is composed of relations among the intermediate terms. . . ." He continues:

> The laws governing this relation are known as political laws, and are also called fundamental laws, not without reason if they are wisely conceived. For if there is in each state only one good way of ordering it, the people that has found it should hold to it, but if the established order is bad, why should the laws that prevent it from being good be considered fundamental? *

The first sort of law, that is, establishes an elementary, indispensable order in society without which all later reasonings, all later attempts at social probity, are doomed to failure. But there follows on on this first law a second, lesser but in its own way more necessary for the *immediate* success and happiness of mankind. This is the civil law:

---

* Tr. Lowell Blair in *The Essential Rousseau* (New York: New American Library, 1974).

The second relation is that of the members among themselves, or with the entire body politic. This relation should be as small as possible in the first case and as great as possible in the second, so that each citizen will be completely independent of all the others and extremely dependent on the state.

But if the second form of law establishes means whereby the members of the state may relate to one another and to the state itself in harmony, it also makes necessary a third variety of law, one which sets boundaries to the possible transgressions of the second type, one which establishes the possibility, that is, of crime and punishment:

> We may consider a third kind of relation between the individual and the law: that of disobedience and punishment. It gives rise to criminal laws, which are actually less a specific type of law than the sanction of all the others.

(Rousseau is never more romantic than here, in insisting that mankind's imagination of sin will always be less sure than its imagination of goodness.)

Finally, more powerful than even the public and legal prosecution of crime, there remains a fourth kind of law which ensures (in Rousseau's system at least) the fundamental sanity and beneficence of society:

> In addition to these three kinds of law, there is a fourth, the most important of all. It is engraved in neither marble nor brass, but in the hearts of the citizens; it forms the true constitution of the state; it renews its vigor every day, and when other laws become obsolte or ineffective, it restores or replaces them. . . . I am referring to morals, customs, and above all, public opinion.

Four varieties of law, then: one that founds, establishes a society, a state in the first place; one that makes the intercourse of its citizens possible or easy; one that, however clumsily, sets boundaries on the mutual impingements of the citizens upon one another; and finally one that, "engraved in neither marble nor bronze, but in the hearts of the citizens," calls forth the full scorn of public opinion against the most outrageous or the most potentially harmful violations of the society's own structure of self-preservation.

But there is one kind of law which Rousseau does *not* describe; perhaps since he himself is one of its prime exemplars, one of its major manifestations. That law is the law of *self-consciousness*. It is the law whereby, after a certain level of self-mistrust and social disintegration, the very structure of society becomes apparent—to one man, to a clique, to a theorist—and thereby reinitiates the whole process of civilization. At this level of "law," of course, the law becomes not a public law but one announced only to the few by the few (we can say that this is also true of the "law" of public opinion, available only to those who happen to hold the same opinion *of* public opinion as you and I). But it has also become the principle according to which we may speak of "the law," or of the other four varieties of "the law," at all.

The great advantage of using Rousseau's concept of law, as opposed to the more conventional system of mythological archetypes, is that it allows us to see how the archetypes themselves are present, at any given stage of history, within a single phase of civilization. It is as if the whole great cycle of the seasons of the earth or of a man's life were present at any single season of such a life. At the moment of founding, the later moments of civilizing, complication, and rejection and re-founding are all implied. But it is only from the viewpoint of the final stage (or phase, or moment) of such a process that we can see this simultaneity. The human mind, that is, tends to think in terms of cycles. But because it thinks in terms of cycles it thinks in terms of both "phases" and "versions," in terms of individual moments both as successive

moments in an overall scheme of cyclic development and as
alternative representations of the same elementary fact or
situation varying according to varying points of view. Each
basic myth is, then, *both* historical *and* atemporal, both a
version of history and a vision of existence as you and I
enjoy it now, at this moment: depending upon our mood,
our desires, and our sense of what we need from the story as
it is told.

Each of Rousseau's four kinds of law involves a sense of
agent, of landscape, and of a possible transgression by the
agent against the landscape. Each type of law, that is, considered as an archetype of story, includes a hero, a variety of
the City that the hero inhabits, and a special sin or crime
that the hero can commit against that City. Rousseau's
forms of law can be easily translated, then, into four elementary forms of storytelling.

In the first form, *epic,* the hero is a king, the City is seen
as it is founded, and the sin is against the gods. Epic is that
form of narrative where we imagine most explicitly how
things must have come to be the way they are, the phase of
storytelling where the story acts out most clearly the origin
of what Rousseau describes as the elementary, indispensable, "political" laws. It is a tale of *beginnings:* Homer and
Virgil are obsessed with the origins of Greek nationalism
and Roman imperialism, Eisenstein with the origin of Russian collectivism, John Ford with the origin of American in-
dividualism. And in each case the storyteller gives us a hero,
a possible self, to incarnate the code of the myth and to im-
pose it—as a truly political law—upon the City he *founds.*
For in the epic world the City is always at the point of
beginning; which is why the hero is always in some way a
king, a man who *begins* the observances which later become
habitual.

In the world of *romance,* the primary, political laws have
been established. The founding figure of the king recedes
into the background, and a new figure—and a new set of

laws, of social problems—comes to be. The hero in the
world of romance is the knight, less than the king but more
than the common man (the marshal in the Western film, the
loyal samurai in Japanese historical films, the gladiator in
Italian Hercules films). His mission is not to establish a political entity, the City, but rather to establish the secondary
though essential human codes of conduct which make City
life *tolerable*. His greatest fear is not so much sin—that has
been obviated by his master the king—but rather a *breach*
of some elementary code of social behavior. We are in the
world, in other words, of what Rousseau calls "civil law,"
that law which makes it possible for us to live together not
only safely, but *decently*.

Once the City has been both established and socialized,
though, there is the possibility of its becoming corrupt, becoming mysterious and threatening even to the citizens
whose lives it is supposed to clarify and dignify. Rousseau
observes that the existence of "civil law" implies the existence of another type of law, "criminal laws, which are actually less a specific type of law than the sanction of all the
others." In criminal laws, that is, the negative implications
of the social code (which is always part of the law) outweigh
its positive implications: Thou Shalt Not, for the first time
in the growth of society, predominates over Thou Shalt.
This is the world of *melodrama*, a world in which the existence of the City has come to be not the end of the hero's
activity, but the originating *problem* of his dilemma. It is
also the world of our most familiar, and perhaps our most
congenial, fictions at the present stage of culture: the world
of detective stories, of "romances" in the cheapest sense of
the word, and of course also the world of the novels of Tol-
stoy, Dickens, Conrad, and Graham Greene.

Rousseau himself implies the essential formula of melodramatic narrative: sin plus indecency equals *crime*. And
suddenly, with this equation, a new vision of the City and of
the hero becomes possible. The City is now the scene of a

conflict between its ostensive morality and its hidden violation of its own laws, and the hero is the conscious *agent*—
descendent of the knight, distant heir of the king—who
strives to understand the real rules governing the operation
of his society, and to bring them, even if by violence, into
alignment with the precepts according to which the City was
founded. Fritz Lang and Alfred Hitchcock, in their quite
complementary ways, have made this version of narrative
one of the richest and, to this point, most triumphantly original varieties of film.

But the hero of melodrama, the detective, the investigator,
the inquisitive person desperate to find out how a confusing
and corrupt society operates, may become a more bitter figure. He may become the investigator who has discovered
that *everyone* is guilty, the detective who finds that the *City
itself* is the criminal he pursues, since the City has failed to
live up to the moral sanctions envisioned by its epic
founders. The hero, in other words, is now the satirist: his
relationship to the community is that of prophetic scorn,
disdain, even visionary paranoia. And the City, the community, is now inimical to the survival of the individual, rather
than a means of that survival. The satirist announces, or, at
his best, acts out just those laws Rousseau calls "the most
important of all," since they are engraved "in the hearts of
the citizens." These are the truly moral laws, since they are
the laws we invoke when all else has failed, the laws which,
without being officially codified, nevertheless remind us of
the original and originating law that brings civilization into
being. Of course, depending upon how many of his audience
share his concern with the decay of the epic foundations of
the city, the satirist will tend toward either the position of
an officially recognized public voice or that of a lone, crazed
prophet crying in the wilderness. And beyond satire, in a
final phase of vision, the hero comes to find the City not
only disappointing or destructive but literally intolerable.
His response to that is to collapse the world into himself, to

take possession of the whole of his society's mythic history and convert it, in the quiet of his own mind (the "smithy of his soul," as Joyce says at the end of *A Portrait of the Artist as a Young Man*) into a new City, a new standard of social and private survival which may be either a radically apocalyptic underground movement or the vision of a new Jerusalem. The hero is no longer public moral voice or crazed prophet, that is, but lives between the riskier alternatives of Messiah or madman. And if the besetting transgression against which the hero-as-satirist shouts is bad faith with the historical inheritance of his City, the besetting transgression of the Messiah or madman is bad faith with his own idea of the direction of history—that is, with *sin*.

But, as the idea of sin implies, the Messiah at the end of story and the epic hero-founder at its beginning fold in on one another. For while story may not describe a historical evolution (*all* its phases, once again, are potentially present at any one level of storytelling), it does describe a great cycle, continually renewing, continually redefining itself. And the new, interior City founded by the Messiah or the madman becomes the City to be civilized by his heirs, beginning again the progression of stories and types I have mapped out. In classical culture, this great cycle is most fully visible in the movement from Virgil to St. Augustine, from the founding of the imperial City in *The Aeneid* to the founding of the holy City in *City of God*. And at this point of comparison, I think, I can, without a blush, speak of *City of God* and Steven Spielberg's *Close Encounters of the Third Kind* as analogous fictions, analogous stories, for both reclaim, from their respective traditions of mythmaking, the possibility of an internalized heroism, a sacrificial heroism-through-defeat, that revises the intolerable public life of their times into a paradigm of survival and triumph.

But this comparison may seem excessive. As a final vision of the forms of narrative we will examine in the rest of this book, let me suggest a comparison between two of the greatest, most perennial, and most instantly comprehensible mythologies the West has produced since the classicial era. Both these cycles of story are so widely dispersed, so universally assumed and understood, that it is impossible to assign their origin or their power to any single author, or even any single *kind* of author. And both of them, with consistent and unerring accuracy, describe the five types of story, the five types of hero I have discussed. They are the tradition of Arthurian legend in medieval writing and the tradition of the American Western in film.

Over its more than four-hundred-year history of development, the Arthurian legend retains a remarkable consistency in the characterization of its major figures—almost as if they form a repertory group or *commedia dell'arte* or "B-movie" set of personalities. Arthur himself, the epic hero, founder of Camelot and the Round Table, is always stately, always withdrawn from the action, always the servant of higher laws and higher purposes than any of even his own knights can understand. Gawain, Arthur's nephew, is the hero of romance, always the *courteous* knight, the valiant and definitively civilized decent man, the pure vassal or loyal retainer who brings civility into the civilization Arthur has established. Lancelot, the adulterous, *failed* perfect knight, is always the man like us, having both a vision of the sublime possibilities of the Round Table and a vision of the human, adulterous but immensely appealing possibilities of loving the king's wife. Modred, the king's bastard son, is the perfect satirist: the mocker, the defomred and weak judge who reveals by his bitter laughter the failure of the society of the Round Table to live up to its own announced and cherished goals, finally a rebel against the power of his own father. And Percival (later Galahad), the Grail Knight, is finally the man whose sanctity, whose holy foolishness (*der reine Tor,* "the perfect fool," is an old name for him) both breaks the solidarity of the Round Table and opens that society to a new revelation, a mystical transport which becomes itself the principle of a new society.

The Arthurian legends, in whatever versions, were the dominant popular entertainment of their time. They retained their popularity, indeed, for perhaps longer than any set of stories in the European tradition. And in the perennial characters of the American Western film we can see, with very little stretching, their analogues and heirs. The king, the founder, is represented by the figure of the frontiersman or the cattle baron (e.g. John Wayne in *Red River*) who carves out from an inhospitable landscape a space that human beings can live in. The town the baron founds or makes possible has to be civilized, however, and this is done by the marshal (e.g. Henry Fonda in *My Darling Clementine*), the delegated agent of a higher authority (*federal*—and this is important) who makes the space of the town a place humans would choose to live in. The federal marshal, though, is superseded by that less hieratic, more recognizably human figure, the *town* marshal or sheriff (Gary Cooper in *High Noon*), the man who has to live out as well as regulate the passions of his town, and who often finds the conflict between his public and private responsibilities a killing one. And the sherifff necessitates, calls into prominence, the figure of the outlaw, the man whose distance from the conventions of the town tests and often annihilates the town's pretensions to decency (Alan Ladd in *Shane*, Gregory Peck in *The Gunfighter*). And out of such decay comes the young-old, sane-insane figure of the new founder, the man who leads society either out of the town that has been spoiled or into a new perception of the realities of the town that needs to be reborn (John Wayne in *The Shootist*). The cycle of story exists with just the same completeness in both cowboy film and Arthurian tale.

But the reemergence of these archetypes is not limited to a single genre. George Lucas and John Dykstra's *Star Wars* is the most successful film in the history of the art; it has passed, quicker than anyone could have imagined, from the status of film to that of legitimate and deeply embedded popular mythology. Children and adults alike (as Gene Shalit discovered when he made the gaffe on the *Today* show) will be quick to correct you if you call the golden, stuffy robot of *Star Wars* "CP3O" instead of "C3PO." R2D2, C3PO's comic companion (an inarticulate Harpo to C3PO's pretentious Groucho?) probably has as high a recognition quotient as Ronald McDonald or Santa Claus. And catchphrases from the film—preeminently, the signature-phrase "May the Force be with you"—have become part of the public repertory of conversation, jokes, puns, and T-shirts.

Naturally, this kind of phenomenal success has generated its own backlash. There are a number, and there are likely to appear a number more, of very funny attacks upon *Star Wars* as a fascist film (the triumphal march at the end reminds people—if they want to be reminded—of *The Triumph of the Will*), as a morally and intellectually empty piece of "escape entertainment" (though no one ever asks, about "escape" literature, the significance of the special kind of world you decide to escape *to*), or as mere "camp" (a phrase used mainly by literary intellectuals to describe works they like but are embarrassed or unequipped to analyze).

But, in terms of the cycle of storytelling I have been describing, we can see that the immense and deep popularity of *Star Wars* is due not to a massive seizure of crypto-Nazism or masturbatory lunacy on the part of the American public, but rather to the way the film taps certain deep expectations we have about the way stories should be told.

The story itself is simple. The young, unsophisticated Luke Skywalker (Mark Hamill), living on an out-of-the-way farm planet in the Galactic Empire, learns from two recently acquired robots or "droids," C3PO and R2D2, that R2D2 has been sent on a special mission to contact the aging, heroic

warrior Obi-Wan Kenobi (Alec Guinness) by the beautiful
Princess Leia (Carrie Fisher), a member of a group of democratic rebels against the Empire's tyranny, in the hope that
Kenobi will join the rebels in their fight against the Empire
and its awesome new tool of destruction, the Deathstar.
Luke finds Kenobi, who tells him that Luke's own father
was a warrior, a "Jedi Knight," and Kenobi's friend in the
early, benevolent years of the Empire. Luke joins Kenobi in
his journey to the rebel base, enlisting along the way the
reluctant, mercenary assistance of Han Solo (Harrison
Ford), a cynical pirate and space-outlaw, and his partner
Chewbacca, a giant apelike creature. Kenobi, Luke, Solo,
and the robots find themselves prisoners on the Deathstar—
where Princess Leia is also being held—and under the dominion of the evil Darth Vader, the Dark Lord and servant
of the Empire who was once Kenobi's protégé but who has
turned his great powers to corrupt uses. They make a daring
escape, during which Kenobi is slain by Darth Vader. And,
finally reaching the rebel base, they all collaborate in a raid
on the pursuing Deathstar and destroy it—though Darth
Vader escapes the destruction.

This study is not designed to move from the "primitive"
to the "sophisticated" in some sort of putative history of the
advance of civilization. The great appeal, and the great
power, of *Star Wars* is that it manages to be both primitive
and sophisticated at once. The plot is both elementary and
complex. For who is its hero? If it is Obi-Wan Kenobi, the
story is the ancient one of the death of the king, the death of
the founder, so that a new order can be born. If it is Luke,
the story is the ancient one of the initiation of the young
man, the potential knight, into the rites and responsibilities
of manhood so that he can carry on the battle for civilization. If it is Han Solo, the story is the ancient one of the discovery, by a private and simpleminded man, of the laws of
conduct and morality that make his life worthwhile. And if
it is C3PO or R2D2, the story is the ancient one of the birth

of heroism out of satire, the way that parodies of human courage and human cowardice can lead back to a perception of what real heroism, and real cowardice, might be.

Kenobi, in other words, is the hero of an epic world; Luke of a romance world; Solo (with his animal twin Chewbacca) of a melodramatic one; and the droids of a satiric one. And, at one point or another in the tale, each of these characters from different worlds of storytelling comes crucially to the aid of the other characters, from other narrative worlds. Which means that *Star Wars* not only recapitulates the cycles of storytelling; it recapitulates them under a single, self-conscious phase: the "fifth phase" of recognition and rebirth of the archetypes. For all these heroic characters are involved in a struggle that is *really* the struggle of the spiritual, psychic power called the "Force" (Kenobi is its positive, Darth Vader its negative side) against the sheerly mechanistic, linear, time-bound power of technology. And the Force wins, but it wins just because the film itself is clever enough to see and to argue that the cycles of heroic myth still have meaning even in the midst of a universe (*our* universe) where technological complexity seems to deny their relevance. "May the Force be with you," indeed. But the Force *Star Wars* at its profoundest celebrates is not clairvoyance or telekinesis, but the ancient, mysterious, and very strong force of our stories to save us from despair at our own complex mortality, and to make us believe in a future—a human future—where stories can continue.

But at this point we need to examine the specific phases of the cycle with specific attention to films and books participating in the distinctive energies and structures of each phase. And to that task I turn in the chapters that follow.

II

The Epic World: Kings

> *The laws governing this relation are . . . political laws, and are also called fundamental laws. . . .*
>
> ROUSSEAU

"If the world is to be lived in, it must be founded": so says Mircea Eliade in his book *Occultism, Witchcraft, and Cultural Fashions,* and it is perhaps the best and simplest formulation of what the epic impulse is about, and what it has to offer us. The world, if it is *our* world, must have at some time become our world: but who did such a great thing for us? It is with these putative, heroic epic founders of the human world that I deal in this chapter, and with the kinds of stories that make them real to us. We begin with the most general, the most undifferentiated, kinds of founding-tales, and we will end with the most finely defined, the most civilized and most self-conscious kinds. This progress is not prejudicial, not organized to move from "primitive" to "sophisticated"; but it is organized to move from one kind of complexity to another, from the self-definition of a whole culture to the self-definition of an individual within that culture. That is the range of epic, and like the range of any other form of storytelling it can contain the entire range of the human experience itself.

Crown and Shadow

The first thing we see in Einstein's *Ivan the Terrible* is a crown. It is held over the head of Ivan IV at his coronation, as he is about to become Czar (king) of Moscow on sufferance by the regional Boyars (dukes) whose territories surround the capital city. The crown, of course, is a symbol: a liturgical, ritual symbol of the greatest solemnity. And the opening sequence of *Ivan,* following that first shot of the crown, establishes the liturgical significance of the central object with overwhelming force by reenacting, in detail, the exotic, sacramental rubric of a medieval Russian coronation (details which would be *almost* as exotic and alien to the Russian audience of the film in 1944 as they are to us). The rest of *Ivan the Terrible* will be an explication, an attempt to humanize and interpret that original object. What does the crown, under all the panoply of ritual investiture, *mean?* What does it imply for the man who will wear it, and for those who pledge it their allegiance? As Ivan, throughout the film, struggles to assert his own independence and the independence of Russia as an autonomous civilization against the Boyar warlords, the story will again and again return to ideas and images of the crown, successive humanizations of it.

For example, as Ivan is waging his successful war against the invading Mongols from the kingdom of Kazan, he encamps outside Kazan in a giant tent which has the unmistakable shape of a crown, but also of a war helmet; the liturgical object is now being turned to use as an instrument of national self-protection. At the end of Part One, Ivan, momentarily thwarted in his attempts to consolidate Russia under a single, visionary kingship, resigns the crown and retires to a monastery outside Moscow to await the choice of the people as to whether he should continue his struggle or not. In the famous concluding scene of Part One the people of Moscow form a gigantic procession through the snow to

Ivan's retreat where they beg him to return—now as not only the Czar of the nobility, but as *their* Czar. And Part One ends as Ivan prepares to return for another coronation, to make real the implications of the first one.

The second coronation is never shown. But throughout Part Two (titled *Boyarskii zagovor,* "The Boyars' Plot," in the original) we are constantly reminded of the *fact* of the crown, the mute but infinitely suggestive presence of the liturgical object, as the theme and central problem of the whole story. Part Two ends with the final attempt of the Boyars to stop Ivan, their plot to assassinate him and put the halfwit Prince Vladimir Staritsky on the throne in his place. An assassin has been hired. But in a drunken feast on the intended night of the murder, Ivan convinces Vladimir, as a joke, to don the robes of the Czar and lead the procession to the cathedral for Mass. The assassin stabs the wrong man—the man, that is, who is not fit to wear the robes of the king—and the plot is defeated, Ivan's total authority finally established.

I shall return later in this discussion to *Ivan,* but for the present it is important to notice that it bears out an observation made in the last chapter about the complementarity of film and written narrative. The epic film (and if any films are "epic," *Ivan* surely and obsessively is) begins with an object, a thing, and throughout its development continually tends toward the elaboration of the human implications of that thing, the crown, the shadow, the landscape. Compare to this the opening lines of the three most definite and influential literary epics in our tradition, the *Iliad,* the *Odyssey,* and *Aeneid:*

> Sing, goddess, the anger of Peleus' son Achilleus
> and its devastation, which put pains thousandfold upon the
>   Achaians,
> hurled in their multitudes to the house of Hades strong souls
> of heroes, but gave their bodies to the delicate feasting

of dogs, of all birds, and the will of Zeus was accomplished
since that time when first there stood in division of conflict
Atreus' son the lord of men and brilliant Achilleus.*

Sing in me, Muse, and through me tell the story
of that man skilled in all ways of contending,
the wanderer, harried for years on end,
after he plundered the stronghold
on the proud height of Troy.
                          He saw the townlands
and learned the minds of many distant men,
and weathered many bitter nights and days
in his deep heart at sea, while he fought only
to save his life, to bring his shipmates home.†

   This is a tale of arms and of a man. Fated to be an
exile, he was the first to sail from the land of Troy and
reach Italy, at its Lavinian shore. He met many tribula-
tions on his way both by land and on the ocean; high
Heaven willed it, for Juno was ruthless and could not
forget her anger. And he had also to endure great suffering in warfare. But at last he succeeded in founding his
city, and installing the gods of his race in the Latin land:
and that was the origin of the Latin nation, the Lords of
Alba, and the proud battlements of Rome.‡

   Each of these epic invocations shows the same characteristics. Beginning with the mention of a man, or at least of a
human force, each moves toward a summary of the passions
and tests to be undergone by the central character, and all
conclude (however indirectly) with a vision of the polity, the
community, the city which the epic hero's agony will help
establish. What the epic invocation presents, in other words,
is the exact inverse of the things—crown, landscape—with

* Tr. Richmond Lattimore (Chicago: University of Chicago Press, 1951).
† Tr. Robert Fitzgerald (New York: Doubleday, 1961).
‡ Tr. W. F. Jackson-Knight (Middlesex, Eng.: Penguin Books, 1956).

which the epic film tends to open. Or, alternatively, epic films open with visions of objects to be explicated which are, in their way, the filmic equivalents of literary epic invocations. One narrative art begins with the image of the primal, the originating man, and proceeds to generate around him the world—of nature and of society—which he organizes. And the other form of storytelling begins with the objects of kingship or dominance, the liturgical symbols of statecraft or the open landscape of the yet-unfounded world itself, and proceeds to articulate the kind of man who might be able to bring those objects into a humanizing, civilizing configuration.

But what are the specific qualities of epic story? What shape does it have, in film or in writing, that differentiates it from other kinds of story, and what sort of world, what sort of people, does it make available to us? As our examples from films and written narratives should make clear, epic, whatever else it is, is the story of a *king*. This gives it a very special quality among varieties of narrative. For kings are peculiar figures, mysterious and potentially dangerous, and a century and more of virtually universal democracy in the West has still not diminished the special power that appertains to kingship, or the special role the king plays in the history and the self-imagination of a culture.

The king is as close to a god as human culture has managed, in its long history, to come. The first cities of Sumeria did not hestitate to identify the king as the representative of a god (or of a great goddess), and Egypt, a few hundred miles to the west, did not hesitate to identify the king *with* god. The immense literature on ancient kingship has, whatever its contradictions and quarrels, established with a kind of thudding authority that the primordial image of the king is very close to the primordial image of the deity, and indeed that the two concepts probably evolved side by side.

The major fact to bear in mind, at least as far as epic stories are concerned, is that the primal king is not only a

representation or an incarnation of the god of the city, but
also an irrevocably *humanized,* which is to say diminished,
form of that godhead. Like a god, like the YHVH of the
Jews, the ruler of Egypt could not be spoken of by his real
name. He was called, therefore, *per-aa,* "Great House,"
Pharaoh. But if that special, stylized name sets the king
apart from other men, it also sets him apart from the divinity whose authority he incarnates. For he is a man *named*
into a divinity—unlike, say YHVH, who is a divinity innately unnameable by men, except through a violation of the
religious and social conventions of language itself. "Great
House" he may well be, and therefore untouchable and un-
approachable, but "great house," even for the Egyptian subjects who stood in awe of that phrase, is nevertheless a
phrase, an appellation given a man who may or may not be
worthy of the weight of the name he bears, but who is
revealed in all his vulnerable humanity precisely by the fact
that the sacralizing, isolating name has to be given to
him—to protect the kingship he carries. (William Golding,
in his story "The Scorpion God," precisely catches this am-
bivalence, this potentially killing tension between the divinity and the human reality of primal kingship.)

The crown implies the shadow, even makes it necessary.
The epic founder, the primal king, is the representative and
the interpreter of the gods. But that role costs him something: the very humanity his founding activity guarantees
for his people. Epic, in other words, is the level of storytelling where myth begins to give way to drama, the level
where stories about gods just begin to be stories about men,
and therefore where men are easily confused with gods, participating in both their omnipotence and their loneliness.

This is perhaps the best way of imagining the epic world,
the world of the founders and of the City in its first manifestation. It is a world of origins, the origin of civilization, the
origin of laws, the origin of standards of heroism, but a
world, for all that, imbued with a kind of deep melancholy.

It is the melancholy of necessary victories rather than of inevitable defeats, none the less melancholy for its triumph.
Every reader of epic, every viewer of epic films, has doubt-
less felt this peculiar quality, a sense that great things have
passed away before the epic action has even begun, a sense
that something has been irrevocably lost—whatever might
be gained by the instituting, formative heroism of the epic
king.

This is a central quality of most of the major epics in the
Western tradition. Think of the *Iliad,* that great and bitter
vision of the birth of one civilization out of the demolition
of another. In an essay on the tragic vision of the *Iliad,* John
Wright points out that Homer imagines the cycle of human
history as a dead round of destruction and rebuilding, endless and murderous. The *Iliad,* that is, celebrates—among
other things—the evolution of a consolidated Greek culture
out of a collection of factional, internecine local kingdoms.
But the price is the destruction of Troy: an older and still
noble, admirable culture whose violent death is nevertheless
necessary to the birth the poem commemorates.

One of the most important aspects of any story is its title,
for the title of a story tells us not only what the story is
about, but—in a subtle way—how the story *feels about*
what it is about. And in this way the title *Iliad* may be one of
the richest and strongest names ever given a story. Why not
Achilleid? The hero of the tale, announced in the first line, is
Achilles. Or why not *Helleniad,* since the most visible and
obviously most important effect of the Trojan War is the
consolidation of a people, the Hellenes, out of a feuding
collection of peoples loosely called, in the poem itself, the
Achaians? Why name the poem for that older, dying civilization, Ilion (Troy), which exists in the poem only to be destroyed? It is like making a film about the American Revolution stressing not the pluck and decency of the American
patriots, but the humiliation, despair, and mutilation suf-
fered by the equally well-meaning British troops those

plucky rebels systematically and (by all European standards of combat) unsportingly butchered.

I have already suggested that the quintessential epic theme is *founding,* establishing the elemental laws by which a great civilization governs itself. But what kind of founding, what kind of splendid march toward a reasonable civilization, does the *Iliad* give us? Of the Achaian heroes (the poem itself does not allow us to call them, at this stage of their history, "Greek"), Agamemnon is a blusterer and a bully, Menelaus a cuckold and an incompetent, Odysseus a clever but somewhat sinister schemer, Aias a well-meaning but not bright strongman, and Achilles, the central figure, a sulker. Nor are these simply flip, modern judgments of the Achaian heroes: each judgment is articulated, at one and usually at several points of the action—by another one of the heroes.

But the more one reads the poem, the more this central foolishness, even childishness of the Achaian heroes seems to be the point. Not that the poem is a "satire" against officially established figures of epic heroism—though, to be sure, the Achaian list of heroes was well established by the time the poem achieved its present state, and though Shakespeare was able, in *Troilus and Cressida,* to turn the *Iliad* against itself in just such a satric fashion. What we have instead is a vision of human possibility, from the sublime to the venal, which depends, for its very assertion of the sublime, upon the full acknowledgment of the venality underlying even our most heroic actions. The Achaian heroes, that is, are heroes not despite, but because of the grasping, unholy passions that impel them to become the conquerors of Troy and the founders of Greek civilization.

This is an important point, not only for the *Iliad* but for the epic frame of narrative. The first word of the poem as it has come down to us is *menin,* "wrath," the wrath of Achilles that causes so much havoc among the Achaian invaders, and that is finally transformed—not into a mystical

acceptance of the universe—but into the bitter and tragic acknowledgment of universal mortality in his final, famous interview with Priam, king of Troy and father of Hector, the
hope of the Trojans, whom he has brutally slain. A later,
Platonist or Christian reading of the poem might argue that
menin is an unruly and murderous passion which is somehow transcended in the course of the action. But I do not
think the *Iliad* is really concerned with transcendence. Such
concerns come later, if not in the history of civilization at
least in the rhetoric of storytelling. For "transcendence" implies purification, leaving behind the things of the earth and
the ego for a larger, cleaner, and less selfish realm of ideas
and actions. But this sort of flight is not really possible until
a social structure has been established and promulgated that
makes such unselfishness feasible. The *Iliad* eschews transcendence because its story is the kind that makes transcendence possible. Like all truly epic wars, the war around
Troy is fought to make the world safe for aristocracy.

What the *Iliad* gives us in place of transcendence is order.
Its invocation and induction begins with the wrath (*menin*)
of Achilles and ends with the resolution of that wrath when
the "will of Zeus was accomplished" (*Dios deteleito Boule*).
And *Boule*, the will of Zeus whose accomplishment signals
the end of the conflict among the Achaians and the effective
doom of Troy, means not only "will" but "advice, counsel,
purpose": all those things, in fact, which can hold in check
or in dynamic balance the unruly passions of individual men
and create out of them, not necessarily a community of
saints, but a polity, a city.

The splendid and undiminished humanism of the poem,
then, is that it manages to suggest to us—actually, to incarnate—the tension between public responsibilities and private
sacrifices, between crown and shadow, which is at the heart
of any social order, no matter how civilized or how puta-
tively "primitive." And no poem, no story, faces as unflinch-
ingly the base of human selfishness upon which the most

sublime accomplishments of civilization and spirituality are founded.

Kingship—the epic kingship of the founder—is a matter not of state ceremony but of positive and often sacrificial *action*. To found his city, to hew out from the hostile rockface of the surrounding world a center for human life, is to engage in violent and largely destructive activity. In terms of a truly primal, a truly first city, this means to clear the land, slay the animals who prey upon man, organize the natural world from a jungle into a garden: or, in terms of the book of Genesis, to move a natural garden (where everything grows of its own accord for man's *benefit*) into a technological garden (where everything has to be grown or, implicitly, uprooted, depending upon whether or not it serves man's *purpose*). One of the great and insufficiently remarked subtleties of literary epic is that it almost never attempts to present us with this first city. There is a secondairness about literary epic, in other words: the sense we have that, however "early," "primal," even "primitive" the epic story may be, there was always something there before the story began.

This, of course, is only to say that there is *no first story*. Epic may be the archetypal tale of the founders, but the founders themselves are always belated, always posterior to some, however rudimentary, form of social organization. Creation stories, like the Babylonian *Enuma Elish,* the Mayan *Popol Vuh,* and indeed the first chapter of Genesis, all give us, to be sure, a vision of the "absolute" origins of things, the moment when god or the gods create the universe—either *ex nihilo* or out of the chaos of the unformed world-stuff. But how "absolutely" original are even these stories? Catholic writers as widely different as G. K. Chesterton in *The Everlasting Man* and Mircea Eliade in *Patterns in Comparative Religion* argue that even the most aboriginal creation-stories point back, implicitly, to an elemental godhead, a preexisting unity whose existence is fragmented in the very moment of narrating its activity. And their argument is corroborated by two great traditions of religious thought. The *Ain-Sof* of Kabbalah and Nirguna Brahman ("Brahman without attributes") of the Upanishads are both versions of a *truly absolute* original deity, so absolute that its nature is betrayed by our attempts to speak at all about it.

This religious paradox doubles, on the level of plot, an important anthropological fact. Of all the world's stories about origins, there are none recorded (at least none I have encountered) about the origin of storytelling. Language can describe everything but the idea of a world without words; culture may encompass any idea except the idea of its own nonexistence. Partly, of course, this is simply to observe that we still live in the aftermath of the Neolithic Revolution: when men began to *plant* the garden of the world rather than merely hunt and gather its bounty, they also became writers and recorders of stories. But how can we neolithic people really imagine the very beginning of the revolution that has made us? (Teilhard de Chardin, in *The Phenomenon of Man*, discusses this evolutionary paradox at length.) But it is also to observe that *all* story, even all epic, is—not accidentally but essentially—belated, secondary, as is the quintessential neolithic art of writing itself. What we write, or what we choose to shoot with the camera (since that too is a kind of writing), is the record of our imprisonment within the secondary forms of language, culture, and story. And this secondariness is profoundly related to the melancholy, the personal and societal shadow, whose presence I have already remarked in the epic world, and also to the nature of epic kingship, and to the form of the *Iliad*.

Put it this way: the shadow is always the shadow of the crown. Or, consciousness of civilization, as soon as it becomes consciousness of civilization, also becomes consciousness of consciousness—and consciousness of itself is always a version of partition, of otherness, of the separation of self from the world and of the separation of the world itself into distinct, humanized, named and written categories. Ontogeny recapitulates phylogeny—if not in biology, at least in literary typology—and we can see a repetition of the central epic activity in watching any child learn to speak. Language, that is, is a partition of the world, a separation of the flux of experience into a number—perhaps an infinite number—of discrete particles of sensation, apprehension, articulation. And in learning to speak, the child learns to separate his world into just such a set of comprehensible, articulable entities. But the price of this separation—the price of consciousness itself—is the loss of that infantile absorption *in* the world, that identification of self with other that Freud called the "oceanic sense." To describe and become conscious of the world around us, we have to partition it, to assign names to things or (since cinema here is quite as primary an act of partition as is language) to assign certain things, certain images, a centrally significant place in our experience. But that act of partition is always, and necessarily, tinged with a certain nostalgia for a *complete* world—that is, a world where there are no demarcations but only the ongoing and unselfconscious dance of ego and id, self and other without discrimination. Hobbes in *Leviathan* and Freud in *Civilization and Its Discontents* are both, in this respect, ideal theorists of epic, indispensable commentators on the dimensions of crown and shadow, respectively. For Hobbes indicates to us how severe, though necessary, is the price of organizing the unformed herd of primitive men into an organized, partitioned, regulated society; and Freud, by redefining this process of civilization in terms of "sublimations," sacrifices of personal desire and their conversion into "socialized" drives, indicates that the price is both public and private.

This price is incarnated also in those mythologies which may be the purest and most ancient source of narrative. A curious detail remarked by cultural analysts as disparate as

Mircea Eliade and Claude Lévi-Strauss is that, at a certain point in their evolution, the gods become wounded. Eliade, in *Patterns in Comparative Religion,* observes that as the original, distant skygod is superseded by more active, more culturally involved deities, those deities take on the aspects of struggle, drama, and sacrificial suffering. Dying and reviving gods like Adonis, Tammuz, or Christ and crucified gods like Odin and, again, Christ are in this respect dramatic displacements, *humanizations,* of an original creative deity too remote to share in our own (quite Hobbesian and Freudian) sacrifices for culture. Lévi-Strauss, in *The Raw and the Cooked,* observes even more pointedly that originating deities tend to be of two sorts: the primally creative, full to overflowing of their own being, and the later, *law-giving* gods who are all significantly *partitioned,* or deprived by sacrificial wounding of the fullness of being. And, as Lévi-Strauss indicates, this ritual wounding participates in the essential "negativity" of language itself:

> Mythological figures who are blind or lame, one-eyed or one-armed, are familiar the world over; and we find them disturbing, because we believe their condition to be one of deficiency. But just as a system that has been made discrete through the removal of certain elements becomes logically richer, although numerically poorer, so myths often confer a positive significance on the disabled and the sick, who embody modes of mediation. . . . "Negativized Being" is entitled to occupy a whole place within the system, since it is the only conceivable means of transition between two "full" states.

Warriors

Returning from this vantage point to the *Iliad,* we can begin to see more fully why the poem is named for the city to be destroyed, not the polity to be born: precisely because the destruction of Troy is the true human cost—for the

Achaians as well as for the Trojans—of epic foundations. Each of the Achaian leaders is a king, undisputed ruler of his little, single city. And Troy itself, though mightier than any of the individual Achaian kingdoms making war against it, is the same kind of political entity. But the Achaians win because they manage to transcend that stage of organization for a larger, more broadly cultural level of cooperation and subordination: because they manage, in the course of the poem, to become Greeks. This is nowhere better caught than in the detail, which Homer mentions twice in the poem, of the contrasting ways the two forces march into battle:

> So thronged beat upon beat the Danaans' close battalions
> steadily into battle, with each of the lords commanding
> his own men; and these went silently, you would not think
> all these people with voices kept in their chests were march-
>   ing;
> silently, in fear of their commanders; and upon all
> glittered as they marched the shining armour they carried.
> But the Trojans, as sheep in a man of possessions' steading
> stand in their myriads waiting to be drained of their white
>   milk
> and bleat interminably as they hear the voice of their lambs,
>   so
> the crying of the Trojans went up through the wide army.
> Since there was no speech nor language common to all of
>   them
> but their talk was mixed, who were called there from many
>   far places.   [IV, 427–38]

A common language: that is all and that is everything, in one way, which guarantees the Achaian (or Danaan) victory over the Trojans. For the common language they speak is the guarantee of their higher level of social force, of subordination (and the word for the "fear" in which the Danaans go of their commanders might also be translated as "subor-

dination" or even "awe"). Kingship, that is, despite all the
shadows of personal ambition and greed which attend it,
becomes more truly kingship as it becomes more truly
socialized, more truly a matter not only of the ancient awe
surrounding the god-king but also of the cohesion of a culture around a single, if destructive, purpose.

But Homer introduces a paradox into this profound piece
of political/cultural theory. The commonwealth of language
shared by the Achaians is expressed in their icy silence, face
to face with the polyglot host of Troy. Homer gives us here
an inversion of the myth of Babel in Genesis. For here we
see a new order emerging, a new social and cultural incarnation of divine favor, of the transcendent order of the primal
skygod, and its sign is the cessation of speech, as in the story
of Babel the fragmentation of the nations is signaled by the
breaking out of speech in a dissonant yammering very like
that of the Trojan host. But what does this mean, that the
surest sign of the founding power of language is silence?

Among other things, it can mean that language divides as
surely as it unifies. And isn't this another way of indicating
the cost of kingship, the necessary partition, loss, sacrifice
that is part and parcel of the king's, the archetypal man's,
organization of his world? On the personal level, the wrath
of Achilles which is at the center of the story of the *Iliad* is
not just rage or resentment but a fully expressed, shouting
anger at Agamemnon and the Achaians. It is disruptive because its overflowing expression is an act of *lèse-majesté,* an
insubordination to the acknowledged leader of the Achaian
expedition. It is the sign of a larger, deeper insubordination,
a refusal to accept limits to power or to accept one's *place*
(which is also, of course, one's displacement) within a cultural organization, a political syntax. And when, at the end
of the poem, Achilles learns his own function not only
within the little society of the Achaian expedition but within
the larger, tragic community of human suffering and mortality, he is silenced. He and King Priam, the father of the hero

he has slain and desecrated, exchange tearful confessions of their mutual vulnerability and then simply weep together; and in this surely most famous and most moving scene of the *Iliad*, the voice of the narrator describing the communion of Achilles and Priam is exactly equivalent to the communal silence of the Achaian nation as it marches into battle, since it is a voice describing the *shared silence* of a deep community. Crown and shadow are reflected, respectively, as language and silence.

Homer's genius, as has been remarked any number of times, is partly manifested in his selectivity. The "matter of Troy," epochal as it is, is compressed into the activity of a few days in the war, an incident—the temporary withdrawal of Achilles from the fighting—which is not even central to the major issues or strategies of the war itself. We may look on this artistic "editing" of the epic as an aesthetic tour de force, a supremely skillful device of storytelling. But it is also an articulation of one of the great themes of primal epic, that of struggle and of world-changing decision: what we might call the epic of the *pivotal moment*. Eliade, among others, distinguishes between two kinds of creator gods, two mythologies of beginnings, namely, those involving an effortless creation from nothing in which the founder-god is imagined as a withdrawn, omnipotent principle of reason and organization, and those in which the creation is the result of a titanic struggle between the vitally male, creative divinity and the forces of chaos which he wrests to the shape of a habitable universe for human beings. Now it is only logical to assume that these two mythologies are expressed in complementary forms of epic narrative—although, to be sure, they are much less clearly differentiated in the human narrative of epic than in their original cultic forms. At any rate, the *Iliad* is one of the fullest versions we have of the second of these two alternatives, the story of a crucial battle, a crucial warfare which establishes a new (for the Achaian culture of the time, we might almost say an "international") order, and which makes the establishment of that order turn upon the violent, destructive and creative activity of a warrior class which is, in its way, the direct descendant of the idea of a primal male warrior-god. Achilles, that is, must learn to accept the counsels of Zeus's order, of the *Boule* of the god, what the god wishes for the fate of Greece and Troy. But in doing so he also recapitulates the creative activity of Zeus himself, who as a young warrior-god rose up against his father Ouranos and the rest of the Titans, binding them beneath the earth and creating the civic order of Olympos and of human culture through the strength of his thunderbolts.

The most obvious analogue to the *Iliad* in film is the tradition of the war movie: a tradition for which our century has provided a massive historical incentive. But, at least if we are thinking for the moment strictly in terms of "epic" varieties of storytelling, it is important to observe that not all war films, not even some of the most famous and most obviously splendid war films, catch precisely the note of the crucial, creative and destructive battle which is at the heart of the power of the Homeric poem. A great number of war films, from *Grand Illusion* and *All Quiet on the Western Front* through *Attack* to the recent *A Bridge Too Far* are, in fact, antiwar films, testimonies of varying subtlety and genius to the futility, the waste, and the often childish inefficiency and cruelty which are the permanent qualities of warfare, and especially of the mechanized, total warfare that is such a permanent feature of our age.

But the *Iliad*, and the epic mode which we may associate with the *Iliad*, is crueler than that. The poem has been read as a bitter indictment of the waste and bloodshed of war (most notably by Simone Weil in her essay "The *Iliad* or the Poem of Force"), but it can be read equally successfully as a hymn to the testing, annealing quality of war, its power to refine and define what is most permanent, most imperishable in a civilization. The fact is that the *Iliad,* like the kind of epic story it incarnates, is almost impossibly daunting, almost impossibly cold in its imagination of the place of war in human life. Destruction, needless bloodshed, the waste of human life, the inevitable collapse of even the most noble civilizations and most heroic individuals—these are not problems the *Iliad* seeks to resolve, but rather the essential conditions of the world whose order, however harsh, it exists to describe. One of the closest—and most shockingly, disturbingly unflinching—approaches in modern writing to the spirit of the *Iliad* is probably the dedicatory page of James Jones's novel *The Thin Red Line,* itself a splendid story of the experience of the infantryman in the Second World War:

> This book is cheerfully dedicated to those greatest and most heroic of all human endeavors, WAR and WARFARE; may they never cease to give us the pleasure, excitement and adrenal stimulation that we need, or provide us with the heroes, the presidents and leaders, the monuments and museums which we erect to them in the name of PEACE.

The reader who is surprised and at least mildly unsettled by the gusto, the enthusiasm of this acceptance of warfare as the greatest of human endeavors is well on the way to understanding the peculiar quality of the sort of epic I am talking about now. And Jones, after all, is being honest. We are delighted with war, at least at the comfortable distance afforded by print or by the motion picture screen. We return again and again to see how the Allies defeated the Axis, how the V-2 base at Peenemunde was sabotaged by American and British commandos, how Guadalcanal was won with courage and desperation against all reasonable odds. And this is not mere bloodthirstiness, not simply an expression of the natural human fascination with gore which also leads us to go to hockey games and crane our necks as we drive past

accidents on the highway. It is rather, I suggest, a kind of
racial memory of the stories of the warrior-gods, an intima-
tion that, at one level or another of our history as a people,
we imagined ourselves as the children and worshippers of a
victorious and transcendently mighty divinity whose distinctive creative act was the destruction of the unspeakable, the
slaying of the aboriginal dragon and the creation of the
world out of that hideous but defeated corpse.

A film like *Sands of Iwo Jima,* for example, may be in its
unsophisticated way much closer to the spirit of the Homeric epic than a number of more self-conscious, more "hu-
manistic" war films. Made in 1949, the film is a quite blatant glorification of the Pacific campaign of World War II,
and especially of the tough, unrelentingly military values of
its hero, Sergeant Stryker (John Wayne). The story traces
the progress of Stryker's platoon from basic training to their
participation in the Iwo Jima landing. Private Peter Conway
(John Agar), assigned to Stryker's platoon, is the son of a
Marine colonel under whom Stryker has served, and resents
deeply the family tradition which has forced him to enlist in
the Corps. Sensitive, aesthetic, a true believer in the arts of
peace, Conway hates the Marines, hates war, and especially
hates Stryker, a surrogate bad father who is trying to turn
him into a soldier. Predictably, as the platoon moves from
basic training to the landing on Iwo Jima, Conway learns
first to respect and then to venerate the values Stryker represents: it becomes obvious that the sergeant's apparent
harshness is really a gruff love and solicitude for the safety
of his men under fire, that what appears to be his coldness is
only the mask of his deep concern for the members of his
command and for the cause in whose name they fight. And
at the end of the film, after Stryker and the platoon have
won the all-important Mount Suribachi (where in fact the
Iwo Jima flag raising occurred), Stryker pauses for that
most cherished of American rituals of male fellowship: he
bums a cigarette from one of his men and begins to share a

smoke with those who are now his friends, his comrades in arms. But at that moment, when it appears that the training has not only been successful but has won for the lonely sergeant a set of companions, he is struck down by a Japanese sniper's bullet. But the war continues. Stryker is dead, and Conway—now no longer the rebellious son of a bad father, but the actual reincarnation of his father the colonel and his tutelary deity, Sergeant Stryker—leads the platoon off the hill and into their next battle.

Much the same effect makes *Battleground* (1949) one of the most powerful earlier war films, still effective in its recreation and mythicizing of the famous siege of Bastogne, defended by the 101st Airborne during the Battle of the Bulge. Unlike *Iwo Jima, Battleground* is an austere, unsentimental war movie, in which the harassed community of the besieged soldiers implies nothing beyond their temporary, desperate togetherness. These men, the film keeps insisting, are not friends. They are something both deeper and more primal, comrades. The siege of Bastogne, like the siege of Troy, is an elemental, brutal situation that matters to us now because it seems to incarnate the special possibilities—for failure and glory alike—of men who are pushed to the limit of their capabilities.

The same effect holds in a film like *The Longest Day* (1961). Here the war—not its heroes or its social implications, but the War itself—achieves a stature, a presence *in the story* which is quite as central as the "matter of Troy," and which it has maintained in more recent films like *Tora Tora Tora, Midway,* and *A Bridge Too Far.*

The Longest Day is, as any number of wags have by now observed after seeing it, "the longest film." A detailed and, apparently, scrupulously exact reconstruction of the Allied landing at Normandy on June 6, 1944, it is a film studded with "stars" and without heroes—or, rather, without any single hero who can overbalance the single, blatant, and overwhelming hero of the film, which is not so much the

Allied Army on D-Day as the historical fact of D-Day itself. In a brilliant way, that is, *The Longest Day* manages to combine elements of documentary and adventurous melodrama in a film which is not so much "historical" as a lyric evocation of an idea of history itself.

The individual officers involved in the D-Day invasion have long since become anonymous to the popular imagination, if their names were ever very widely known. But of course the stars of the American film—John Wayne, Richard Burton, Henry Fonda, Robert Mitchum, Edmund O'Brien, Red Buttons, Sal Mineo—cannot, because of the nature of film "stardom," be anonymous. They are the most known, the most familiar public personalities in our culture. And a film like *The Longest Day* does become almost Homeric in the way it manages to project upon one another those two varieties of heroism: the real, historical heroism of the men who actually participated in the invasion of Europe and the stylized, ritual heroism of the stars whose charade of courage has been such an important part of the imaginative life of this century. In the context of this film, indeed, the idea of a "cameo" appearance by a known and established actor takes on a new significance.

We can remember that the Achaian warriors (who must, at one time or another, have had some sort of historical reality) are converted by Homer into the giant forms of a quasi-allegory of statecraft; and we may also remember that one of the chief means of this conversion is the celebrated technique of the "Homeric epithet," whereby an individual becomes mythicized by being assimilated to one of a set of standardized, conventional, but nonetheless powerful linguistic forms of heroism: thus, "Menelaus of the loud war cry," "glorious Diomedes," and preeminently among the Achaians, "Achilles who breaks men in battle" (this epithet is reserved, throughout the *Iliad*, for Achilles alone). In *The Longest Day*, the representation of historical figures by star actors has much the same effect. We can say, that is, that the *identity* of each star in this film is the direct equivalent of the Homeric epithet: it idealizes, mythicizes, and at the same time preserves the historical reality of the figure represented by it. As the great invasion fleet is launched for Normandy, Edmund O'Brien, playing the skipper of an American destroyer, ·advises a young ensign on his ship to "remember this day": perhaps that sentiment was uttered by thousands of participants in the actual invasion, but what matters here is that, *in this film,* an actor acting the part of a historical participant utters the line, and thereby seals the legendary quality of this day which sees the final, determinative struggle of the forces of civilization against those of egoism, chaos, and brutality.

The vantage point of myth, indeed, even allows the film to be charitable toward the conquered, just as Homer nearly displaces Achilles as hero by making the Trojan hero Hector so appealing. The film ends, after the first great day of the invasion, somewhere in France with the trio of a dead German soldier, a perhaps terminally wounded RAF flyer, and a GI who has lost his outfit. Surveying the carnage and the eerie quiet of the day's end, the American asks the Englishman, "Who do you think won?" It is a splendidly ironic last line for this narrative, since of course we do know who won—*we* won—and yet the question, by being asked, allows us to glimpse underneath the triumph of this crucial battle the uncertainty, the doubts and venalities which underlie all human enterprises, and which in their way make the distinction between victor and vanquished trivial. We have won, says the film; and since we have won we can afford to admit that decent men fought and died on both sides of the conflict; but of course that admission can only, or most easily, be made by us since we *have* won.

Judges

The victors can afford to be tolerant of the enemies they have defeated. The winner can always afford to say that the game doesn't really matter. But what if we were to ask the victor about the reason for the game he plays? Achaians and Trojans, Americans and Germans in the narratives we have discussed so far all admit the same fundamental conventions of civilized conflict. But how do these conventions, this mass psychology of civilization, come into being in the first place? This is either an earlier or a later idea of the "founder": earlier, since the founder of the conventions must logically precede the man who succeeds through those conventions, and later, since we cannot recognize the real nature of a game (or a civilization) until we have played it and won or lost a few times. At any rate, this kind of epic narrative brings us to the fiction, not of the epochal and determinative battle establishing the authority of the race, but of the origin of the race itself.

Eliade suggests two kinds of skygods, pre-epic deities, who correspond to the two kinds of epic we encounter. The warrior-gods (Zeus, Thor) are creators-through-struggle, heroes who forge reality through their own strength and resistance to the constantly disruptive forces of chaos and disorganization. But the other skygods, perhaps earlier, perhaps later, are simply establishers of the law, not warriors for its sake. They are the creators *ex nihilo,* the heroes whose heroism is not so much their prowess as their need of no prowess, their supreme and sublime incarnation of civilization, order, and rationality.

The form appropriate to this second kind of epic should, properly, be the story not of a single battle or a single warrior, but rather of a series of battles or heroes, each of whom represents in one form or another the evolution of the civilized ideal, the hypostasized godhead, which is the epic's end. And there exists such an epic, perhaps the only book in the world which can really stand against the *Iliad.* It is the story contained in the books of Genesis and Exodus.

In the *Iliad* Zeus, Achilles' divine double, represents the values of creation-through-effort, power-through-violence that Achilles must learn to balance and hold in a human proportion. But the heroes of Genesis and Exodus are not warriors of that sort. They are rather quiescent, passive characters, often unwilling even to participate in the drama of salvation for which they are chosen. From Adam through Abraham, Isaac, Jacob, Joseph, and Moses, the first two books of the Bible describe a double movement which is one of the most complex and moving counterpoints in the history of storytelling. It is the history at once of the birth of the Law, and of the succession of unwilling heroes who became, in spite of themselves, the agents of the Law's self-revelation to men.

The history of the folktales which eventually became the book of Genesis is too difficult and too controversial to trace here, but we can observe that the tale is deliberately organized *against* the story of the virile warrior-hero-god whose presence we have traced already. That mighty figure appears in the Babylonian creation story, the *Enuma Elish,* which narrates how the god Marduk went to war against his mother the dragonness Tiamat, slew her, and out of her body created the world as we know it and all the dwellers therein. But it is by now common knowledge that the first chapter of Genesis is, in part, a satire *against* this Babylonian cosmology. The memory of the warrior-god Marduk is undercut by the serene and transcendently powerful God of Genesis 1, who creates not by battle but by *fiat,* by simply speaking His Word. "And God said, Let there be light: and there was light." This is a god whose distinctive quality is the rationality, the inevitability of the order he brings to the world: unlike the Zeus of the *Iliad,* who constantly intervenes to alter or readjust the shape of events, and who himself consults higher "Fates." But the God of Genesis is a *combination* of Zeus and those mysterious Fates.

For the God of Genesis and Exodus is not only, as He describes himself, a "jealous god." He is also an especially historically minded god, a god who recognizes and ensures that His people recognize the congruence of individuality and collectivity, single heroism and racial destiny, in the world He makes for them. He is a god, that is—perhaps the most definitive god of His sort in the world's literature—of the *Law*.

The course of the first two books of the Bible describes the gradual disappearance of God from the scene of human action as a personal participant, and His replacement by the Law, the Word, the *writing* which is the books of Genesis, Exodus, etc. And the patriarchs from Adam to Moses are not only "heroes" in the simplest sense of the word, they are also witnesses to this process. Adam before the Fall walks with God in the cool of the day; Abraham, summoned by God to His service, responds with all the simplicity and sublimity of ecstatic vision, *hineni*, "Here I am." But Isaac and Jacob know God only as a voice, not as a face-to-face presence. And Joseph knows Him only as a god of symbols, the unknown power that allows him to interpret the dreams of his Egyptian captors. But as God withdraws Himself from the personal knowledge of these earliest patriarchs, He also refines, tests, establishes His central idea of a *people,* a community organized not under His direct intervention, but under His virtual presence, His Law. This is the point of Genesis: it prepares us, with any number of anticipations, structural parallels, subtle foreshadowings, for the advent in Exodus of the great lawgiver, the Prophet, the Just Man, the man who for the last time in human history looked upon God and lived, Moses.

It is important to understand Moses, for he is not only the crucial man in one of the great religious traditions of the world, he is also the representative of a richer kind of heroism than the one we have been tracing so far. The heroes of the Homeric battle may wrest history to the shape of their own wills, and may even create history—or the history of a single culture—in their defeat of a primordial monster or an earlier, inhibitive culture. (Thus oriental Troy symbolically inhibits the birth of occidental Greece; and thus, in innumerable war films, the German or Japanese enemy is imagined as not only inimical but subtler—i.e. more culturally ancient—than the rowdily democratic GI's.) But Moses does not wrest history into a contrary shape. Rather, he is the central figure in the historical emergence of a culture. Not a tragic victim like Achilles, he is rather the point at which the withdrawal of God from human events becomes the presence of the Law as meaningful, *directed* history. He suffers, of course, the representative "wound" I have already remarked as essential to founder-figures: this first and greatest of the Prophets is a stutterer and must rely upon his brother Aaron for transmitting his messages. But, reinvoking the terms with which I began, Moses' stutter is shadow *and* crown. He is, above all else, the receiver and promulgator of the Law. He receives the text that initiates history as the self-revelation of a deity against whom no enemies can possibly stand.

This self-revelation, though, is also the deity's withdrawal from history. The Law is His human form, and once that form has been established, there is no more need for his presence. The last verse of Exodus is, in this way, a perfect conclusion to this epic of the creative disappearance of God:

> For throughout all their journeys the cloud of the Lord was upon the tabernacle by day, and fire was in it by night, in the sight of all the house of Israel.

Cloud and fire, the same elements which have led the Israelites through the desert, are the signs of the divine presence. But they are *signs*. Without paradox, we can say that only in a world from which God has withdrawn are miracles possible, since only in a world like that is the human norm firmly enough established ("Things like that just don't happen!") to be the appropriate background for signs and wonders. And this, too, is an aspect of the world Moses establishes. His first sight of God is as the bush which burns *and is not consumed,* and which must be approached with reverence, unshod: the first *true* miracle in the Bible, since it is the first theophany, the first manifestation of the divine, which identifies itself as a violation of a natural order of things which is just nascent with the advent of Moses himself. And when Moses finally, upon Sinai, is allowed to gaze upon the Lord as He passes, it is the Lord's "hinder parts" which he sees—that is, a vision of farewell and departure. Here as everywhere Moses stands precisely at the juncture of two worlds, a world (like that of Genesis) brooded over by the constant presence of God, and a world (Exodus and the whole future of the Chosen People) humanized and ironically exalted by the loss of that brooding presence. Moses, in other words, is the archetypal *king* in his role as law-giver and founder of the line of *judges.*

The earlier heroes I discussed are all warriors. And perhaps the best way to imagine the difference between Moses and these others is to realize that he is a *writer.* He is the legendary author of the very books, the Torah, in which his exploits are narrated: the narrator, that is, of his own and his People's epic story.

The Law itself, in what may be one of the richest single details of Exodus, has to be written not once, but twice. First it is written on tables of stone by the finger of God. But Moses, carrying the tables down from the mountain, discovers that the people have given themselves over to idolatry, and in his wrath and disgust he shatters the tables. And the second time the Law is delivered, it is written not by the finger of God, *but by Moses at God's dictation.* Writing itself is being established as the indispensable, and indispensably human, link between men and the divine. Moses repeats the act of God in writing down the Law, but repeats it in a significantly different key.

The Interpreter's Bible comments upon the name "Moses": "The Hebraic form of the name was *Mosheh* which could be the active participle of the Hebrew root, *mashah,* 'to draw out.' If the Hebrew form of his name is to have any meaning, it must be 'the one who draws forth,' i.e., he was *mosheh 'ammo . . .* the drawer forth of his people."

This drawing forth is primarily the drawing forth of the people from Egypt. But we can also think of it as a *with*drawing: not only of the People from Egypt, but also of the People from the mythic immediacy of their God into history, a *leading* of the People out of cult into culture. And "to draw forth" can also be taken in the sense of "to bring out of obscurity, out of hiding," and, by metaphorical extension, "to make explicit," that is, to write.

If we think of epic narratives in film and literature, and specifically of the epic figure of Moses, it is inevitable, I suppose, that the names C. B. DeMille and Charlton Heston will come up. DeMille's *The Ten Commandments* (1956) seemed to many a faintly absurd period piece even when it was first released; and of course Charlton Heston—an actor of real, if limited, talent—has spent twenty productive years suffering jokes about his wooden portrayal of Moses in that film. But Heston's woodennness is, at least partly, due to the pomposity of DeMille's direction: in something of an inverse miracle, DeMille even manages to make Edward G. Robinson (as the sycophant and idolater Dathan, a kind of Bronze Age Little Caesar) boring. But the interesting thing about *The Ten Commandments* is just this epic pomposity—for if there is one thing the epics I have so far discussed are not, it is pompous. Things appear pompous to us when their form seems somehow in excess of, or at variance with, their content. And the problem DeMille's film shares with any number of biblical "epics" from the fifties is that while they try to recreate the myth of Torah or the Gospels, they do so in terms of a narrative which is really more appropriate to the barbaric warrior-heroism which those sacred stories *replace* and against which they are structured.

Moses in DeMille's film is the nexus of a set of personal, sexual, and political conflicts which require a violent, individualistically heroic solution—but not the passivity, the diffidence, the *writer's* withdrawal that characterize the biblical Moses even at his most impressive. The director delights in manifestations of raw power. And the best scenes of the film, the building of the pyramids and the parting of the Red Sea, are as complete incarnations as film has achieved of a violently creative and destructive energy. But since the point of the original story is that such energy is *departing,* to be replaced by the sublime syntax of the Law, *The Ten Commandments* finds itself in the embarrassing position of telling one story while showing its opposite. Significantly, the film gives us only one writing of the Law: a dazzling science-fiction visualization of the finger of God striking the Commandments onto stone. But the later, essential, human writing of the Law it does not show. Finally, the film is "influenced" less by the biblical narrative than by the grandiose visualizations of that story by Gustave Doré. That human writing will have to wait some time to be manifested. But, as we shall see in Chapter V, it will finally appear. In Steven Spielberg's *Close Encounters of the Third Kind,* a sequence from *The Ten Commandments* will be shown, precisely to illustrate the true capability of filmmaking for transcendence.

But a much closer analogue to the cultural epic of Genesis and Exodus than *The Ten Commandments* is a silent film that strives toward the complexity and polyphony of sound. Although D. W. Griffith's *Intolerance* (1916) is one of the greatest films ever made, it can seem more dated than the *Iliad.* This is a measure of how much closer we are to its world than to Homer's, just as the dress styles of 1916 appear to us "old-fashioned" while those of Minoan or Etruscan culture appear simply different. But *Intolerance* offers an important analogue to some of the themes I have described in the Homeric poems. The entry in the *Oxford*

Companion to Film is as good a summary of the involved plot as one could want:

> Griffith attempted to abstract and universalize the theme of intolerance by intercutting four illustrative stories from different worlds. "The Mother and the Law," set in the present, contrasts the treatment of capitalist and worker by the law; "The Nazarene" recounts Christ's crucifixion; "The Medieval Story" recounts the massacre of the Protestants of Paris on St. Bartholomew's Day, 1572; "The Fall of Babylon" the betrayal of Prince Belshazzar to the Persians. The symbolic image of a woman rocking a cradle which punctuates the film is intended to unite the separate episodes. This complex structure disconcerted audiences of the time and the overblown grandeur of the Babylon story upset the balance of the film.

There is a kind of diffidence in the last sentence of the entry: for it is not simply "audiences of the time" who have been disconcerted by the multiple story-lines of *Intolerance*. Even the most hardened film students find it difficult to take the film at its own self-evaluation, and any showing of it in a film class is usually accompanied by repressed giggles or outright laughs at some of the more blatantly sentimental sections; or at least by sardonic grunts at the crudity of the cutting among the four plots.

But this laughter is really wasted on *Intolérance*, which finally triumphs over any degree of sophisticated distaste we bring to it. It is a remarkably sophisticated film. Griffith, to be sure, possessed a Victorian imagination: sentimental, melodramatic, in hopeless awe of the immitigable innocence and vulnerability of woman and profoundly suspicious of all male motives. It is not despite, but because of these qualities, however, that he made *Intolerance* a vision of origins, of the dialectic of crown and shadow, public and personal tensions, which we can call "epic" in quite the same way we use the word for Homer.

As the *Oxford Companion* also indicates, Griffith was impelled to make *Intolerance*, among other reasons, because his earlier masterpiece *The Birth of a Nation* was widely attacked as "racist" (which, in fact, it is). But, leaving such questions aside, we can say that the titles themselves, *The Birth of a Nation* and *Intolerance*, give us a precise distinction between the two aspects of epic kingship I have been discussing. The function of the king, that is, is to supervise the birth of his nation, his city. But the underside, the shadow, of that public role is a failure of community that—at least in Griffith's own lexicon—we can call "intolerance." It is the failure of the people to understand the order offered them, their failure to understand the humanity that the heroic founder tries to act out for them.

"Intolerance," after all, is a fairly fuzzy concept. What can it mean to build an expensive, elaborate, three-hour-plus film on a concept of "intolerance through the ages," ranging from the fall of Babylon to the near-execution of a contemporary young man for a murder he did not commit? "Intolerance" is not simply prejudice, social snobbery, or class hatred. It is, rather, the breakdown of communication, the failure of speech to achieve meaning. In the Babylonian story, the "Mountain Girl" who is so desperately and hopelessly in love with Prince Belshazzar races to warn him of the incipient attack of the Persians, but is kept from his presence until it is already too late and the Persians are at the gates of the city. In the "Medieval Story," the young lover of "Brown Eyes," the beautiful Huguenot girl, races to warn her of the massacre on St. Bartholomew's Day but arrives at her house only to find that she has already been killed by the rampaging Catholics, and to die himself. In the modern story, "The Mother and the Law," Griffith creates one of his most famous and effective chase sequences as the wife of the young man condemned to die on the scaffold races by car, with the evidence that will save her husband, to the prison where he is about to be hanged.

All three of the "non-canonical" stories, in other words, are nominally about intolerance (the intolerance, presumably, of Persians for Babylonians, Catholics for Protestants, and capitalists for working-class folk) but actually about something that goes deeper, the impossibility of explaining ourselves, the hopelessness we all feel when called upon to voice the reasons we exist as and where we do. It is a film, that is, about *language:* all the more compellingly so since it is a silent film, where speech exists, if at all, as the dramatic, visual and visible communion of human beings without—or beyond—words. (Griffith, one feels, could have filmed as well as anyone the final interview between Achilles and Priam.) Civilization is founded upon the word. And how appropriate it is, in this massive vision of the failure of civilization, that the word is present only in the forms and events of its failure.

Griffith, of course, is a master of the last-minute reprieve, of the rescue-in-the-nick-of-time which is such a cliche, for us, of early, melodramatic filmmaking. But, in all but one of the four plots of *Intolerance,* he systematically inverts this habit of storytelling: except for the modern story, all the last-minute rescues fail. The saving word is not spoken in time, the anger and hatred—which we could also call the irrational, insubordinate *menin*—of society is not resolved. Civilization, implicitly, is frustrated in its attempt to be born: the Mountain Girl is slain in the court of Belshazzar, Brown Eyes is slain by militant Catholics, Christ is crucified. It is only the young man in the modern story who is saved: his wife arrives at the prison just in time for her to confront the governor with the evidence of her husband's innocence, and the execution is canceled. But it is a happy ending which, against the overwhelming weight of the film in which it is embedded, seems cold comfort indeed. The word has for once been spoken and received in time. But how much faith can we put in its efficiency, for all that—especially when we have seen, throughout the film, how often the word is defeated in the very moment of its articulation, drowned out by the cries of the mob or deformed by the interpretations of the corrupt? The audience of the film, of course, knows at all times the proper interpretation of the events on the screen. But *Intolerance* is a great film—and a great *silent* film—just because it makes its own silence such an indispensable part of its meaning. In fact, since so many epic foundation stories are concerned with the foundation or invention of *writing* as well as of the state, it is worth noting how much care Griffith takes with writing in *Intolerance*. The captions of the film are, as it were, *double* writing. Not only are they—as in all silent films—interruptions by the static, printed word into the flow of visual narrative, but they insist on their "written" quality, imitating the physical form of Babylonian tablets, Renaissance books, and a modern printed page. Writing itself is a silent language—a freezing of the flow of speech that, nevertheless, gives that speech a fuller, *institutionalized* reality.

I have already said that the *later* gods, those who replace the original sky divinities, are always wounded, always in one way or another living symbols of the separateness, the partition of man from nature and of man from man which is the essence of culture. They incarnate the primal wound which is language itself. And thus at the center of Griffith's film is the story of "The Nazarene," which incarnates the filmmaker's admittedly sentimental, but nonetheless still noble, interpretation of the Gospel message.

We can fault that message as a watered-down version of an already watered-down variety of Christianity: that latitudinarian and vaguely liberal Protestantism of the late nineteenth century against which thinkers like Rudolf Otto and Karl Barth were already reacting when *Intolerance* was made. But to say this is to misunderstand the real subtlety of

Griffith's film. "Intolerance" means, in the film, misinterpretation, misunderstanding, the failure of speech: that failure of communion which it is the task of the epic founder to remedy. And it is both natural and brilliant that Griffith, with his nineteenth-century religious imagination, centers this history of civilization upon the figure whom he thought of as the *Word*. But the Word, the idea of the word, is not only the central plot of the four plots in *Intolerance*. It is also the central force in the narrative of this wordless film. Each of the four plots hinges upon the detail that a message which must be delivered either is or is not delivered in time: the most familiar structure of all melodrama, perhaps, one from which Alfred Hitchcock, for instance, has forged his whole career. But here it is raised to a level of self-consciousness which transforms it from a plot detail into a vision of human relations.

"That Was a Good King"

I have so far described two varieties of epic story, two types of epic heroism, as complementary versions of the "foundation" of the world which is the major theme of epic: and complementary, in many ways, they are. The creator-god as warrior and the creator-god as speaker of the Law cannot really cohabit in the same aboriginal myth. But they can, and often do, coexist in later stories. And here we enter a level of storytelling more immediately accessible and familiar, and yet perhaps more complicated than the primal epics so far examined. I have remarked that a film like *The Ten Commandments* generates a kind of aesthetic and psychological dissonance by telling the story of a lawgiver-king as if he were a warrior-king. But the stories we are about to examine are stories whose heroes are at once warriors and lawgivers.

I have already said that those two functions, warrior and lawgiver, are derivations, deflections, projections of aboriginal ideas of godhead. For them to be combined, then, it is necessary to imagine a substantial change—really, a quantum leap—in the humanness of the epic hero. Here we confront those kings who, for all their stature, are most like us in their individuality, their sensitivity to the psychic perils of kingship, and their dramatic incarnation of the idea of the hero. After the austerities, even the impersonality, of the *Iliad* or of Exodus, their stories seem to us more comprehensible, mor comfortably and recognizably *stories*.

"Secondary epic" is a convenient term for the stories we are about to examine. "Secondary" here does not mean "inferior" or "derivative" or even, necessarily, "later in time." But it does imply that, if these epics still imagine the world (or the archetypal city) as in need of being founded, they nevertheless imagine that world as having been already humanized: the gods, that is, have already made way for men to establish their own civilization, with only their occasional advice or subtle assistance. Epic battles remain to be fought, epic laws remain to be established; but the *very first* battle, the *very first* law, are both already decided. And, we might also observe, the mythical *very first* story has been told, so that secondary epic has the leisure to refine, psychologize, make more elegantly self-conscious its own narrative. The city itself, as far as we can reconstruct its evolution, begins as the center of a local cult, the shrine of a god, and grows into a political, bureaucratic entity. Just so, the transition from primary to secondary epic leads us from stories that are visions of the birth of religion to stories that are first forms of political theory. Some examples will make these details, and their importance, clearer.

"Don't sign up for any class with *Beowulf* on its reading list," Woody Allen advises Diane Keaton in *Annie Hall.* And generations of English graduate students, coerced into reading it in Old English before they have mastered either its language or its subtle and melancholy rhythms, can applaud that sentiment warmly. But that is a pity. For *Beowulf* is one of the most remarkable stories we have, and one of the most representative of a crucial phase of the epic imagination. It is a sign of the poem's neglect that, while it narrates three major struggles, three tests of its hero, only the first of those struggles is usually remembered. Even John Gardner, in his brilliant novel on the Beowulf theme, *Grendel,* acknowledges that accident of memory, though he manages to compress the whole mythic range of the epic into that first struggle.

Briefly, the poem tells us how King Hrothgar of the Danes builds a splendid and mighty hall, Heorot, for his subjects to dwell in. But the hall is terrorized by the monster Grendel, a man-eating creature bearing the mark of Cain and outraged by the joy he hears from afar in Heorot. To Hrothgar's kingdom comes Beowulf, a young man from the land of the Geats in Sweden who promises to kill Grendel for the king. He does so, wrestling with Grendel, to universal rejoicing. But the next night, Grendel's mother, seeking vengeance, attacks the hall, killing one of the men. Beowulf tracks her to her lake, swims to the bottom and finds her in her lair. He kills her with great difficulty, finally only with the aid of a magic sword he finds in her cave. Having cleansed Hrothgar's realm, Beowulf returns to the land of the Geats, where after some years he becomes king. At the end of his long and successful reign, however, a monster arises to terrorize his own kingdom, an ancient dragon whose treasure-hoard has been plundered by one of Beowulf's subjects. The old Beowulf, knowing that this will be his last battle, nevertheless assembles a band of warriors and goes to slay the dragon. He succeeds, but at the cost of his own life, and only after all his followers save one, the faithful soldier Wiglaf, have deserted him in panic. The dragon dead, the poem ends with Wiglaf's bitter funeral oration on the courage of the late king and the cowardice of his survivors, and with the immolation of Beowulf on his funeral pyre:

> Thus the people of the Geats, his hearth-companions,
> lamented the death of their lord. They said that he was
> of world-kings the mildest of men and the gentlest, kind-
> est to his people, and most eager for fame.*

It is easy to see in the story of Beowulf the elementary
shape of what I have already described as the most ancient
of myths, that of the godlike hero in his battle with the
primal monster of chaos. And it is this elementary form
which has led so many critics to write of the "primitive"
quality of the poem. But the poem is not primitive. As a
paradigm for what I have termed "secondary epic," it takes
this elemental material and transforms it into an elegant, intricate parable about kingship, political responsibility, and
the evolution of culture. In secondary epic, culture not only
is founded, but explains its foundation to itself. And one is
not far from the mark in reading Beowulf as an implicit, and
remarkably subtle, anthropology.

The poem probably dates, in final form, from the first half
of the eighth century, an age which modern parochialism
still calls "dark." But the culture the poem describes is already well consolidated and self-conscious about its secondariness, its derivation from an earlier and harsher civilization. I have already, at the beginning of this chapter,
referred to this sense of secondariness as characteristic of all
epics. But in secondary epic it is not simply an elegaic undertone to the action; rather it is an essential part of the action
itself. Thus Beowulf begins with a long catalogue of the
founder-kings who have preceded Hrothgar, *placing* the action of the poem within a tradition of founders who have already performed the quintessential activity of humanizing
the world. Out of this line of primal kings comes Hrothgar;
and when he finally establishes the great castle, mead-hall,

---

* Tr. E. Talbot Donaldson (New York: W. W. Norton & Co., 1966).

human space of Heorot, *that* act of founding is presented as, not the rough beginning, but the supreme and supremely civilized *culmination* of the king's organizing power:

> It came to his mind that he would command men to construct a hall, a mead-building larger than the children of men had ever heard of, and therein he would give to young and old all that God had given him, except for common land and men's bodies.

This splendid passage exactly catches the ideal of kingship and civilization that the epic as a whole tests and examines. The king is a "giver"—a ring-giver, in the famous phrase—and Heorot is planned as the human space, the enclosed, walled place where he will give gifts to his retainers. The hall, moreover, is founded on a vision not only of the prerogatives of the king, but also of what we might call his "constitutional" limitations. It is for "the children of men." This phrase might seem merely decorative until we remember that the threat to Heorot will come from Grendel and his dam, Cain's cursed brood; i.e. representatives of the savage world *outside* the hall, populated by creatures who are not the children of men.

So what is left for the king to "found," with this much already founded? What is left, of course, is the quality of his own kingship, the morality of politics, that "political law" which Rousseau in *The Social Contract* identifies as the indispensable relationship of ruler to state. One of the most frequent phrases in the poem, applied to the numerous model rulers from the past whose example is a constant counterpoint to the action, is "That was a good king." The simplicity of the phrase is eloquent.

Beowulf, then, is the story of the education of a king to kingship. And when Beowulf does become king of the Geats, after returning from Hrothgar's land, a curious and revealing thing is said about him:

Thus Beowulf showed himself brave, a man known in battles, of good deeds, bore himself according to discretion. Drunk, he slew no hearth-companions. His heart was not savage, but he held the great gift that God had given him, the most strength of all mankind, like one brave in battle.

All the things said about Beowulf as king fit in fairly well with our preconceptions about the dignity appropriate to royal position, except for the shortest sentence in the passage: "Drunk, he slew no hearth-companions." And what surprises us about the sentence is, I think, that, like the rest of the passage, it is obviously meant as high praise. It is no disgrace to Beowulf that he gets drunk; rather it is to his credit that when he is drunk (and the adjective implies nothing about the possible frequency of this condition) he does not kill any of his friends. But is this the kind of praise befitting a king?

It is, as the whole poem exists to prove. Like Hrothgar's original vision of the founding of Heorot, this detail of Beowulf's reign implies an idea by no means "primitive," but highly sophisticated, an idea of civilization as a strenuous battle against the disorganization of the universe, against the entropy not only without, but within the human soul. Men will get drunk: so much is our concession to mortality, the dues we pay for the Fall. But the best men, even when drunk, will not violate the elemental bonds that hold culture together; hostages to the chaos of the heart, they will nonetheless kill no hearth-companions.

Furthermore, "hearth-companions" is an important phrase. It is the basic concept of the feudal, prechivalric society which *Beowulf* describes (the society, of course, of the author of the poem, not of its possibly real, possibly unreal heroes). It is the society of the *comitatus*, the band of warriors and retainers whose loyalty to the sovereign is absolute, but also absolutely based upon a sense of the sovereign's duties toward *them*. The kingdom, in other words, is in *Beowulf* a tightly knit organization of loyalties and responsibilities, but is not yet that later, more problematic version of society—the scene of romance narrative—the court. One may still get drunk without loss of face, and one may still make of one's self-control while drunk a boast.

It is difficult not to read *Beowulf* as a highly self-conscious parable about just this essential, originating phase of culture. The hero's three battles are, to be sure, the main activity narrated in the poem, but before and after each battle Beowulf is exposed to long monologues by various speakers on the idea of kingship, on the exemplary activities of great kings, great protectors of the people before his time. And, perhaps more importantly, the three fights of the hero describe a putative history of civilization, a mythic anthropology in terms of the tool-using capability of men.

The first tool was probably the first weapon. Stanley Kubrick's *2001: A Space Odyssey* establishes this as convincingly, and as intelligently, as any number of studies of the nature and talents of Paleolithic man. And, indeed, we might elaborate the formula, and observe that tools, at whatever level of culture we examine them from stone axes to computers, are always weapons, always to some degree instruments whose function is to extend the reign of the human over the inhuman: the axe extends our reign over potential enemies and potential game (not always distinguished from each other in the earlier stages of civilization), and the computer extends our reign over the world of numbers and chance. A primal hero-king, then, should be a man who understands and incarnates this most indispensable of human capabilities, the use of the tool/weapon.

Thus it is not an accident of the plot, but central to the power of the poem, that Beowulf in his three fights advances toward kingship at the same time he advances toward the human, civilized use of weapons. His name itself may be the remnant of an original animal totem: Beowulf = bee-

wolf = bear. And Beowulf's prowess as a wrestler supports
the idea that he originated as a figure in folktale or cult
myth: the bear-man or the bear-god who can appear as a
man. But this origin is altered, transformed by the narrative
into which it enters. Not only is Beowulf within the poem
educated, drawn toward kingship, but *Beowulf,* the poem itself, grows from its mythic origins into the eloquent essay
on human fate which it is. Thus in his first fight, with Grendel, Beowulf scorns weapons: he will destroy the monster
with his bare hands, he boasts, and does so. In the second
fight, however, with Grendel's mother, he uses a weapon;
and this is curious, since the poem carefully points out that
Grendel's mother, though terrible, is "less terrible by just so
much as is the strength of women, the war-terror of a wife,
less than an armed man's. . . ." Nevertheless, Beowulf accepts the loan of a sword as he descends into the lake to
fight the monster. And when the sword breaks against the
monster's flesh, he defeats her only by the happy accident of
finding the magic sword in her den, which melts after it has
killed her. And in his final fight with the dragon, he not only
uses conventional weapons but also relies on the help of his
friends, his warriors—his *comitatus* (even if that *comitatus*
is reduced, tragically, to one friend and fellow-warrior).

Clearly the progression of fights is organized not in terms
of the escalating horror of the monsters, but in terms of the
technology through which civilization constitutes itself and
banishes chaos (or the monstrous) to its borders. From a
primitive wrestling match to a phase of magical, consecrated
weapons to a phase—our phase—of ordinary weapons and
community aid: that is the progress of Beowulf, as representative of his whole culture's progress. And it is, in this most
mature of poems, a progress tinged with an inevitable melancholy. For in the transit from the mythic world of the
gods to the epic world of men there is a loss, a death: just as
in the movement from pretechnological to tool-using culture
there is an inevitable diminution of force. In becoming a

community we grow individually less so that we can grow collectively stronger. And the king is the incarnation of the melancholy of this diminution, this descent into culture. Beowulf in his mortality and his acceptance of death incarnates both civilization *and* its discontents, for—as the author of *Beowulf* and Freud both know—those terms are not opposed, but are articulations of a single experience, the experience of culture coming to consciousness of itself.

In the vision of secondary epic, then, tools play almost as important a role as do heroes. For heroes in this world are defined by their command of tools, of the technology which makes founding possible. At the beginning of this chapter I discussed the way *Ivan the Terrible* transforms the crown from a symbolic, decorative object into an object of *use,* a sign of power. But before discussing Ivan more fully, and the great literary epic to which it bears so startling a structural resemblance, the *Aeneid* of Virgil, it makes sense to consider a film which develops a mythology of tools quite as "primitive" and complex as that of *Beowulf:* Robert Flaherty's 1934 documentary, *Man of Aran.*

The documentary film, Béla Balász observed, is a special version of the art of the film. It claims to employ the camera simply as a recording instrument, a clear window onto the "real world" around us, with a minimum of authorial intervention. But, as filmmakers and theorists have said, and as Flaherty understood, this "objectivity" is no more possible in documentary film than in any other recording medium. The "objective" newspaper reporter becomes a narrator, a creator of *fiction,* simply in deciding which "facts" of his story he will record as significant. And the camera, after all, has to be aimed—like a gun, or like consciousness itself. The phenomenologists speak of the "intentionality" of consciousness: of the way consciousness is always consciousness *of* something, the way consciousness always constructs what it perceives. The history of the documentary film is, among other things, a demonstration of the intentionality of film narrative as a version of consciousness.

But we have come to expect that "documentaries" will be satiric—or, at least, skeptical of the dignity or humanity of their subjects. The documentaries of Frederick Wiseman (*High School, Titicut Follies, Meat*) and the Maysle brothers (*Salesman, Gimme Shelter*) are parables of an "intentionality" of the filmmaker's consciousness that aims its attention at hypocritical, brutal, or sleazy phenomena (the vapidity of the American high school, the crass inhumanity of the meat-packing industry, the life of a door-to-door Bible salesman, etc.). These films owe a debt to the great British theorist of documentary, John Grierson. Grierson, the first man to apply the term "documentary" to film, was head of the celebrated Documentary Unit of the General Post Office from 1933 to 1937, and an eloquent proponent of the power of the documentary film to further general education and social justice by recording various aspects of the problems and the small heroisms of the modern urban working class. It is a short step from Grierson's ideal of documentary as propaganda for social responsibility to the later idea of documentary as negative propaganda, an acid revelation of the multiple forms of social irresponsibility. Both attitudes assume that "reality," once revealed, will have a corrosive effect upon the myths (of privilege, hierarchy, or naturalness) with the aid of which we normally interpret the world.

But these observations only underscore the special, eccentric quality of *Man of Aran,* and the irony of the fact that Grierson was one of the people who lured Flaherty from Hollywood to Great Britain to make the film. Flaherty was a painstaking "realist" (with important reservations) in his filmmaking technique, but an unrelenting and unabashed romantic in his purposes. From his first, great film of 1922, *Nanook of the North,* he was concerned with images of what I must call, in the context of this discussion, "primal man," with images of men in their aboriginal, founding struggle against the environment. He possessed a truly epic imagination. And in the three years he spent in the Aran Islands filming *Man of Aran* he created a work which, though "documentary," disturbed many of his socialist colleagues precisely because it is so unabashedly, courageously epic in its scope, subject, and intention.

The Aran Islands, off the coast of Galway in Ireland, have a total area of approximately eighteen square miles and a total population of less than a thousand. They are one of the most uninhabitable places on earth. And yet they are inhabited, and have been for centuries, by fishermen whose survival is not simply miraculous, but a dramatic model of the idea of "primal civilization." It is to this sort of civilization that Flaherty was drawn, and *Man of Aran* is his fullest, most thematically complex examination of its allure. He enlisted three Aran Islanders—man, woman, and boy—to represent ("acting" is not a word that really applies here) the archetypal Aran family in its daily, perennial struggle to establish a human space in the midst of that chillingly inhospitable environment. And the word "archetypal" is exactly appropriate to Flaherty's presentation of their life. As the title of the film itself indicates, there is something deliberately statesque, self-consciously "universal," in its treatment of the subject. "Man" of Aran is not only an abstract object of anthropological study, it is also the more ancient mythic generalization, *Man* of Aran.

We are back at the complementarity between film and literary narrative I noted before. As *Beowulf,* in developing a myth of good kingship, becomes a complex analysis of the progressive roles played by tools and technology in the human warfare against chaos, so *Man of Aran,* in its loving examination of the minimal technologies through which the Aran Islanders stave off the encroachments of chaos, becomes finally a parable—fully as mythic as *Beowulf*—of the nature of kingship. Man, wherever he marks out a human space against the surrounding rockface of the universe, has already become man the civilizer, man the king. (It is an accident, impossible to pass, that the fisherman Flaherty chose to "play" his Man of Aran was called Colman "Tiger" King.)

The film contains three major episodes, each introduced by a series of shots of that chaos, the sea, against which the inhabitants of the Aran Islands struggle. In the first sequence, the fishermen return to their island in a high sea, and we follow the attempts of the Man of Aran, his two fellow fishermen, and his family to salvage their battered net from the surf. The rapid alternation of very close shots of the struggling humans and long shots of the towering sea emphasizes the difficulty of even the simplest, elementary tasks in such a violent element. At one point the mother slips and falls into deep surf, and as men turn to reach for her she shouts, "Get the net, don't mind me!" Whether "staged" or not, the incident and the line provide an epigraph for the whole film: in this world, where tools are handmade and absolutely essential for individual survival, they finally become, not a substitute for, but a symbol of the survival of the community as a whole.

The crucial question in *Man of Aran* is: "What can be reclaimed from the sea?" And the second sequence continues the examination of that question. It opens with a long shot of the fishermen's village, clustered within sight of the sea whose presence and noise are a constant undertone in the film. And in this slower, domestic section, the daily activities of the family take on the same seriousness, if not urgency, of the original retrieval of the net. The mother and son laboriously carry baskets of kelp from the shore to fertilize their tiny potato plot. The father attempts, with growing frustration, to sledgehammer a large rock out of the way of a new line of planting. And finally, in an unusually long sequence, the father mends a hole in his damaged boat with cloth, tar, and a smoldering stick of driftwood. Merely to

describe these activities, of course, makes them sound flat;
almost like a parody of some of the "proletarian" subjects
favored by other documentarists of the thirties. But each
task, in context with the other sequences and in constant
counterpoint to the theme of the unyielding sea, takes on the
quality of epic arduousness. Flaherty's achievement is
not—as in many socialist and Marxist documentaries—to
"dignify" labor, for the vision of Man of Aran implies that
labor is already, innately "dignified" as the quintessential
human activity (we can remember, along with the Man of
Aran's arduous and heroic clearing of rocks from his little
potato plot, the beautiful and excruciating patience of Nanook in the ice-fishing sequence from Nanook of the North).
It is rather to uncover, by simply aiming the camera at it,
the mythic, founding quality of all labor. When the Man finally loosens the great rock, he lifts it over his head and
throws it far out of his path. But Flaherty (using a technique
perfected by Eisenstein) *expands* that moment of triumph
far beyond its "real" duration, intercutting four or five shots
of the man lifting the rock, from different angles, before he
finally casts it away. It is a moment which splendidly con-
nects the mythic with the quotidian, for it catches the sense
of exhilaration, of "God, *that's* over," that anyone has felt
who has ever labored hard and long at a task (building a
city or digging a ditch), and has finally finished it. That elementary sense of accomplishment, lovingly expanded by the
editing of the film, is perhaps the feeling which most con-
nects us with the larger world of the epic founders.

Man of Aran, that is, can be viewed as a long hymn to
man the toolmaker and tool-user. But to say this much is to
say that the film touches a very deep level, indeed. A distinctive feature of *Beowulf* is the "kenning," the basic metaphorical (or imagistic) unit of Old English verse. On the surface, the kenning seems to be simply a kind of
circumlocution, a way of describing an object in terms of its
aspect or its significant features: the kenning for *king* is

"ring-giver," for *queen* "peace-weaver," for *sword* "battle-flash," and for *sea* "whale-road." In most Old English poetry, the kenning has just this ornamental, embellished function. But in terms of the mythic anthropology of *Beowulf* itself, as an epic about the birth of civilization through technology, the common device of the kenning takes on a new and quite special force: for it is the description of objects in terms of their use. Thus, at the elementary level of language itself, the imagery of *Beowulf* acts out the essential civilizing activity of its hero.

Much of the same force is present in the basic shots of *Man of Aran*. The entire film may be taken as a "kenning," an assertion that the world becomes meaningful only when humans can turn it to use, that the world becomes perceptible as it becomes *technological*. Language itself, as I have already indicated, is the first of human technologies, the first medium through which consciousness takes stock of itself *as* consciousness and, at the same instant, takes command of the world by organizing it around a perceiving subject, a self. But this is only to say that language, like consciousness, like the "documentary" language of the film camera, is *intentional*, that all three of these elements *make* a world in the very act of perceiving it. And what modern phenomenology describes as intentionality is described with equal perception by Old English prosody, since the word *kenning* derives from the Old English *cennen* or *kennen*, "to know," and is therefore *itself* a metaphor for knowledge, or an implicit assertion that to know a thing is to know its human use, its human function.

This etymology helps make sense of the middle, "domestic" section of *Man of Aran*, where the world of the Aran Islanders is viewed in terms of its orientation around the central activities and tools of survival; and it also explains the special power of the final section of the film, which returns to the sea itself and to the theme "What can be reclaimed from the sea?" more explicitly and more tragically than either of the other sections. This third section involves two major incidents, a shark-hunting episode, in which a shark is sighted off the coast of the island and successfully harpooned and brought to beach by all the fishermen of the village working in concert, and a storm at sea echoing the storm of the film's opening—with the difference that in this storm the Man of Aran loses his boat, and barely escapes to shore with his life.

The shark, as the caption to the final section of the film makes clear, is hunted by the Aran Islanders for the oil he provides for lamps and cooking fires. And, as if the archetypal overtones of the situation were not evident enough, one of the men fishing for him exclaims—again in one of the few clearly heard lines of dialog in the film—"He's a big monster." The shark is, indeed, a monster, a personalized representative of the chaos of the sea: and we do not need to have been exposed to all the folklore of the shark surrounding the recent success of *Jaws* to understand this. Flaherty was faulted and sometimes ridiculed, on the first release of *Man of Aran,* because the Aran Islanders had not in fact hunted sharks with hand-held harpoons from open boats since the eighteenth century, and he himself had to instruct his subjects in the "authentic" hunting method he wished to film. But this objection only makes sense if we want *Man of Aran* to be "documentary" in the narrow way of a scientifically faithful record of a "primitive" way of life. And that it manifestly is not, on two counts: it is not scientifically faithful, but rather faithful to the truth of heroic myth; nor is it an examination of a "primitive" way of life, since it insists that the distinction between "primitive" and "sophisticated" labor is merely one of the observer's own prejudices about what is "sopnisticated" (and in this respect, of course, the film anticipates the insights of structural anthropologists).

The shark, if we want to continue the idea of the film as kenning, would be something like "oil-monster" or "sea-oil": that is, a manifestation of the primal monster imagined absolutely in terms of his relationship to human use, and to human control. The shark-hunting sequence, then, is far from a "cheat." It continues the central theme of the film, and raises that theme—man's survival against the over-whelming odds of the hostile universe—to its highest pitch of danger and urgency. And most significantly, the shark is hunted (in this reconstructed eighteenth-century method) not by the Man of Aran singly, but by the whole community of fishermen. All the able-bodied men of the village partici-pate in the hunt. There is even a scene in which the Boy, not yet having crossed the initiatory threshhold into manhood, is sent back from the epic quest. And as the killed shark is brought back to shore, we see—for the first time in the film—the *whole* community, men, women, and children, gather on the beach to render the monster into usable prod-ucts. Against the threat and the promise of the monster, in other words, the *comitatus* defines itself and is defined by the heroism of its warriors. No literary epic I know of goes further toward defining this aboriginal sense of community than the scene in which the village marches down to the shore to claim the flesh and the oil of the shark.

But if the shark is an optimistic answer to the question "What can be reclaimed from the sea?" *Man of Aran,* such is its honesty, does not stop at that optimistic answer. As all epics make clear, the king is our founder and our father, and the king must die. The founding act, like every human act, is tinged with an irreducible aura of loss and melancholy. Beo-wulf slays the dragon, but dies in the course of that saving act on behalf of the community. And the end of *Man of Aran* recapitulates the storm at sea of the opening sequence: but this time the sea reclaims the artifacts of man, the pri-mal chaos triumphs over the technologies we have devel-oped to organize that chaos. The net was saved at the beginning, but now the boat is lost. And the entire film pre-ceding this sequence, of course, has emphasized the central importance of the boat, the crucial importance of the tools of his trade, for the Man of Aran. It is, indeed, a symbolic death, an image of inevitable and cosmic defeat in exactly the same fashion as is the death of the good king Beowulf in his own poem. For it establishes that the struggle against encroaching chaos, the war with the sea, is never either fully won or fully lost. The last shots of the film show us, first, a tight closeup (one of the few in the film) of the Man as he looks back at the sea which has claimed and now is battering his shattered boat; then the boat itself, indispensable tool for mediating between man and the flood, being beaten to pieces against the rocks; and then the triad, Man, Woman, and Boy, in profile, making their way home across the rocky landscape of the shore. And in both the bitterness and the grandeur of his conclusion it is difficult, once we have made the association, not to remember the simple and eloquent epitaph which *Beowulf* assigns its own epic examplars of the warfare against chaos, "That was a good king."

"Till He Founded His City"

I have said that "secondary epic" is conscious of its own epic quality, epic narrative that *knows* it is epic narrative. In terms of *Beowulf* and *Man of Aran,* this is to say that the epic story becomes a kind of anthropology, a "documentary" myth about the origins of civilization shown through the activity of a single hero who acts out the ascent of his whole race or whole tribe to the status of organized community or *comitatus.* And there is a certain inevitable and complex degree of self-consciousness implied in any narrative of this sort: whether it is the primal epistemology of the Old English kenning or the subtle but indispensable "intentionality" of the documentary camera. In the two works I have examined, and in any number of similar works (the Babylonian *Gilgamesh,* say, or *October* or *Storm Over*

Asia) there is still something missing. But it is foolish to speak of something "missing" from works of art as rich and as deeply humanizing as these: let us say, rather, that there is a *possible* resource of storytelling which these works do not employ—a resource which, indeed, would alter and not necessarily enhance their power if it were employed, but which nevertheless they conspicuously avoid. And once we have examined that special, and revolutionary, resource of storytelling, we will have surveyed the full expanse of epic.

One way of describing this last, most subtle variety of epic narrative is to say that it is epic narrative which uses the first person pronoun. Earlier in this chapter I cited the opening lines of the *Aeneid* of Virgil. But that famous opening is *not*, in fact, the opening of the poem. The actual beginning of the poem is:

> I am that poet who in times past made the light melody of pastoral poetry. In my next poem I left the woods for the adjacent farmlands, teaching them to obey even the most exacting tillers of the soil; and the farmers liked my work. But now I turn to the terrible strife of Mars. This is a tale of arms and of a man.

The four lines of Latin before *Arma virumque cano,* "This is a tale of arms and of a man," were for centuries assumed to be a later interpolation, a summary of Virgil's literary career tacked on at the beginning of the *Aeneid* by an admiring copyist. But recent scholarship indicates that they probably are authentic. And if they are, then the *Aeneid* is not only the greatest of Roman poems, but also the fullest articulation we have of a crucial stage in the evolution of consciousness. The *Aeneid* is the incarnation of that moment in history when the epic vision becomes internalized, when the epic bard learns that he is the epic poet. If the poem begins, that is, with the words *Ille ego,* "I am he," rather than with *Arma virumque,* than we can say that the poem is not simply a latter-day reconstruction of the Homeric world, but a deliberate translation of that world into the urbanized and more morally complex language of Augustan Rome. We have said that in epic civilization becomes aware of itself. But in secondary epic, and particularly in the level of secondary epic represented by the *Aeneid,* epic itself becomes aware of itself.

This is the implication not simply of the first four disputed lines of the poem, but of the shape and pressure of the entire narrative. As is well known, the emperor Augustus commissioned Virgil to compose a poem which would celebrate the manifest destiny of Rome to rule the known world and rival the majesty and beauty of the Homeric epics. (Augustus may also have insisted on the excision of the first four lines, realizing their antiwar character.) The very circumstances of its conception, that is, indicate to what degree it is a deliberate act of secondary mythmaking, a founding-story by a civilization already founded and already sophisticated. And throughout the poem, Virgil is at pains not only to rival the Homeric epics, but to invoke and overcome their memory. Again and again he narrates episodes with strong parallels to the *Iliad* or the *Odyssey.* But in each case he converts the Homeric episode into an assertion of the Roman values which, in his mind, complete and transcend the values of Greek civilization; order, authority, and the vision of history as a pageant of Rome's imperial destiny. The trials and wars of Aeneas, that lonely and distraught wanderer through Homeric times, are all directed toward and justified by his great, divinely impelled mission, all undergone only until he can found his city—*dum conderet urbem*—the city which will, centuries later, make possible the Augustan Age, the *pax Romana,* and the *Aeneid* itself.

Harold Bloom has lately argued that the central impulse of modern literature is what he calls "the anxiety of influence," the attempt of poets to create by assimilating and symbolically overcoming the poets who have been the strongest influences on them or, as Bloom says, their "pre-cursors." It is an unimpeachable insight into romantic and postromantic writing. But the example of the *Aeneid* helps us see that it is more than that: an insight, in fact, into the nature of writing itself. Virgil, in his struggles with the specter of his own strong precursor, Homer, can be regarded in many ways as the first major *writer* (as opposed to storyteller) in the Western tradition.

But the kind of self-consciousness implied by the opening *Ille ego* extends from the character of the poet himself to the character of his hero. Aeneas is the man driven by fate—*fato profugus*—whose destiny is to become a king on the great model of the king of the heavens, Jupiter himself. This Jupiter, however, is not simply a Roman version of the Greek Zeus. He is the supreme, lawful, and absolute authority over heaven and earth, not (as in Homer) a strongman in uneasy control of a factional community of gods. Jupiter, that is, is imperial, the heavenly double of the Augustus who is the patron and inspiration of the poem. And Aeneas is the agent of his will.

Pius Aeneas, Aeneas the True or Aeneas the Faithful, is Virgil's favorite epithet for his hero, and the epithet implies a great deal for the story of the *Aeneid.* Unlike the Homeric heroes Achilles and Odysseus, Aeneas' great talent is his piety, his ability to trascend his own personal, passional identity for the sake of the destiny assigned him by god. There is even something unheroic about Aeneas, at least in terms of the Homeric convention of the hero: the first time we see him in the poem, he is caught in a storm at sea raised by his enemy the goddess Juno, and is bemoaning his fate in the most despairing, most unheroic of fashions. But this is just the point. Aeneas is not heroic because of his physical courage or his personal valor (though he does possess those qualities). He is heroic, rather, because he recognizes and accepts his divine mission to found the central city of Rome, because he takes on the burden of history itself. He is the epic founder as fated man, as *fato profugus,* and his heroism in the poem named for him is a deliberate inversion of the athletic heroism of the Homeric poems. He lays waste no cities, slays no monsters, embarks on no marvelous journeys. Rather, he remains true to his fate, and manages—even at the cost of his own desires—to found his city, becoming thereby the quintessential and quintessentially self-conscious epic man. Aeneas is the king who not only acts out, but understands, the dimensions of his kingship.

No sequence of the poem makes this clearer than the story of Aeneas and Dido, queen of Carthage (Books II–IV). Shipwrecked on the coast of North Africa, Aeneas wanders into the kingdom of Dido, who is just then building the first foundations of the city of Carthage. Welcomed by her as a famous hero of the Trojan War, he tells her the story of his wanderings after the defeat of Troy. And as he speaks, Dido (urged by Aeneas' mother Venus) falls madly in love with him. After an intense struggle with herself, Dido confesses her passion to Aeneas, and they become lovers, with Dido willing to share half her kingdom and half its reign with the Trojan hero. But fate insists that Aeneas' destiny is not simply to be the half-ruler of an Asiatic, woman-founded country, but rather the founder of the line that will lead to Rome. So he is commanded by the gods to abandon his Carthaginian lover and pursue his course toward the land which is his destiny. And, although reluctantly, he obeys the gods, abandoning Dido, who, in a seizure of madness, kills herself while cursing Aeneas and his future.

The Dido episode is probably the most famous, and certainly the most touching, episode of Virgil's great poem. But it is important to realize that this episode is also a crucial, perhaps the crucial, moment in Aeneas' own growth into his destined role as founder of the race of Romans. It is in Dido's court that Aeneas recounts his wanderings after the fall of his beloved Troy—a clear reminiscence of Odysseus' flashback narrative of his travels in the *Odyssey,* in the is-

land kingdom of the Phaiakians. And it is after the interlude
with Dido that Aeneas goes on to the final accomplishment
of his quest, his landing on and possession of the Italian territories where Troy is destined to be reborn, greater and
eternally, as Rome. So far this is a technique of storytelling
which owes a gigantic debt to Homer: the hero is first
glimpsed in the middle of his travels, is taken to a banquet
hall where he recounts the adventures he has had up to the
present moment, and proceeds thence to the fulfillment of
his journey. But Virgil's genius converts this already brilliant
device of storytelling into a profoundly moral fable, by the
simple device of having the auditor of the hero's tale fall in
love with the hero. Dido and Aeneas love each other, and
yet Aeneas must—cruelly and even, according to some
readers of the poem, heartlessly—abandon her for his own
imperial destiny. During his idyll with the queen of Carthage, Aeneas is deprived of his characteristic epithet; only
after he has determined to leave her, and announced his
decision to her, is he once again referred to as *pius Aeneas.*

The elements of crown and shadow to which I referred at
the beginning of this chapter have in the *Aeneid* achieved
their fullest and most complex expression. For at the elementary level we can say that the cost of founding Rome is
abandoning the comfortable, reassuring love of Dido. But
this level of reading is inseparable from the historical sense
of the poem, a sense which involves the knowledge that the
Roman and Carthaginian civilizations were to clash,
hundreds of years after the Dido episode, in the Punic Wars
which were in many ways the consolidating force of the
Roman Republic. And at yet another level it is impossible
not to regard Dido—Eastern, exotic, seductive, and devoted
to foreign gods—as a surrogate for Cleopatra, who had only
recently shocked conservative Romans by introducing (with
great success) the fantastic gods of the East into the pantheon of Roman deities and who, by perverting the hero
Marcus Antonius to her side, had very nearly wrecked the

unity and imperial peace of the newborn empire. It was only Augustus who, in his sublime coldness, managed to counteract the divisive influence of the Egyptian queen and her spoiled Roman lover and restore the illusion of historical continuity to the political life of the sacred City. Dido, then, represents not only passion, the comforts of the sensual life, the relaxation from the arduous quest; she is also, in spite of herself, the seductress who for all her fascination and even for all her sincerity and paradoxical innocence represents a threat to the divine order of history.

Aeneas, that is, is never more heroic than in his renunciation, his acts of self-control and self-discipline. It is this which makes him so distinctively an anti-Homeric hero, and also this which makes him Virgil's perfect metaphor for the Roman Imperium he loves so deeply. In the center of the poem, Book VI, Aeneas visits the underworld to learn from his father Anchises the full destiny of the new Troy he is about to found in Italy. Anchises shows him a splendid and powerful pageant of Roman history up to the time of Augustus, when the history of Rome literally becomes the history of the civilized world, and concludes with this great vision of the Roman mission:

> Others, for so I can well believe, shall hammer forth more delicately a breathing likeness out of bronz, coax living faces from the marble, plead causes with more skill, plot with their gauge the movements in the sky, and tell the rising of the constellations. But you, Roman, must remember that you have to guide the nations by your authority, for this is to be your skill, to graft tradition onto peace, to show mercy to the conquered, and to wage war until the haughty are brought low.

The immense power of this passage, and of the whole poem, does not depend upon our agreement with Virgil's patriotic love of his empire, for his genius transmutes that love into the stuff of major myth, a universal vision of the possibility of a truly just and decent civilization which can communicate with and humanize, one feels, any system of political or religious belief. Indeed, without the *Aeneid* it is doubtful whether Virgil's fourth-century A.D. admirer, St. Augustine, would have articulated in the same way his own seminal, internalized epics of the soul, the *Confessions* and especially the *City of God*.

The last six books of the *Aeneid* narrate the fulfillment of the quest, as Aeneas arrives in Italy, is betrothed to the princess Lavinia, daughter of the king of Latium, and then is forced to wage war against Lavinia's disappointed suitor Turnus. These books are more austere, more violent than the first six (it is often observed that Virgil rewrote the *Odyssey* in the first half of his poem, and the *Iliad* in the second). But here, too, the theme of heroic restraint predominates. Aeneas is actually absent from much of the action of this half, away to the north arranging bonds with important allies. This is partly, to be sure, a reminiscence of the *Iliad,* where Achilles is so conspicuously absent for so much of the action. But Achilles withdrew from battle out of an anarchic, finally mad insistence on his own individual rights, a tragic selfishness which the whole poem exists to purge. And Aeneas' withdrawal is, characteristically, for the highest and most provident reason of state. It even helps assure the correct succession of rule, for while Aeneas is away the Roman defenses are commanded by his untested son Ascanius, who demonstrates that he, too, is a responsible and humane—a *pius*—leader of men. And when, in the last book, Aeneas and Turnus finally engage in a single combat upon which the whole war for Latium depends, we are meant to think of the climactic battle between Achilles and Hector in the penultimate book of the *Iliad.* But here the ironies of literary influence and allusion are paramount. For in the *Iliad* the ultimate battle was between Achilles, the egoistic hero who had been chastened into tragic bitterness, and Hector, the glorious but impetuous Trojan hero; whereas in the *Aeneid* the final battle is between Aeneas, Trojan hero of the new values of authority, subordination, and civilization, and Turnus, who represents in his anger, his excessiveness, and his disruptive egoism the values of both Achilles and Hector—that is, the values of the world which the world of the *Aeneid* (and of the Roman Empire) is destined to supplant. The victory, then—the only time in the poem we actually see Aeneas in combat—is a victory for precisely that system of values, of elementary laws, which will render combat unnecessary, a curious fossil from an overpassed time. Aeneas is reluctantly bloodthirsty so that his heirs can be gentle.

Eisenstein's *Ivan the Terrible* bears a number of striking resemblances to the epic narrative of the *Aeneid,* not the least of which is that Ivan, like Aeneas, is a man caught in and crucified by his own heroic role. "This is the story of a man, not a legend," says the printed legend which introduces the film. But Ivan IV, Ivan the Terrible, or as the Russian has it, *Ivan groznyi,* "Ivan the Magnificent" or "Ivan the Awesome," is precisely a man who has become a legend; just as Aeneas, the minor Trojan warrior mentioned in Homer, had become a strong folk legend in Roman history before Virgil made him a major literary myth. And Eisenstein throughout both parts of *Ivan* is at pains to indicate how the Czar is driven not by personal ambition but by an obsessive, sometimes almost mystical, sense of mission.

Like Virgil, Eisenstein was commissioned to make his great narrative by a nationalistic sovereign. Josef Stalin was the patron of *Ivan,* as Augustus was of the *Aeneid.* And both works are, at least on one level of reading, equally uncritical exercises in patriotic propaganda which become (on another level) central myths of the sacrificial, civilizing king.

Ivan's mission is to consolidate Russia for the first time in its history into a single political entity, to rid the sacred Russian soil of foreign occupying forces, and to supplant the feudal dictatorships of the Boyars by a centralized, modern, bureaucratic rule. His mission, in other words, is to turn medieval Russia into a Russia which can be imagined as the possible seed-ground of the communist revolution, the dictatorship of the proletariat. *Ivan,* that is, is highly self-conscious secondary epic since it attempts to turn the stuff of national legend into the stuff of contemporary political argument. It is a "founding" story in the fullest sense of the word, for it "founds" the origins of Soviet populism in the activities of a sixteenth-century absolute monarch.

Stalin, who understood propaganda but perhaps did not understand mythmaking quite as well, was angered at seeing himself represented as not only *groznyi,* "awesome," but *groznyi,* "terrible." He knew that the figure of Ivan was a thinly disguised metaphor for his own rule over Russia, but did not comprehend that Eisenstein really meant to celebrate Ivan's ruthlessness and cruelty as necessities of history. This is one way of saying that real, as opposed to narrative, kings, vastly prefer the crown to its inevitable shadow, and tend to be embarrassed (and retributive) when reminded too forcefully of the presence of the latter.

All this aside, *Ivan* is a great film—perhaps the only film that deserves to be compared (as do almost no other literary works) to the *Aeneid.* Especially in Part One, Eisenstein creates out of the "legend" of Ivan the story of a man whose sense of mission and dedication to the future are in fact as powerful in their effect on his behavior as would be a religious vocation. If, indeed, we remember that the primary meaning of "vocation" is *calling,* then we can see that Ivan in the course of Part One of the film is discovering precisely what he is called to do—i.e. consolidate the Russian land by enlisting the aid of the common people against the nobility. His heroism, in other words, is a heroism of organization rather than of violently creative or destructive activity. And, just as Aeneas is contrasted throughout his poem to the chaotically self-assertive Homeric heroes, so Ivan throughout Part One of the film named after him is contrasted to the figure of Andrei Kurbsky, a historical figure who serves as a counterpoint to Ivan's self-contained, bureaucratized ideas of heroism and kingship. Kurbsky is a highly self-conscious allusion by the filmmaker to the standard of heroism which his own hero is meant to supplant. More conventionally handsome than the Czar, Kurbsky stands for all the values of individual self-aggrandizing accomplishment which Ivan's reign will convert into state service.

At the siege of Kazan, Ivan's first major triumph after his coronation, it is his friend Kurbsky who objects to Ivan's use of gunpowder to destroy the Mongol battlements. Their quarrel about military techniques is in fact a quarrel between two different worlds—we might say, the worlds of primary and of secondary epic—which Ivan wins by demonstrating the success of his own less heroic but more efficient methods. As he remarks to Kurbsky, with eloquent scorn in his voice, "Fighting on horseback is beautiful!" But beauty is not the point of warfare: victory is, and victory with the least cost of human life. If Kurbsky is the prime objector to Ivan's use of gunpowder and mines, he is also the man who, to Ivan's disgust, crucifies Mongol prisoners before the walled city of Kazan and urges them to cry for their city to surrender. He represents, in other words, the full elegance and the full barbarity of the precivilized ideal. And it is just this ideal which Ivan replaces and transcends.

At the beginning of the film, Ivan is betrothed to the princess Anastasia. It is the one human attachment which sustains him throughout his early struggles against the Boyars, the one loyalty on which he can count. Kurbsky too is in love with Czarina Anastasia, and as an early sequence in the film makes clear, her love and loyalty is exclusively for Ivan and for his mission to liberate Russia from her foreign occupiers. But if the beautiful Anastasia (played wonderfully by Ludmilla Tselikovskaya) is an image of happiness and normality in the first part of the film, she is also an image of personal loyalty, personal affection, which the Czar of all the Russias cannot, finally, afford. She must die, as Dido must be abandoned, for the epic founder in his role as lawgiver must undergo a sacrificial wound, perhaps a sacrificial castration, which involves the loss of his passional self for the sake of his rational, legal authority.

And so it is that the plot of *Ivan the Terrible,* Part One, is largely the story of Ivan being systematically deprived of every affection that might keep him from the realization of his mission to consolidate the Russian land. First he loses his friend Kurbsky, at the siege of Kazan where Kurbsky wants to wage war in a more picturesque and less efficient form, and later at the Moscow court where Kurbsky is constantly jealous of Ivan's success. And later in his career Ivan loses his bride Anastasia, poisoned by Countess Efrosyne Staritsky (played by Serafima Berman), who wants her own son, the idiot Vladimir Staritsky, to win the throne.

We may take *Ivan groznyi,* in fact, as a parable about the growth of epic self-consciousness, even more self-aware than Virgil's poem. For Ivan learns, in the course of Part One, that his nationalistic mission precludes any personal attachments: learns, that is, that the shadow is part of the crown. The death of Anastasia, like Aeneas' desertion of Dido, is a kind of purification of the hero for later tasks that also represents a dehumanization of him. "I will be an abbot of steel," cries Ivan at Anastasia's deathbed, determined to place his trust from now on only in the people. The Russian word for steel is, of course, *stalin,* and the pun was certainly deliberate on Eisenstein's part. Much like Virgil's hero, Eisenstein's Ivan demonstrates his heroism nowhere so much as in his acceptance of the agonies of his role. But this is not to say that Ivan is passive. He is passionate for the consolidation of the Russian land, and passionate also for the consolidation of his own reign. He is capable, as the second part of the film indicates, of ordering mass executions to preserve the order he has established, and even capable (as his interview with the Metropolitan in Part Two indicates) of employing the techniques of religious hypocrisy to further his ends. What he is not capable of is abandoning his quest to make Russia a national, cultural entity. And this is the point of the film, as well as the point of Ivan's whole historical career. We can even observe that Ivan's struggle (in Eisenstein's film) is to establish a progressive, male kingdom against the claims of a regressive, fragmentary, female ideal of government, that represented by Countess Efrosyne and her son Vladimir. In the second half of the film, Ivan becomes more violent, more grimly self-assertive in his establishment of a unified rule for all the Russias. And, as I have already said, in the famous last sequence of the film, he averts an assassination plot against himself by clothing the halfwit Vladimir in his royal robes. After Vladimir is mistakenly killed, Efrosyne (instigator of the plot) discovers her mistake and collapses, mad and ruined, while the now-triumphant Ivan strolls out of the frame. It is one of the most affecting endings in film history, for it not only humanizes Efrosyne, but also humanizes Ivan himself, who in his last glance at the now-mad Efrosyne understands her loss, her pathos. The point, though, is not lost: the king, in order to become king, must assume his own shadow, must assume the defeats and the losses of personality that attend his kingship.

With *Ivan* and the *Aeneid,* we enter a realm of storytelling where the function of the king is not only to found, but to civilize his kingdom. We enter a realm, that is, very like the realm of romance, the second of our narrative forms. And it is to that second form that I now turn.

III

The Romance World: Knights

> *The second relation is that of the members among themselves, or with the entire body politic.*
>
> ROUSSEAU

From Patriarch to Priest

One of the greatest of medieval romances, *Sir Gawain and the Green Knight,* opens with an explicit salute to the epic tradition out of which romance narrative develops.

> Since the siege and the assault was ceased at Troy,
> The walls breached and burnt down to brands and ashes,
> The knight that had knotted the nets of deceit
> Was impeached for his perfidy, proven most true,
> It was high-born Aeneas and his haughty race
> That since prevailed over provinces, and proudly reigned
> Over well-nigh all the wealth of the West Isles.
> Great Romulus to Rome repairs in haste;
> With boast and with bravery builds he that city
> And names it with his own name, that it now bears.
> Ticius to Tuscany, and towers raises,
> Langobard in Lombardy lays out homes,
> And far over the French Sea, Felix Brutus
> On many broad hills and high Britain he sets,
>   most fair.

Where war and wrack and wonder
By shifts have sojourned there,
And bliss by turns with blunder
In that land's lot had share.*

Medieval Europe was obsessed with identifying its historical continuity with the Roman Empire founded by Aeneas. And it is no accident that the distinctive narrative mode of the High Middle Ages, which we call (as did they) "romance," should center on the exploits of knights in the service of a king——Arthur of England—whose kingdom was established by the mythical "Felix Brutus," a lesser companion of Aeneas.

But if the romance world is self-consciously continuous with that of the great epics (and the Middle Ages, of course, knew only Virgil's epic in its entirety, with Homer a dim and inaccurately transmitted memory), romance is also highly conscious of its distance from that world and the increased complexity of its own political, social, and religious universe. The City has been founded by the king. It remains for the king's delegated authorities, his knights, to settle and civilize the City whose walls have been built. And, as we shall see, this civilizing act, this substitution of duty for original creative freedom, is often more important for the special, morally instructive defeats its imposes upon the knight than for the victories it might make possible. Gawain, in the poem I have quoted, is the perfect knight, a model of courtesy, loyalty to his king and religion, and gentleness toward women. But in the course of *Gawain and the Green Knight* he finds that his multiple loyalties and perfections are coming apart from each other, pulling him in different and contradictory directions. And at the end, in his final confrontation with the mysterious, benign/malevolent Green Knight, he discovers that he is *not* perfect, and that means that no man in the complex society of Arthur's court *can* be perfect. There is an inevitable sense of

* Tr. Marie Borroff (New York: W. W. Norton & Co., 1967).

diminution about the romance world: the knight is not a king, and must learn that he is not a king. But the test which the knight must always undergo and must always, to some degree, fail, is also the realization by a culture that its own best gifts and powers are founded upon a principle of order, of limitation, whose price must be paid if the culture itself is to survive.

> The second relation is that of the members among themselves, or with the entire body politic. This relation should be as small as possible in the first case and as great as possible in the second, so that each citizen will be completely independent of all the others and extremely dependent on the state.

That is how Rousseau defines the second essential law of civilization, the law which follows the elementary act of the epic founders, and which completes that founding act by making the ideal City not only tolerable but habitable. This is the romance world, the world of the civilizers whose activity follows, is less than, and paradoxically more than that of the founders themselves. Each citizen under this dispensation should be "completely independent of all the others and extremely dependent on the state": and what is the relationship described in this phrase if not courtesy, civility? The king, lord of the epic world, is the man who by main force calls the City into existence from the disorganized, chaotic world of preculture. The knight, hero of the romance world, is the man who—less than the king, drawing his authority from the founding act of the king—civilizes the society which the king has created. It is a delicate relationship, for the knight is always almost a king, always threatens to displace the king from his eminence (the warfare of Lancelot and Arthur in Arthurian legend is a perfect example) and substitute his own, later values for those the king has won from the cruelly unsympathetic circumambient universe. But it is also a relationship crucial to the growth of the City, and hence a relationship which develops, which reaches fruition. The knight's function, that is, is not only to establish and act out elementary laws of courtesy and civilization, but to recognize his own belatedness, to realize and accept the fact that he will never be king. He is, that is, still more than we are but definitively less than divine.

As we shall see, the romance world revalues or transvalues a number of elementary concerns of the epic world. Action, which the epic vision tolerates only insofar as it is destructive or creative, becomes in the romance world neither destructive nor creative, but expressive: what a knight does in a given situation is a symbolic expression of where he stands in relation to a given set of moral problems. Sexual passion is in the romance world the primary paradox with which the knight has to deal: love has been made possible, in other words, by the founding act of the king, and must now be faced head-on as the quintessential problem of a nascent civilization. How can a man love a woman and simultaneously remain faithful to the City, the political entity, from which he draws his own manhood, his own individuality? This is the central problem of "courtly love" and one about which I will have a great deal to say later in this chapter. And finally, in the romance as opposed to the epic world, the paraphernalia of individual identity—tools, weapons, clothing—take on a new and complicated quality. In the epic world, as we have already seen, the founder-king is the man who converts the accouterments of his rank to use, who turns the crown into the instrument of war, the scepter into the tool of power. But if in the epic world you use what you have, in the romance world you are what you wear. The knight is the first figure of allegory, the hero whose armor is not so much for protection against enemies as it is the expression of his total relationship to the world of his civilization.

All this is a way of saying that, in the romance world, civilization is imagined in a state between its founding and its consolidation, the state in which we learn not only not to kill each other without a good reason, but also to be kind to each other unless there are good reasons not to be. The knight of romance may or may not be officially delegated as such, but he is always, in terms of the elements of storytelling, the representative of the king within the City the king has founded, the carrier-out of the king's elemental laws in the more complicated, more richly human world of social interaction.

One way of looking at the relationship between the epic and the romance worlds is to think in terms of the relationship, fairly well established by now in anthropological studies, between the functions of the shaman and those of the priest. In terms of the evolution of religion, the two functions play a complementary and perennially adversary role, the shaman being the founder, or prophet, of divine revelation and the priest being the regulator, the socializer of the truth the shaman reveals.

In psychoanalytic terms it is easy enough to identify the shaman as a schizophrenic (the man who hears voices from another world and invents a counter-reality to substitute for the reality he sees around him) and the priest as a primary form of paranoia (the man who accepts and elaborates the idea of a hidden, unified explanation for the welter of his experience and puts himself to great pains to explain it to all with whom he comes in contact). And in terms of a putative history of storytelling, it is easy enough to distinguish the shaman as the originating (and probably half-mad) teller of the primal tale from the priest as the later, embellishing and elaborating re-teller of the myth the shaman has uttered. But these distinctions are reductive. It is truer to the details of cultural evolution, to say that the shaman is the originating Voice of God and the priest the interpreter and ritualizer of that Voice's utterances.

Whether he is an Eskimo healer, an African witch doctor, or an Old Testament prophet, the shaman stands in a unique position between the community which shelters and venerates him and divine order which calls that community into being, and which the shaman announces to it. He is daemonic, that is, his special gift is his openness to possession by the god—or, in terms of a later, skeptical civilization, his predisposition to madness. Contemporary versions of shamanistic religion like mediums or like the speakers-in-tongues, glossolalists, still found in many fundamentalist Christian churches may be the butt of pointless irony by the half-educated. But they are an important and a still-noble survival of what may well be the earliest and most inexhaustible of all religious and civilizing impulses, the impulse to discover a dimension to life outside the visible perimeter of this life, the impulse to learn a language that speaks to us not of this world, but of a world which justifies and makes this world real by making it holy.

The activity of the shaman, the prophet, is a variety of the action of the epic founder. But shamans, though essential, are notoriously unstable. Once the founding act has been performed, once the saving word of the god has been uttered, it becomes, almost immediately, institutionalized. Cult becomes culture, speaking in tongues becomes language. The revelation must be preserved, but it must also be made communicable to, and in the deepest sense habitable by, those for whom it is intended. It must be humanized, in other words, and this is the function of the priest/knight.

Nikos Kazantzakis, in his novel *The Last Temptation of Christ,* imagines the crucial moment of transition from the world of the founders to the world of the preservers in terms of the shaman-priest relationship we have been examining. The Christ of the novel is a radical, tortured mystic, as much the victim as the medium of his apocalyptic vision. And as he hangs on the cross he thinks about the possibility of renouncing his messianic role, confessing to the charges of his persecutors, and escaping to live a humble, "normal" life. This much we can recognize as the truly last and first temptation of the founder, political or religious—the temptation to renounce the crown and thereby escape the human cost of its shadow. But Kazantzakis takes us further. In his last vision, Christ sees himself as having escaped from his mission, settled in a comfortable life as a carpenter, married to Mary Magdalen. But one day there comes to his shop a man named Paul, a man who insists on calling him Savior, the Light of the World, and who with his fanatic's devotion promises that he, Paul who once was Saul, will preach the word of Christ until the whole world becomes his church. And Christ, in both panic and exaltation, learns that he cannot escape the spiritual kingship he has instituted; that his knight, the soldier of Christ Paul, will carry out his message even if he himself were to recant.

It is the most profoundly ironic moment in Kazantzakis's book, and it makes the central point that the mission of the knight/priest completes the mission of the king/shaman, even to the dissolution of the latter's own identity. Founders, kings, and skygods alike always, in the history of culture, are superseded, become unimportant precisely in realizing their importance, their true effectiveness as founders. In partial substantiation of Kazantzakis' ironic vision, we can observe that Christ was not a writer, while Paul was. The Savior of the world left behind him no documents, but only a vision and a message for his followers to record at second and often third and fourth hand. But the greatest preacher of that vision left written texts in abundance, the Epistles, which include the very earliest of Christian texts—much earlier than the Gospels—and which not only explain, but institutionalize and humanize, the apocalyptic, eschatological message of the Messiah himself. There is even some large room for doubt as to how much of so-called primitive Christianity is a preservation of the original message of Christ, and how much is the Pauline interpretation of that message. I have mentioned glossolalia, speaking in tongues, as a prerogative of the shamanic vision out of which the later idea of a socialized "church" is formed. And Paul is especially subtle in his First Letter to the Corinthians, who apparently were much given to speaking in tongues and to other ecstatic modes of behavior. He writes:

> For he that speaketh in an unknown tongue speaketh not unto men, but unto God: for no man understandeth him; how be it in the spirit he speaketh mysteries. But he that prophesieth speaketh unto men to edification, and exhortation, and comfort. He that speaketh in an unknown tongue edifieth himself; but he that prophesieth edifieth the church. I would that ye all spake with tongues, but rather that ye prophesied: for greater is he that prophesieth than he that speaketh with tongues, except he interpret, that the church may receive edifying [1 Corinthians 14:2–5].

This epistle is one of the earliest Christian documents, and it is important to notice that Paul is careful here to distinguish between speaking (in tongues) and prophesying (to the church). The first kind of speech is proper to the relationship between the believer and God, the second to the relationship between the believer and other believers: and "greater is he that prophesieth." We may remember (as Hans Küng observes in *The Church*) that in the Gospels themselves, the recorded sayings of Christ, Christ almost never uses the word "church," *ekklesia,* for the community he comes to establish, but rather uses the work "kingdom," *basileia.* Paul's role, then, a necessary one in the history of any culture, is to transform *basileia* into *ekklesia,* to socialize and historicize the apocalyptic message of the god whose revelation he both preaches and interprets. The king, in other words, remains the king, but his radically originating kingship becomes diffused and socialized through the activity of his emissaries to history, his knights.

There is something innately lesser about the romance world. I have already examined the secondary, melancholy quality of even the greatest epic works, their sense that something larger, perhaps transcendent, has been left behind by the time they begin. But the melancholy of romance narrative is more focused, more specific. It is the explicit knowledge, on the part of the romance hero himself, that he is subordinate. To be a knight, after all, means to be grander, more civilized, more noble and more fully human than the great mass of human beings, a carrier of culture and decency to the otherwise savage herd: but it also means to be not a king.

Nowhere is this elementary irony better caught or expressed than in the thirteenth-century *Quest of the Holy Grail,* a part of the long prose romance usually called the *Lancelot,* composed probably by Cistercian monks. The *Quest* repeats the story of how the knights of Arthur's court set off in search of the Grail, that mysterious sacramental substance, in order to find it and in finding it restore health and vitality to the wounded Fisher King, whose land suffers from the same lingering impotence as he does. And, as every version of the Grail Quest makes clear, the adventures of the knights in search of the sacred object are the end, the breaking of the round table: simultaneously the purpose for which Arthur was impelled to found his splendid kingdom and the dissolution, the transcendence by a higher order, of that kingdom (and we may recognize in this detail a very self-conscious expression of the displacement of the king by the later, lesser, but necessarily more civilized knight). A poignant detail repeated in version after version of the story is that as soon as the Grail is mysteriously revealed to the knights of Arthur's court and as soon as the mission of the court—the Quest—is announced to them, their first response, king and knights alike, is not to rush enthusiastically to the fray, but to weep—to weep for the aboriginal, secular world which has been forever shattered by the irruption into it of a more humane, but also a more complicated, order of belief.

This order, the order of romance, is also the order of allegory, that is, of actions and details whose "true" meaning is other than their surface meaning. For the romance world is always explicitly secondary, always explicitly the acting-out, the socialization of the founding act of the epic kings. I may remark in this context that it is Paul, the knight of Christ, who invents one of the great and controlling allegories of Western civilization, the idea that though the Savior himself in his physical form has departed from this world, he remains here in his "mystical body," that is, the church itself. But the Cistercian *Quest* is even more fully conscious of itself as allegorical, and as the sort of fiction which makes allegory possible. The *Quest* relates how three of Arthur's knights succeed, in varying degrees, in finding the Grail. Percival (who in his Welsh incarnation as "Peredur" was probably the original Grail knight) is a living allegory of something like innocent emotion deprived of the aid of mature reason, the pure fool whose goodheartedness makes up for the multitude of his errors in judgment. Bors, Percival's antitype, represents a mature, sometimes gloomy rationalism that finds its salvation within the mazes of thought rather than through the childlike transports of enthusiasm. And between Percival and Bors stands the perfect knight, Galahad, the ideal balance of reason and emotion, the human double of Christ himself, destined in his search for the Grail to recapitulate the whole range of Christ's own gospel, but to recapitulate that gospel in an explicitly lower, later key.

The same rhythm occurs in all the adventures of the Grail knights: the knight encounters a mysterious test, passes or significantly fails that test, and then meets a holy hermit or a wise old man who explains to him the moral allegory and the scriptural allusions of his adventure. Stated baldly like this, the story sounds absurd, childishly reductive. But it is not. The rhythm of the knights' adventures finally establishes itself with an undeniable, highly self-conscious authority. We are aware that we are reading not only a tale about, but a disquisition upon, the inevitably secondary nature of the romance world. Early in the *Quest,* one of the apparently myriad hermits explains it this way to Galahad:

> For just as folly and error fled at His advent and truth stood revealed, even so has Our Lord chosen you from among all other knights to ride abroad through many lands to put an end to the hazards that afflict them and make their meaning and their causes plain. This is why your coming must be compared to the coming of Jesus Christ, in semblance only, not in sublimity.*

It would be difficult to find a more concise or elegant summary of the characteristic action of knightly romance than this passage, or one which more firmly makes the point that the romance narrative is precisely that story told *after,* and in civilizing clarification of, the epic story of the founders (be they kings or messiahs).

Of course, the *Quest* is itself a "secondary" romance, a deliberate revision and purification of the often adulterous matter of earlier courtly love romances. But even the earliest and—from the Cistercian point of view—most "pagan" romances are definitively secondary in the way I have been describing. One of the most brilliant and most complicated of the lays of Marie de France is the tale of Gugemar, a heroic knight who scorns the gentle, civilizing emotion of love and places his whole joy in the exclusively manly activity of hunting. And the plot of this short romance is designed to chasten Gugemar for his inappropriate (can we say, pre-neolithic) emphasis on primally heroic rather than courtly, knightly behavior: he is miraculously wounded by one of his own arrows, and can only cure his pain by undertaking a mysterious voyage, falling in love with a beautiful

* Tr. P. M. Matarasso (Middlesex, Eng.: Penguin Books, 1969).

lady, losing her and winning her again from the power of the epic rapist king Meriadus. Gugemar, that is, has to learn that he lives in a romance world and that the epic energy of the founders and warriors needs to be channeled and sublimated into the energies of courtship—courtly, courteous behavior.

We can say, indeed, that the relationship of the romance knight to the epic king is always one of "diminished doubling": the knight is the image of the king, but in a universe of story that can no longer tolerate the disruptive, founding, but chaotic presence of the king himself. For the knight to be born, the king must die; or at least, his work done, retire to the noninterfering passivity of chairman of the board. Thus in the Cistercian *Quest* the doubling between Galahad and Christ is a complementary and creative one, while in *Gugemar* the doubling between Gugemar and Meriadus is murderous, for Gugemar must learn to slay the epic, hunting, unromantic king within himself.

The film version of *The Prisoner of Zenda* (1937), based on Anthony Hope's famous novel, has become stereotyped as the perfect example of that thirties blend of costume, swashbuckling, and ultimately prurient petting called "Ruritanian Romance." But in its way, and much more so than the original novel, it makes significant and witty use of the characteristics I have identified in my more general idea of romance as a prime variety of storytelling. The motif of doubling between king and knight, for example, is expressed in the film by having the two pivotal characters, Rudolph Rassendyl and King Rudolf V, both played by Ronald Colman. Rassendyl, a virile and thoroughly competent Englishman, arrives in Rudolf's kingdom for a fishing trip only to discover that he is (except for his beard) the very image of the king who is about to be coronated. But Rudolf has been a frivolous, irresponsible prince, and is furthermore being plotted against by his evil brother, Black Michael (played with fine nastiness by Raymond Massey). The king is ab-

ducted on the eve of his coronation—a disgraceful derelic-
tion of etiquette that will ensure Michael's coronation in the
king's place—but Rassendyl is persuaded by the loyal old
Colonel Zapt (C. Aubrey Smith) to take the king's place
until he can be rescued. The masquerade goes on, with Rassendyl actually behaving better, more nobly, as king than
anyone would have expected the real Rudolf to act. He even
falls in love with the princess Flavia (Madeleine Carroll),
who has been reluctantly betrothed to the king, and she
with him. But the imposture is suspected by Michael, and by
his dashing, totally amoral and totally admirable henchman
Rupert (Douglas Fairbanks, Jr.). Things become complicated to the point that a daring rescue of the real king has to
be attempted, with of course Rassendyl leading the attempt.
Black Michael is killed in the course of the rescue mission,
and the film reaches its climax with a long, brilliantly
choreographed swordfight between Rassendyl and Rupert—
at the end of which Rupert escapes by diving into the moat
surrounding the castle where the king languishes in prison
and swimming to freedom. The rightful king restored to his
rightful place, Rassendyl must return to his own proper
identity and to England, leaving behind the beautiful
Princess Flavia, who in the penultimate scene of the film
declares her love for Rassendyl (whom she now knows to *be*
Rassendyl) while nevertheless insisting that she must remain
loyal to her country, her royal role, and the fate that assigns
her to be the bride of the feckless, but now chastened, King
Rudolf V.

A summary of the action of *The Prisoner of Zenda* as short
as this is bound to make the film seem more improbable,
more cliche-ridden than it actually is. But we can extract
from this summary a number of important and definitive
"romance" elements. Rassendyl's masquerade, like the action of any good knight of romance, is a flurry of civilizing
activity whose essential result is the clarification of personal
relationships and the purification of relationships between

the sovereign and his people: the education, that is, of the king. For that is what the action of the film comes to. The king, finally, will be crowned, will assume the duties of his office—but only after having been educated by and, in some sense, translated into the less self-assertive, more humane figure of the knightly Rassendyl.

Rassendyl himself, of course, has to learn the perquisites and responsibilities of his knightly role. Like Gugemar, like the Percival of the original Grail stories, he begins his career as an unselfconsciously "natural" man, an unassuming Englishman on a vacation fishing trip (we may remember here Gugemar's original passion for hunting). He first meets his double the king in one of the very few "outdoors" scenes of this exclusively sound-stage film as he has begun fishing. As he proceeds with his masquerade as King Rudolf, though, he also progresses toward a fuller understanding of his own possibilities for decency and heroism. Falling in love with Princess Flavia is the crucial experience, for Rassendyl, of the charade on which he has embarked. For once he has fallen in love with her, it is impossible for him to take the imposture simply as a game anymore. It is also impossible, though, for him to carry the game-turned-serious to its logical conclusion by bedding or marrying the woman with whom he has fallen in love.

I have already remarked on the presence of "courtly love" or, more simply, "romantic love" in romance narrative. And without getting involved in the complicated debate over the precise nature and origin of the idea of courtly love, one can at least observe that it is usually adulterous, usually suggests that the life of the passions is the most important and most problematical area of human existence, and usually involves the love of a knight for the wife of a king (Lancelot and Guinevere, Tristan and Isolde, Gugemar and Meriadus's lady, Rudolph Rassendyl and Flavia). There is probably some point of seeing this perennial courtly love situation—a knight-queen gambit behind the king's back—as in itself a parable of the latter-day civilization of the romance world. For courtly love, in this reading, insists not just that heroic action makes sense only in terms of the hero's dedication to his lady, but also that the hero of the later world, the secondary world of the court and courtesy, must come to terms in some way with his passion for the bride (the soul? the erotic projection?) of that very epic king whom he serves and supplants.

In this respect, at any rate, the essential situation of courtly love is not simply an accident of medieval psychopathology casting its malign shadow over even the less enlightened lovers of our own time, but an ancient and quite profound, quite inexhaustible myth: the myth of Oedipus and his mother/lover Jocasta, or of any of the revolutionary, civilizing deities of primitive religion who establish their reign by supplanting their larger, more violent progenitor gods and then wedding the father's bride, the great goddess who is simultaneously earth, kingdom, and eternally desirable, eternally humanizing and civilizing woman. *Das ewig Weiblich / Zieht uns hinan,* writes Goethe in the last great chorus of *Faust:* the eternal feminine leads us upward. It might be the epigraph for the entire romance tradition.

The Prisoner of Zenda is an especially innocent and therefore especially instructive version of romance narrative in film. It is literally packed with doubles, with good knights striving to be bad kings and bad kings unaware that they are good knights. Foremost among these is Rupert, the accomplice of the pretender Michael, a jaunty, witty killer. Douglas Fairbanks, Jr., not only looks like Ronald Colman (who is already, of course, doubled in the film), he talks like Colman. Rupert is the bad knight or the overambitious king who represents not only the greatest danger to Rassendyl in his charade, but in fact the negative side of Rassendyl, the shadow-projection of his own potential worst characteristics (gaiety become inhuman frivolity, insouciance become cruelty). The climactic scene of the film, then, is naturally a

battle not between Rassendyl and Michael, but between
Rassendyl and Rupert—between Rudolph, twin of Rudolf,
and Rupert. It is a central aspect of the story's subtlety that
Rupert is defeated in this last swordfight, but not killed: for
the shadow is never really killed, only suppressed in the in-
terests of civilization.

In *The Prisoner of Zenda* the relationship of knight to
king, priest to shaman, is imagined in terms of doubling,
twinship, lighter or darker mirror reflections between the
two narrative worlds those two archetypal figures imply.
But in a film like Howard Hawks's *Red River* (1948) the
relationship is both more complex and more potentially
murderous. If *Zenda,* that is, gives us the romance world at
its most immediately attractive and its most comprehensible,
Red River shows us the deep risks underlying that surface
myth of civility and courtesy. For king and knight, shaman
and priest in this story are not simply twins, the one humanizing the other, but more problematically father and son,
originator and continuator, the one humanizing the other at
the possible cost of his own individuality, his own life. In
Zenda the warfare is between the true king and true knight
and their false doubles, but never between king and knight
themselves. In *Red River* though, the warfare *is* between the
true king and the true knight, the father and the son, locked
in a struggle whose history is the history of the form we are
now describing, and also the history of society's image of itself.

Adapted by Borden Chase from his novel *The Chisholm
Trail, Red River* is the story of the founding, growth, and
final triumph of the cattle empire begun by Tom Dunson
(John Wayne) and carried on by his adopted son Matthew
Garth (Montgomery Clift). As the film begins, the young
Tom Dunson is about to leave a westbound wagon train to
search for a piece of land of his own. He takes with him his
grumbling sidekick Groot (Walter Brennan) but leaves behind, promising to return to her, his lovely young fiancée,

Fen (Coleen Gray). Dunson and Groot have traveled a day's journey when they discover that the wagon train has been ambushed by Indians and every member of it, including Fen, slaughtered. Every member, that is, except the young Matt Garth, a boy who has witnessed the massacre of his parents and whom Dunson takes along with him on his journey to the promised land. Dunson finds his land, south of the Red River, and defends it from threatening Mexicans with sudden and brutal efficiency.

So far, the film is a perfect model of the epic paradigm: the founder of the land, the man who walls in and defines the human space of a given culture, must be both deprived of his "natural" passional life (the death of Fen, in this respect, is almost a ritual sacrifice) and trained to a seemingly heartless, mythically inhuman disregard for his own or others' lives. But this is only the first episode of *Red River*. In a dissolve which is among the most eloquent sequences in film, we move from Dunson, Groot, and the young Matt immediately after the final winning of the Red River territory to the older Dunson, the yet older Groot, and the now-mature Matt twenty years later, after the Red River ranch has become a gigantic success and at the moment it is about to be driven into bankruptcy by Dunson's own refusal to move with the changes of the times. The dissolve catches the three men—sidekick, founder, and heir—in exactly the same position, posed against the massive background of the American West. But, as the rest of the film exists to indicate, twenty years have shifted the center of that dynamic triangle: it is now the younger man, Matt Garth, the knight come into his inheritance, who will dominate and finally justify the action of the film.

As the title of Chase's original novel indicates, the story of *Red River* is based on a historical fact of some importance in the opening of the west. It is the story of the first herd of cattle to be driven along the Chisholm Trail from Texas to Abilene, Kansas—a cattle drive that opened a new route for the movement of livestock from the West to the eastern markets, and therefore played an important role in the consolidation of the United States as an economic and social entity. Thus at heart the story is about trade routes and their effect upon human culture: one of the oldest and richest themes of storytelling. But in this film the finding of the right trade route is also the establishment of the right inheritance for the kingdom, for the Red River brand.

Dunson, as befits an epic king or founder, is a hard man, closed to passion (except for his kingdom) and incapable of bending. And his adopted son Matt Garth is at once his complement and his completion, sensitive, open to new suggestions, amenable to the suasions of love and courtesy—and a better man. It was an accident of history and casting that created the dominant tension of *Red River*, between Wayne and Clift. For Wayne, after nearly twenty years in second-rate Westerns (excepting *Stagecoach*) was finally allowed here to act out that archetypal role which has since been forever his, the role of founder, of savior, of primal civilizer; while Clift, whose first film this was, established here better than in any of his other films the special vulnerability, sensitivity, near-femininity that were to be the hallmarks of his screen personality. Wayne as Dunson speaks in Wayne-ese, in that flat and nasal speech which thousands of nightclub imitators have tried to mimic, while Clift as Garth speaks in the hesitating, almost-but-not-quite-stammering tones that he bequeathed to a whole generation of actors (Dean, McQueen, Brando, Newman). And the conflict between the acting styles, between the speech habits of the two stars of this film is almost a sketch of its fundamental mythic situation. For the film insists that the king must not simply die, but be transformed into his complement and completion, the knight. Which is to say that, with regard to the primal and perennial battle between the father and the son, the son, the knight, the weaker member of the team—at least in *this* fable of identity—wins.

In terms of the plot of the film, the central quarrel between Dunson and Garth is how to lead their cattle to Abilene, where the railroad waits to pick up the cattle and ship
them east at a gigantic profit. Dunson has staked his entire
fortune on one last cattle drive north, attempting to win
through inhospitable land and hostile Indians by sheer force
of will and guns. But Garth has heard of a new cattle trail,
blazed by a man called Chisholm, that might save the men
on the cattle drive a great deal of trouble and might also
allow a great deal more cattle to survive the journey from
Texas to Kansas. Dunson, naturally, does not want to follow Garth's suggested plan, since it is both a violation of established custom and, more important, an infringement of
Dunson's own authority.

As the trail drive progresses, however, it becomes clearer
and clearer that Dunson is wrong, and that Garth is right.
Dunson begins to drink on the drive, and to bully the men
he has hired to accompany him. When a stampede occurs,
causing the death of one man, Dunson is unrelenting in his
effort to humiliate and punish the cowboy who inadver-
tently began the stampede. Finally, Matt Garth can no
longer tolerate the injustices of his symbolic father. When
three cowboys attempt to escape from Dunson's control he
sends his henchmen after them. But as they are brought
back before Dunson, who intends to kill them, Matt Garth
intervenes, saving their lives and thereby jeopardizing his
own: Dunson—drunk, helpless, and universally hated—
swears to pursue and kill Garth.

The rest of the film is a lengthly chase sequence. It is the
story of Matthew Garth's following the Chisholm Trail with
his cattle and of Tom Dunson's pursuit of Garth along the
same path. But Dunson never really realizes how crucial or
how epochal is the road he follows. The king, in other
words, is here not murdered, superseded, or doubled, but
educated. And he is educated by being led along the same
road the knight has previously traveled. Matt Garth's jour-

ney leads him to a chance encounter with a wagon train
besieged by Indians: a recapitulation both of his own original orphanage and Dunson's aboriginal loss of love. But
time—mythic time at least—is here reversed. For here, in the
midst of an Indian attack, Garth meets the beautiful Tess
Millay (Joanne Dru) with whom he falls in love and who finally aids him in his own struggle against Tom Dunson.

But that part of the film is yet to come. Tess Millay is not
a simple girl, but rather a prostitute (or, in that hallowed
circumlocution of Western films, a dance-hall girl) whose
place of business, in transit on her wagon train, has been
saved by the virginal Matt Garth. She is, in other words, a
whore whose heart of gold is to feature as the chief narrative device of the story yet to be told. For she does fall in
love with Matt—and, as Matt proceeds northward toward
Abilene with his cattle, Tess stays behind to meet his neme-
sis, Dunson, and to try and convince Dunson to abandon his
insane quest for vengeance. Her pleas are finally unavailing,
though, and Dunson follows Garth to Abilene, where Garth
was already sold, at a gigantic profit, all the cattle of the
Red River brand. In the final scene Garth, supported by the
whole town, walks out to meet Dunson, who enters town
alone. And after Dunson fails to force Garth to draw his
guns—for the knight, whatever the faults of his king, remains loyal to that primal authority—the two men begin a
fistfight that only ends when Tess fires a gun between them
and hysterically tells them that, since they obviously love
each other, they should begin to act as if they loved each
other. And at this point, perhaps the last sixty seconds of
the film, what had threatened to be the murderous conflict
between the founding father and the gentle son turns to
comedy, as Wayne and Clift stare bewildered at each other
and exchange appreciative comments about the woman
Matt is obviously going to marry.

The end of *Red River* disappoints some viewers, since it

seems to transmute the stuff of epochal tragedy into domestic comedy. But, of course, that is just the point of romance narrative. At the end of Borden Chase's original novel Dunson is fatally wounded—though not by Garth—and Garth and Tess take the dying patriarch back to Texas where he dies just after crossing the Red River. The original ending was changed because—so goes the folklore of Hollywood— John Wayne, a good friend of director Hawks, did not wish to die at the end of a movie in which he was starring. True as the reason for it may be, though, the film's variation from the novel actually makes the film a better story. For the relationship between Dunson and Garth is not the tale of a revolution, but rather of a natural growth and even of a profound complementarity. Garth is the humanization of Dunson, and as such the completion of the empire which Dunson founds.

We may even describe this complementarity in terms of the image of the wagon train—the little community of men on a perilous journey into the inhuman wilderness—as it affects the lives of the two central figures. The wagon train is civilization on wheels, the possibility of family life, of solidarity, of human survival outside the cosmic risks of epic struggle or romance questing: it is, in other words, an image of the *ordinary* life whose stability is ensured by the activities of the king and the knight. There are, furthermore, two wagon trains in *Red River,* and both of them are attacked by Indians. Both, that is, are threatened by whatever it is that lies outside the border of civilization, whatever is conscious but not yet fully human (the appalling racism of this element of the story needs no comment, but is nevertheless, within the conventions of the Western, a crucial feature of the plot). At the opening of the film, Dunson, the epic figure, leaves the wagon train—and his lady love—in order to found his empire. But the empire, once founded, has to be humanized. And at the second turning point of the film,

Garth, the romance quester, finds a wagon train—and
thereby finds his own lady love—in order, ultimately, to
continue the empire founded by Dunson.

Dunson's world is a world of minimal enclosure—the
ranch, the cattle range which has just been fenced in to distinguish it from the chaotic expanse of unclaimed nature.
But Garth, Dunson's heir, is at home also in the more fully
consolidated civilization of the city itself. And the pursuit
which makes up the second half of the film is also, importantly, a journey *toward* a city—a city which is also located
along that crucial artery of modern trade and civilization,
the railroad. So that Matt Garth's journey to the city with
his (and Dunson's) herd of cattle is not just a demonstration
of his maturity and fitness to inherit from the patriarch, but
also a journey toward his own appropriate context, his own
proper allegorical locale. This is nowhere better caught than
in the eerily moving scenes after Garth has reached Abilene,
where there is not enough corral space for his herd. The
cattle are driven into the streets of the town, and a sequence
of shots shows us the cattle standing, sleeping, and lowing
among the streets and stores of the city: a truly mythic meeting of two worlds, two narrative universes whose conflict
and reconciliation is the plot of the whole of *Red River*.

The Lost World

Wayne's performance in *Red River* is complex, alternating
between regal authority and violent, crazy frustration at his
loss of control. And as such, it teaches us something important about the special melancholy of the epic king in the
romance world.

I have already mentioned, in Chapter 1, the strong importance, for the story-cycle I am tracing, of the Arthurian
legends of the Middle Ages. The creation of a multitude of
storytellers, largely anonymous, the Arthurian cycle is the
most complex and complete story sequence we have, rang-

ing through almost every level of story, every variety of archetypal plot. But the Arthurian stories are most firmly associated with the romance world of knights who act out and thereby render practical the civilizing laws of a single, heroic founder.

And more than any genre of American film—or any tradition of film—the Western reduplicates the possibilities and the abiding concerns of romance. Its perennial subject is the City already founded on the edge of the frontier; the world between the world of the kings and our world, the indispensable middle phase in any myth of civilization, the phase in which the wisdom of the god-kings is transmuted into a human standard of courtesy, in which the world is made safe not only for human survival, but also for love. (It is interesting, in this respect, that both Arthurian legend from the vantage point of the High Middle Ages and Western romance from the vantage point of twentieth-century America are set in "olden times"—times, that is, significantly earlier than the times in which the stories are produced, but also times significantly closer to the era of the producers than the aboriginal, time-instituting age of the founders themselves.)

In a way, then, the king, the central figure of epic myth, is still importantly present in the romance world, but present in his decline, or rather in his moment of passing, ceding the world to the later, lesser, but necessary figure of the knight. This is clearest in Arthurian romance itself: Arthur, the great king, gives his name to the cycle of stories built around his court, but Arthur himself in the stories plays the role mainly of spectator to the adventures of his knights, and of course the role also of cuckold, since his queen, Guinevere, is involved in an adulterous liaison with Lancelot.

The same situation exists in the story of Tristan and Iseult, perhaps more subtly: Tristan, the perfect knight of King Mark's court, is the lover of Mark's bride Iseult. His perfection, in other words, masks an imperfection, a sin, which makes him not less but rather more a knightly figure, since it casts him and his mistress into a moral dilemma whose complexity Mark's world does not admit. Tristan and Isolde have remained two of the most perennially fascinating figures of Western myth precisely because their romance (in both senses of the word) is not so much a simple tale of adultery as it is the discovery of the sociology of the passions. They are betrayed into their love for each other by a magic potion, and while they cannot struggle against their passion, they can and do analyze it, talk about it, and attempt to find a space for it in the preexisting world of their loyalty to the king. They attempt to be true, in other words, both to each other and to the sovereign whom their love betrays. It is literally a murderous dilemma for them, but one that represents an important phase in the history of the human City. Adultery, after all, is not merely a sin, but the lyrical acknowledgment of the growing tension, in the romance world, between private and public responsibilities. It is the love which challenges the absoluteness of the king's epic order, and which introduces into culture another level of moral choice, fidelity not to the idea of the state but to the idea of the court, the assembly of individuals whose passions, by becoming civilized, form a kind of counter-institution to the earlier, official institution of marriage and kinship. Or, put another way, we can say that only in the romance phase of story does love itself become possible.

But, again it is only against the institution of marriage that the romance "institution" of faithful adultery can define itself. It is only against the shadowy but agonized and affecting figure of King Mark of Cornwall that the passion of Tristan and Iseult makes sense. From the viewpoint of romance, the king's world is a lost world, or a world in process of being lost, of disappearing. But it is important that enough of it remain visible for the romance world, the knight and his lady, to remember whence they embark on their own perilous journey of civilization. Shakespeare's *An-*

tony and Cleopatra, for example—though a much greater work than either Gottfried van Strassburg's *Tristan* or *Red River*—does not operate in this way. The illicit passion of Antony and Cleopatra is more daringly, more problematically realized than that of the other lovers, just because it exists independently, corrosively, with its own dark brilliance apart from any real relationship to the world of kings or the world of authoritative moral orders against which it can define itself. Antony's rival, the soon-to-be emperor Octavius, and Cleopatra's Egyptian deities are weak, remote figureheads in the moral universe of the play; they may destroy the lovers but they cannot command the lovers' serious regard. And thus the play, for all its brillance, is, unlike the structured adulteries of the romance world, a moral chaos.

Wayne in the American Western plays much the same role as does the figure of Arthur or Mark in medieval romance. He is the aging king whose reign is in process not so much of dissolution as of transformation into the later, more morally complicated and dangerous world of the knight. Wayne's assumption of this role begins in *Red River,* as I have said—and in a more interestingly "Arthurian" fashion than the film alone indicates. For in Borden Chase's original novel, Tess Millay is not only the dance-hall girl whom young Matthew Garth—the passionate and introspective knight—eventually marries, but has also previously been the mistress of the aging patriarch Tom Dunson. Because of the Oedipal implications of this state of affairs, Chase excised that detail from his screenplay for *Red River.* But, indeed, the love of the knight for the king's bride is always fraught with Oedipal implications. Or, looked at the other way around, the Oedipus story itself is a kind of paradigmatic romance: out of the austere universe of gods and founders emerges, in the Oedipus legend, the figure of the rational, civilizing hero whose passions lead him to a cataclysmic confrontation with that older authority, and also to the discovery of a new, internalized moral imagination of the self.

Wayne's incarnations of the lost or disappearing world of the epic founders continue from *Red River* to his most recent Westerns. In *The Man Who Shot Liberty Valance, Rio Bravo, The Searchers, True Grit, The Cowboys,* and *The Shootist* he portrays, with an authority that finally does become truly mythic, the king as seen from the vantage point of romance. In each of these films Wayne is paired with another figure, either younger or more vulnerable, more fallible; e.g. James Stewart's eastern lawyer in *Valance,* Jeffrey Hunter's sensitive young man in *The Searchers,* Glen Campbell's callow Texas Ranger in *True Grit.* And in each film, to one degree or another, Wayne's benevolent patriarchy saves, reforms, or initiates the younger figure. The king's phased withdrawal from his role, in other words, clarifies and creates the function of knighthood.

This aspect of Western romance, moreover, has played an important part in the recent political history of America (as the central myths of storytelling always do in a given culture, however complicatedly). "John Wayne," during the years of America's involvement in the disastrous Southeast Asian war, was not only a proper name but a common noun, an adjective, a projectile word fraught with political implications. Indeed, I think it is fair to say that a whole generation of war protestors probably had to wait until the end of the Vietnamese adventure before they could really *see* a John Wayne film. And this is not simply because Wayne himself, in his public statements during the sixties and early seventies, established himself as one of the Hollywood hawks. It has to do, rather, with his definitive role in our national mythology and with a cognitive dissonance between that role and the state of chaos into which the war cast the mythology itself. For surely, one aspect of the war was the way its savagery and waste undermined the nation's confidence in its "kings," the way it revealed an elementary bankruptcy in a presidency which, throughout the sixties, was significantly referred to as "imperial." But it was a decade when the Emperor's clothes were increasingly regarded as, if not nonexistent, at least disgracefully shabby. One president was assassinated, another driven from seeking re-election, and a third finally forced to resign in the most severe scandal of the century: not an age for kings, nor for the knights of the Pentagon and the Senate who attempted to carry out their bidding. So that Wayne's mime of authoritarian and withdrawn patriarchy was bound to become, even if he had not involved himself in the debate over the war, a metaphor for what was wrong with us rather than what was best about us. Even before the height of the debate and the most violent of the protest marches, soldiers in Vietnam were referring to acts of battlefield bravura in this absurd cause with the contemptuous phrase "John Wayne-ing it"; and the final collapse of the "student revolution" from political protest to a despairing escape into the privacy of pharmacological and erotic obsession, the decay of the "Movement" into Woodstock Nation, can remind us of that other vision of erotic chaos in the moment of the king's departure, *Antony and Cleopatra*.

But such moments of chaos, however bright or outrageous, cannot last. The human mind naturally orders its experience, naturally imposes a form and a sense on the world around it: language and storytelling are species-specific instincts with us. And so it is, also, with cultures: they cannot choose but recapitulate the archetypes, for the archetypes are the very way in which cultures exist. All I have been saying about the romance hero indicates how much the world of romance is a world of moral dubieties, of confusions between private passion and public responsibility, and of the attempt to resolve those confusions through an ideal of knighthood where power and courtesy are held in balance.

The Perils of Heroism

Another way of looking at the relationship between the epic and the romance worlds is to think in terms of the transition from *comitatus* to court. We have seen that the society, the minimal City, surrounding the king is a kind of military or paramilitary fellowship of warriors—the *Mannerbund* or *comitatus*—whose ethics is one of energetic and ferocious individual prowess combined with energetic and ferocious individual loyalty to the king. This loyalty, though, as the *Iliad, Beowulf,* and *Ivan the Terrible* all make clear, is a loyalty won on strictly personal grounds by the aboriginal king or (to use again the suggestive kenning of *Beowulf*) "ring-giver": it is the moral equivalent of the barter phase of primitive economics. But as the world of epic foundations is considered it merges imperceptibly into the romance world of a more abstract, more generalized order, where individual loyalty is replaced by the more difficult but also richer concept of fealty.

The two words, to be sure, mean much the same. But "fealty," laden as it is with associations of abstract faith and oaths of observance, accurately catches the special moral universe of the romance hero. Loyalty may be pledged to a person, but fealty is sworn to an idea: the idea of the state, of the culture, the idea which is the bequest of the founding king to his heirs and to history itself. If the loyalty of the warrior-band to its chief is the equivalent of barter (I shall remain constant if the king provides for me), fealty is the equivalent of the idea of currency or symbolic wealth (I am constant because the king represents the state's promises for me). Whatever is functional, emergent, or practical in the *comitatus* becomes—through a necessary social and mythic evolution—symbolic, ornamental, instituted in the court: and this is true whether we are thinking of the hero, his weapons and armor, or the idea of the City itself.

We saw the beginnings of this transition, to be sure, in the last works examined in the preceeding chapter. Both the *Aeneid* and *Ivan the Terrible* show us founder-kings whose loyalty (or fealty) is to an abstract idea of the state whose full range of implication is far beyond that of the most primal epics. If it is only at the romance phase of story-telling that love becomes possible as a centrally motivating factor in human behavior, then surely it is significant that both the *Aeneid* and *Ivan* treat love more fully than any other epic narratives. Aeneas' doomed love for Dido and Ivan's doomed love for Anastasia are, in this way, nearly transitional elements of storytelling, indications both of what is forbidden to the founding kings (the life of private passion within the life of public responsibility) and of what the king's own sacrifice makes possible for his heirs and executors, the simultaneously heroic and loving knights.

But if, as we have said, the king must learn courtesy, gentility, and civilization from the knight, the knight must also learn: must learn that he *is* a knight, not a king, and the limitations of his prowess and possibilities that difference implies. With the emergence of the figure of the knight, in other words, the idea of initiation itself becomes possible, because the king his symbolic father has established a culture, a system of symbols, for the younger man to be initiated *into*. A remarkable number of romance narratives, both literary and film, are concerned primarily with the education of a young man into the symbols and duties of his cultural role: since, at the romance level, culture itself becomes institutionalized, the culture hero of this phase of storytelling will naturally be the man whose main activity is learning the degrees and complexities of that institution. The "lost world" of the king, that is, is regained, found again, in the symbolic universe inhabited by the knightly initiate.

But the learning process itself can be a bitter one. *The Song of Roland* is one of the earliest of the great narratives of the Middle Ages, and possesses almost none of the qualities of grace, fantasy, or charm we usually associate with the term "romance." And yet, for all its harshness and "primitiveness," it obviously belongs to this phase of storytelling. In fact, it can almost be taken as a paradigm of the romance world, an archaic, preliminary summation of the concerns which obsess this kind of narrative.

I have discussed *Beowulf* as a complex essay on the idea of kingship. *The Song of Roland* may be taken as its completion and complement, an archetypal examination of the idea of knighthood—an idea which the poem's hero does not fully understand himself until the end of the poem, when it is too late.

G. K. Chesterton described the poem as "the glorification of failure." But the failure *Roland* glorifies—or commemorates—is precisely the failure of its hero to comprehend the world he inhabits, to understand the transition from *comitatus* to court. As Charlemagne and his army retreat north from Spain after their successful campaign against the Moors, Roland, the greatest of Charlemagne's warriors, is given the difficult and dangerous task of marshaling the rear guard of the army. This task has been assigned Roland by Ganelon (or Guenes), his vengeful and traitorous kinsman, who out of envy for Roland's prestige has agreed to help the pagan king Marsilie ambush the Christians at the pass at Roncesvalles. The ambush occurs, with the French army massively outnumbered, and Roland—in one of the most famous and foolhardy decisions in world literature—decides to make a heroic stand against the Moors without summoning aid from the rest of the king's army by sounding the alarm on his mighty horn. The decision is at once foolish, noble, and suicidal, for after a day's bloody fighting the Christian knights are decimated. Finally, after repeated urging by his close companion Olivier, Roland does sound the alarm—but it is too late. Charlemagne and the main body of his troops race back to the pass only in time to see the last of the heroic rear guard slaughtered, and to wreak vengeance on the Moorish warriors.

Such is the basic story of *The Song of Roland:* an odd, grim tale upon which to construct a national masterpiece. The bleakness of the poem can seem, especially on a first reading, almost too unrelieved. At the very end, in the last stanza, after Charlemagne has returned to France and executed the traitor Ganelon, there is still no rest, no peace for the beleaguered king. A vision comes to him in sleep calling him to take his army and wage holy war in yet another foreign land:

> And now that King in's vaulted chamber sleeps.
> Saint Gabriel is come from God, and speaks:
> "Summon the hosts, Charles, of thine Empire,
> Go thou by force into the land of Bire,
> King Vivien thou'lt succour there, at Imphe,
> In the city which pagans have besieged.
> The Christians there implore thee and beseech."
> Right loth to go, that Emperour was he:
> "God!" said the King: "My life is hard indeed!"
> Tears filled his eyes, he tore his snowy beard.*

End of poem: but what sort of end *is* this, anyway? Roland is dead, Ganelon is dead, and Charlemagne is off on another, to him deeply depressing, mission of salvation. The depression, though, is largely the point. For the depression is occasioned by the melancholy of the romance world itself, the world in which an ethics of individual accomplishment and individual prowess is supplanted by, transformed into, an ethics of duty, honor, and fealty to an abstract cause—here, the cause of the Christian Empire—which makes men sad just because it reminds them how much their individual wills are in conflict with the larger and more important, impersonal will of the state itself.

The poem both ends and begins not with Roland but with Charlemagne. It opens, "Charles the King, our Emperor the great/Full seven years hath sojourned in Spain." And, both in the poem and in the history of Europe, Charlemagne is the king who consolidates society into empire, into a self-

---

* Tr. C. K. Scott-Moncrieff (Ann Arbor: University of Michigan Press, 1959).

conscious image of the grandeur that was Rome. He is an almost impersonal force, a man whose kingship resides not so much in his individual prowess as in his organizational genius and his fidelity to duty, to the idea of the Christian Empire. One can say, in fact, that Charlemagne represents in the historiography of Europe much of what Arthur represents in its mythography, the king whose greatness makes possible the rich civilization of romance, the civilization based upon his own withdrawal from creation into politics.

But Roland does not realize this. The most heroic and perfect of Charlemagne's knights does not learn, until the very end of his life, the terms of his own knighthood. And this, I think, is the heart of the poem's grim brilliance. I have been insisting that the idea of the City in romance is somehow more "abstract" than it is in the epic mode. And it is surely important, in this respect, that the crucial act of betrayal in *The Song of Roland* involves a transition from loyalty based on kinship to loyalty based on a more generalized idea of political expediency. The traitor Ganelon is Roland's uncle. And when Roland, through Ganelon's machinations, is assigned the duty of guarding the rear of the army, Roland reacts to that assignment in three famous mutually contradictory stanzas, with pride, acceptance, and outrage—but in all three stanzas he is conscious that the duty has been given him, not only for his liege lord Charlemagne, but *by* his kinsman Ganelon. Ganelon, however, has not merely betrayed the elemental ethics of loyalty to kin, he has transcended those ethics for a more complicated—and, in his case—much more evil sort of activity, treachery to the state.

As I said in Chapter I, one way of distinguishing types of story from each other is in terms of the kinds of sin they describe. And if the besetting evil of the epic world is cowardice or betrayal of the divine injunction to create a city, the besetting evil of the romance world is discourtesy—i.e. un-courtliness—or the betrayal of the royal command to preserve the city that has been created. When Ganelon agrees to help the pagan king ambush Charlemagne's army, he undergoes a ritual exchange of arms that seals his transfer of loyalties by making it symbolic, liturgical as well as practical. A series of pagan warriors comes forward, each one offering Ganelon a Moorish weapon in exchange for the Christian weapons, the weapons of Charlemagne's cause, which Ganelon has rejected in agreeing to the treachery:

> In haste there came a pagan, Valdabrun,
> Warden had been to king Marsiliun,
> Smiling and clear, he's said to Guenelun,
> "Take now this sword, and better sword has none;
> Into the hilt a thousand coins are run.
> To you, fair sir, I offer it in love;
> Give us your aid from Rollant the barun,
> That in rereward against him we may come."
> Guenes the count answers: "It shall be done."
> Then, cheek and chin, kissed each the other one.

One of the most common and distinctive features of medieval romance is its emphasis upon symbolic—heraldic—weaponry and costume. In romance, as I have said, you are what you wear. And it is by no means a minor detail of romance narrative that the knight and his major adversaries usually have emblematic names for their swords, their horses, even sometimes for their already heraldic shields. As the liturgy celebrating Ganelon's treachery helps us see, this emphasis upon the symbolic nature of weaponry is itself symbolic, an outward sign of the increased self-consciousness of the state *as* state. Allegory and liturgy, that is, are also institutions. An element of culture becomes symbolic or allegorical—a hero's sword, his coat of arms, the flag, the Washington Monument—by being inserted into a broader, already established system of meanings and significations which determine its own specific signification and which it, in turn, reinforces and develops. Unlike the shield

of Achilles or the weapons of Beowulf, which include or
create their own meanings, and thereby initiate the "meaning" of their respective cultures, the shields and weapons of
the heroes of romance imply or allude to meanings and values that are already central to the very culture which makes
such narrative possible.

Ganelon and the pagan knights understand as much: the
betrayal of Charlemagne's authority is not complete until
there has been a corresponding betrayal or symbolic rejection of the arms that signify Ganelon to be "in the service of
Charlemagne." The glory and the tragedy of Roland, however, is that he still believes in the system of personal, non-
political ethics which his lord's very power and civilization
have transformed. The stand at Roncesvalles is thus, in a
way, both his and his culture's initiation into the new order.
Near the very center of the poem, in the midst of the battle,
Roland finally realizes that the cause is lost without aid
from Charlemagne, and decides to blow his horn. But it is
too late. His comrade Olivier has urged him twice previously to do so, and Roland has proudly refused. And now,
in the crucial stanzas of the poem's moral universe, Olivier—the lesser, but the wiser knight—tells Roland what he
has misunderstood.

CXXX

Then says Rollant: "Strong is it now, our battle;
I'll wind my horn, so the King hears it, Charles."
Says Olivier: "That act were not a vassal's.
When I implored you, comrade, you were wrathful.
Were the King here, we had not borne such damage.
Nor should we blame those with him there, his army."
Says Olivier: "Now by my beard, hereafter
If I may see my gentle sister Alde,
She in her arms, I swear, shall never clasp you."

CXXXI

Then says Rollanz: "Wherefore so wroth with me?"
He answers him: "Comrade, it was your deed:

Vassalage comes by sense, and not folly;
Prudence more worth is than stupidity.
Here are Franks dead, all for your trickery;
No service more to Carlun may we yield.
My lord were here now, had you trusted me,
And fought and won this battle then had we,
Taken or slain were the king Marsilie.
In your prowess, Rollanz, no good we've seen!
Charles the great in vain your aid will seek—
None such as he till God His Judgment speak;—
Here must you die, and France, in shame be steeped;
Here perishes our loyal company,
Before this night great severance and grief."

Oliver's speech is unrelentingly honest. "Stupidity" is the word he applies to Roland's misguided heroism, and in the context of the poem he is, of course, quite right. But Olivier is also careful to give Roland his due. He does not deny or denigrate Roland's prowess, but simply observes that in that bravery "no good we've seen!" Because the function of the knight (or the "vassal," as Scott-Moncrieff's translation has it) is precisely to mediate between the primal, raw courage that makes warriors and the social responsibilities that make a civilization. Indeed, if we substitute sexual passion, that other most primal of emotions, for courage in Olivier's speech, we can see that he could equally well give advice (which would, of course, be equally unheeded) to Tristan.

Roland helps us to see another and crucial romance aspect of that most perennial and stylized of commercial film genres, the American Western: its emphasis upon costume and social function. In the great bulk of Western films, both in the theater and on television, the central character is not the cowboy or the rancher but the marshal, or the marshal's dark double the gunfighter. And marshal and outlaw have a ritual correspondence, defined mainly in terms of their relationship to the established and delegated authority which creates the minimal civilization of the town. The marshal—whose title itself has associations of medieval military organization—is not the maker of the law, but the enforcer, the knight of the law. And, especially in those Westerns which are closest to the elementary formula of the genre, his role is established not only by the way he behaves but by the way he dresses, and the *special,* liturgical quality of his tools—guns, badge, horses with proper names. However the historical Wyatt Earp may have dressed for his daily job, it is impossible for us to think of him, or of his numerous mythic cousins in Western films, without a string tie, a vest, or a western-style suit. And this generalized uniform serves precisely to mark, to allegorize, his social function. In John Ford's *My Darling Clementine,* perhaps the best and certainly the least historically accurate film about Earp, the symbolism of clothing is one of the major elements of the plot itself.

In *Clementine,* Earp (Henry Fonda) and his brothers come to Tombstone on a cattle drive; Wyatt has given up marshaling after Dodge City and is determined to return to the "natural" life of the cowboy. But their cattle are rustled by the Clanton brothers, who also kill James, Wyatt's youngest brother, in the cattle raid. So Wyatt accepts the job offered him as town marshal of Tombstone, finally winning his revenge against the Clantons in the famous gunfight at the O.K. Corral. After the gunfight Wyatt leaves Tombstone, to return to his father's ranch and once again attempt to live the life of the cowboy.

The whole film, not unusually for a John Ford Western, is an elegant essay on civilization and the discourtesies—ranging from murder to faithlessness—that threaten civilization. Nature itself is both the sustaining force of and the permanent threat to Ford's idea of culture. Disciplined and humanized by gentleness and charity, it is the motivating force and the very center of a truly human culture. But undisciplined, unorganized, it becomes the Darwinian rapaciousness which turns men into killers. Earp is the man who strikes the balance, and the film contrasts him to two figures who incarnate the failures of civilization.

As Pa Clanton, Walter Brennan acts out a savagery which has never known order. His role is that of the undisciplined, disastrously "natural" man, as one of the most effective scenes of the film makes clear. On the morning of the gunfight at the O.K. Corral, the camera shows us a landscape of pure horizon broken only by an indeterminate mass which may be either a mountain peak in the background or a human figure in the foreground of the shot. As dawn breaks we see that it is Pa Clanton waiting for the Earps to enter the corral, but the point of the shot has been made: Clanton, older than and quite as impersonal as the rocks with which he is confused, is the agent of natural force without civilization, without the disciplining and humanizing rein of charity. But Earp's ally in the gunfight is, in his way, an opposite number to the unselfconscious barbarity of Pa Clanton. Doc Holliday, here played with rare brilliance by Victor Mature, is a figure of civilization gone rotten as opposed to Clanton's civilization not yet begun. This Doc Holliday—as opposed to the violent, tubercular dentist of history—is a sensitive surgeon from the East (always the direction of culture in the Western) whose fatal disease has cast him into a despair for which only hard drinking, gambling, and cynical whoring offer any alleviation. Holliday, in other words, is civilization *attempting to escape* its own responsibilities, civilization acting out a ghastly parody of the instinctual, "natural" life of the outlaw Clantons. Doubling the scene in which we first confuse Pa Clanton with a piece of the inhuman statuary of Monument Valley, the film gives us a scene in which Doc Holliday, disgusted with what he has made of his life, stares at his reflection in the glass covering his medical degree and finally, in despair, throws a whiskey glass at it.

Between the totally unselfconscious bestiality of the Clantons and the unhealthy, suicidal involution of Doc Holiday, then, stands the mediator, Marshal Earp. And while the Clantons throughout the film are dressed in the ragtag, cowboy style which befits their parts and Doc Holliday alternates between that style and elegant, overstylized gambler's clothes, Earp himself not only performs but dresses to his mediatory role. When we first see him on the cattle drive, he is wearing a nondescript ensemble not significantly different from the Clantons' own: since nature, as I have said, is both potentially destructive in this film and the potentially creative force of civilization itself. After he agrees to become the marshal of Tombstone, however, he dresses in the tailored grey suit and carefully blocked hat which has, since the release of *Clementine,* become part and parcel of the Wyatt Earp iconography—and which offers an important contrast not only to the Clantons' costume but to the overemphasized elegance of his uncomfortable ally, Doc Holliday.

I mention this not to reduce a splendid film like *My Darling Clementine* to a mere exercise in haberdashery, but to indicate how important and how perennial is the function of costume in romance narrative. *Clementine* details that function, though it does so self-consciously, with a minimum of tension. Characters dress the parts they play in the moral, nature/culture allegory of the film, and do so without any apparent resistance to those parts. Compared to *Roland,* that is, a film like *Clementine* is relatively uncomplicated, innocent romance, since *Roland* is much more concerned with defining and examining the boundaries of the moral claims upon the true knight. The real equivalent of *Roland* would be a film where the "knight" and "king" come into conflict with each other, where a central figure finds for himself which moral universe he belongs to, where the legendary quality of romance is tested against the claims of the ordered, subordinated civilization that romance celebrates. Ford himself, in the darker "late phase" of his filmmaking, began an exploration of this sort, reexamining the myth of the American West in terms of the violent, often shabby reality of its history.

In *The Man Who Shot Liberty Valance,* for example, the idealistic young lawyer from the East, Ransom Stoddard (James Stewart) brings "law and order" to the frontier town of Shinbone and eventually becomes a famous and powerful figure in the politics of the state by killing the savage outlaw Liberty Valance (Lee Marvin). But we learn at the end of the film that Ransom's whole career has been based upon a deception—a benevolent one, to be sure, but a deception nonetheless. For Liberty Valance was really shot by Tom Doniphon (John Wayne, once again), a rough-edged cowboy who grudgingly protects the greenhorn Ransom from a world whose chaos the lawyer is not really adequate to face. The whole story is told in a long flashback. Senator Stoddard, many years after the events, returns with his wife (formerly Doniphon's sweetheart) to the town of Shinbone for the funeral of Tom Doniphon, who has died a lonely old man and is about to be buried in a pauper's grave. Sitting in the local newspaper office, Stoddard relates to the editor and a young reporter the real story of his success for the first time. All the elements of romance I have been discussing are present in the tale, but oddly mutated.

Ransom Stoddard, whose first name itself is blatantly allegorical, does bring civilization and courtesy to the already founded town (he even teaches his wife-to-be, Doniphon's girl, to read poetry); Doniphon, the primal founder-figure, lives outside the town he helped begin, but invests the young Ransom with some of his own authority; and Valance is as convincingly frightening, explosive a human monster as any knight ever had to conquer. But as the flashback technique itself establishes, the principals are all either dead or old now. And the story itself is legend that betrays the facts of the matter. However, in the famous summary line of the film, when asked by the young reporter if they should publish Stoddard's surprising revelation, the editor replies,

"When the facts conflict with the legend, print the legend."
It is a bitter but not a cynical line. For the legends of civilization—Stoddard's heroism, Roland's courage, Gawain's courtliness—are, in their way, the reality of civilization more than the disruptive "facts," even though the legends themselves mask an often confused and painful human reality of loss and defeat.

A number of war films carry on the same romance reevaluation of the nature of heroism, placing the "heroic" within the context of a richer and more problematic civilization. They are not necessarily "anti-war" films, though, unlike the war films discussed in the last chapter, they do take a view of war which emphasizes the human, social context in which it is fought. The titles of many of them—*King and Country, What Price Glory?, Grand Illusion, Paths of Glory,* and *King Rat*—indicate, with varying degrees of bitterness and irony, their consciousness of the official, "epic" ideal of warfare against which they suggest a more dubious truth. But two of the most complete versions of this sensibility are named simply for their central characters, men whose historical careers actually do seem to call into play many of the confusions, triumphs, and clarifications of the more problematic romance heroes. And they are both films which are also, in subtle ways, expansions of flashbacks, films that retrospectively fill in the human costs of men who became "printed legends." I refer to *Lawrence of Arabia* and *Patton.*

Living Legends

Outside film and popular fiction, the twentieth century has not really produced many undisputed heroic figures. In a century where war itself is more global, more mechanized, more chillingly mass-produced than in any previous one, and where the business of statecraft appears so often to depend upon the slimier aspects of bribery, secrecy, and espionage, heroic figures are not likely to emerge. Or, when they do emerge, they are likely to be de-mythologized rapidly by the same mechanism of information retrieval and transmission, the "news," that creates their initial fame. Allenby was callous, MacArthur was an egotist, Roosevelt a mama's boy, Churchill a vindictive drunkard, Kennedy a satyr; so goes the by now predictable process of innuendo and half-truth by which we demolish the images we set up for ourselves in the desert. We know, in a way, too much about the ills of the psyche to trust the ability of any man to transform those debilities into the stuff of victory.

Except, perhaps, in the case of T. E. Lawrence, Lawrence of Arabia, whose permanent fascination for our age is that his heroism was compounded self-consciously out of the details of his own psychosis. Almost from the beginnings of his legend, it was an open secret that this was a complicated, not entirely stable man: and no one was more flamboyantly disingenuous, more openly secretive about the matter than Lawrence himself. Samuel Hynes, in his book *The Auden Generation,* summarizes the special appeal of Lawrence to British intellectuals of the thirties. He was the type, Hynes suggests, of the Truly Weak Man who becomes, through his own efforts, the Truly Strong Man:

> He was an intellectual and a homosexual, a shy, undersized Oxford archaeologist who made himself into a man of action as though by an act of will, and then withdrew again into himself . . . a divided man, an adolescent who had never matured, and a man who "suffered, in his own person, the neurotic ills of an entire generation."

The last phrase, from an essay on Lawrence by Christopher Isherwood, may indeed be the central insight into Lawrence's appeal. For however many studies appear arguing that he was a pathological liar, an obsessive flagellant, an exhibitionistic blusterer, we continue to be amazed and obsessed that a man like Lawrence could become heroic not despite but precisely through such flaws. David Lean's film *Lawrence of Arabia* (screenplay by Robert Bolt) is a perceptive and, finally, tragic examination of just this phenomenon. It begins with the death of its hero, with a suitably vague version of the mysterious motorcycle accident in which Lawrence was killed. The next scene is a series of interviews with the mourners leaving Lawrence's funeral at St. Paul's. Asked for a comment on Lawrence, General Allenby (Jack Hawkins), his commanding officer in Arabia, snorts, "What, more words?" and then resignedly delivers a brief summary of public cliches about Lawrence's role in the war, ending with the suggestive comment, "I didn't really know him very well." The journalist Jackson Bentley (Arthur Kennedy)—a thinly disguised version of Lowell Thomas, Lawrence's "discoverer"—obliges the questioning reporter with shopworn phrases about the "mighty warrior" and then mumbles to his companion, "He was also the most shameless exhibitionist I've ever met." An unnamed man overhears Bentley's comment and challenges him, insisting that Lawrence was "a great man—a very great man indeed!" "Oh, did you know him well?" sneers Bentley. "No, sir, not well," replies the man. "But I did once have the honor to shake his hand. In Damascus."

With the word "Damascus" the film cuts to an Arab city during the First World War. But not to Damascus, where Lawrence's long journey ended and his hopes of a free, united Arab state were finally disappointed. The scene is Cairo, where Lieutenant T. E. Lawrence (Peter O'Toole) is about to be sent on the mission to Prince Feisal that will make him the famous and reviled figure we have heard about for the first five minutes of the film. The first scene has established not only the fascination and contradictoriness of the heroic Lawrence, but also the ambiguities of "legend" and "reality" which are at the heart of the narrative as well as at the heart of Lawrence's own riddle. But if the film is a flashback, whose flashback is it? Not Lawrence's, since he has already died into legend and controversy. And not really that of any of the three characters whose observations introduce the story, though they all reappear within it. Rather (and I am indebted to the David Lean scholar Louis Castelli for this insight), the film is a "flashback" of the whole culture which creates, celebrates, and finally defeats the heroism Lawrence seeks to attain.

We will find, as "Lieutenant Lawrence" becomes "Lawrence of Arabia," that each of the three mourners plays a crucial part, not only in constituting the public myth of Lawrence, but in contributing to the personal agony which finally makes that myth uninhabitable for the man. Allenby, recognizing the strategic importance—for the British war effort—of an Arab revolt against the Turks, flatters and cajoles Lawrence into continuing his desert campaign although Lawrence himself fears, as much as he is drawn to, the opportunities for cruelty and savagery that the campaign offers him. Bentley, looking desperately for a good story and a bona fide hero, makes him world-famous but at the same time cheapens, renders tawdry, his passionate quest for an authentically pure existence. And the unnamed man who "had the honor" to shake Lawrence's hand in Damascus dramatizes the same paradox in one of the film's subtlest ironies. For we do see him shake Lawrence's hand, just as Lawrence is leaving British headquarters to be sent back to England, his hopes crushed and his usefulness to British and Arabs alike outlived. But the day before, Lawrence—in Arab garb, his face partially covered—has visited a Damascus hospital housing wounded Turkish soldiers, horrifyingly filthy, overcrowded, and mismanaged by the Arab occupiers of the city. And while Lawrence collapses in hysterical, revolted laughter at the suffering he has helped cause, the man who later shakes his hand, a medical officer in the British Army, arrives at the hospital, explodes in rage at the conditions, and, cursing Lawrence as a "filthy Wog," strikes him.

But the ironies of the film go beyond the simple ironies of the tension between public role and private appetite. It is important that the medic strikes Lawrence while he is wearing the celebrated and theatrical Arab clothing in which he is most recognizably "Lawrence of Arabia," and recognizes him the next day as "Colonel Lawrence" when he is back in British uniform. For the unasked question with which the film opens, "Who was Lawrence?," is one that not only puzzles the characters surrounding him in the Arab campaign, but centrally puzzles and obsesses Lawrence himself. Throughout the film his British commanders, his ranker admirers, and his Arab companions ask him, in various ways and for various purposes, who he is, where he comes from, what he *wants*. But, as Lawrence himself says after his torture and humiliation in the Turkish garrison at Deraa, though you can be whatever you want, "you can't *want* whatever you want."

What Lawrence wants, very simply, is to bridge the gap between two worlds. His attempt to "become" an Arab is an attempt to live in the austere world of a primary, epic kingship, a world of tribal loyalties and individual freedom to which his antiquarianism, his cultural nostalgia, impels him as the only appropriate theater of action. "Loyal to England *and* to Arabia. Is this possible?" asks Prince Feisal of Lawrence at their first meeting. It is not possible, as the film and Lawrence's own tortured experience make clear. For in attempting to live in the mythically *earlier* time of Arab tribalism, while at the same time serving the aims of the British war effort in all its mechanized, globally engineered complexity, Lawrence is caught between not only two worlds but two masters: Feisal, the archaic and noble king of a congeries of tribes that has not yet become a nation, and General Allenby, the military and social executive of a nation-state. And ultimately this conflict of political loyalties is the parallel to Lawrence's own intense personal confusion of identities.

T. E. Lawrence writes, early in his massive and brilliant memoir *Seven Pillars of Wisdom*, of the special psychic problem of living as both Arab and British serving officer, of living two selves, "Sometimes these selves would converse in the void; and then madness was very near, as I believe it would be near the man who could see things through the veils at once of two customs, two educations, two environments."

Whether or not we choose to accept the historical Lawrence's estimate of his own proficiency in Arab language and culture, this is precisely the dilemma of the myth of Lawrence, and of the Lawrence of the film. And the special madness involved in the dialog of those "two selves" is, as the film makes clear, a madness generated by the attempt to *live* in the two identities at once. Lawrence's quest is not simply to "become" an Arab, but to lead the loose federation of Arab tribes into nationhood. He is forever separated from the purity of the culture he wishes to assimilate himself into by the very imagination—modern, anthropological, self-conscious—which leads him to desire such an assimilation. It is our nostalgia for the Edenic state of epic clarity which separates us from that state. At the beginning of the second half of the film, Prince Feisal explains to the journalist Bentley the difference between his own idea of mercy and that of Lawrence: "For Colonel Lawrence, mercy is a passion; for me it is simply good manners. You may decide which motive is the more trustworthy." But the distinction, of course, between good manners and obsession is precisely the distinction between primary, unselfconscious society and latter-day, profoundly self-conscious civilization. Lawrence tries his best to become an Arab. But at the moment he is given his all-white Arab garb by his desert friends, he rides away from them into the desert, salaams his shadow with a

mocking smile on his face, and—with suitably heroic pan-
ache—draws his dagger only to look laughingly into its surface for his own absurd reflection, a scholarly and frail Englishman in his dress-up robes. It is at once the most private
and most public moment of the film. Private, since it may
"really' never have occurred, and public, since it catches, in
all its ironies of performance and reality, the puzzled position of Lawrence caught between the two political and
moral worlds he is trying to mediate.

That the attempt at mediation fails is the judgment of history and of Lawrence's own autobiography. But the film,
like the literary myth of the man, gives us an image of the
profound importance of that failure, the profound ambigu-
ity and historical necessity of the grasped-at and lost
heroism of the modern man who aspires to knighthood,
kingship itself. Lawrence is a hero not so much of the imperial self as of the modern imagination of the imperial self,
encumbered by all its weight of self-consciousness and dubi-
ety. And had Lawrence lived into the Second World War he
might well have grown to be the hero of the next "romance" film I will examine, *Patton*.

Released at the height of the American involvement in
Vietnam, *Patton* managed, remarkably enough, to please
both hawks and doves, to be taken both as an essay on the
glories of armed conflict—a mechanized *Iliad*—and as a satire on the megalomania of the professional soldier—another
Catch-22. In fact it is neither of those things. But it is one of
the subtlest and most moving examinations we have, in either film or literature, of the terrible seduction of the heroic
ideal and the terrible price that ideal requires of those who,
at their peril, attempt to live as if it were attainable in an age
which will not allow it to be attained. At the very center of
the film—emotionally as well as in terms of running time—
George C. Scott as Patton, accompanied only by his aide,
surveys the scene of a pitched battle between American and
German tanks. The field is littered with wrecked war ma-

chines, corpses, wounded men and still-burning fires. And as
Patton observes the wreckage he says, half to himself, "I
love it. God help me, I do love it so."

It would not be difficult to extrapolate the vision of the
whole film from this short speech and its immediate context.
The battlefield is a wasteland, and Patton recognizes it as
such. But it is not the wasteland he loves; rather it is the
energy and the exultation of war which has left the wasteland behind it, testimonial to its passage. Keats once observed that though a fight in the street is not admirable, the
energies released therein are; *Patton*—and George Scott's
Patton—is both more honest and more problematic, insisting that we canot really distinguish between the fight and
the energies the fight incarnates, cannot know this violent
dance from its dancers. The speech is also a shocking one.
What sort of man *loves* war? we may want to ask. But the
real shock is that the speech, like the film in which it occurs,
forces us to the admission that *all* men love war, though few
are either brave or foolish enough to admit that love as Patton does. We usually civilize our love of warfare by translat-
ing it into the activities of social or sexual competition—that
is precisely the legacy of the romance world. Patton knows
this too, yet insists upon trying to live in the purer, austere
world of primal combat from which our later, civilized com-
bats arise. Like Roland's attempt to substitute courage for
policy, to translate *court* back into *comitatus,* it is foredoomed.

"God help me, I do love it so." The screenplay, by
Francis Ford Coppola and Edmund H. North, is studded
with lines of brilliant dialog, but none more moving than
this one. There is something not only old-fashioned but romantically sentimental about the turn of phrase "I do love it
so." It is the kind of thing a man with a late-nineteenth-
century education and late-nineteenth-century literary
taste—a man like Patton, in other words—might write or
say to a woman. And as such it signals the degree to which

Patton's love *is* love, not the simple (and largely imaginary) bloodthirstiness of the professional killer.

We would not be wrong, indeed, to view *Patton* as a love story, a story, like *Roland* or *Tristan and Isolde,* of a man's passionate commitment to a world, a set of values, that torments him with the impossibility of its attainment. "All real Americans love to win," Patton snarls in the famous address to his troops that opens the film. It is the most quoted, most remembered, and most often parodied line of *Patton,* and also one of the most rightly ambiguous. What, after all, does "winning" mean? In his films *The Godfather,* Parts One and Two, and *The Conversation,* Coppola devotes much talent to examining the complexities and dubieties of "success" or "winning" in American society. But his screenplay for *Patton* begins that examination at a more primary, almost allegorical level.

"Winning," of course, is most basically winning the war. "Nobody ever won a war by dying for his country," Patton announces in his opening speech, "he won it by making the *other* dumb sonofabitch die for *his* country." And as he says later in the same speech, "We're going to go through those Germans like crap through a goose!" Like the sense of the Second World War in *The Longest Day,* though at a much higher level of energy and brilliance, this much of Patton's quest is the pure, uncomplicated, heroic vision of warfare as the ultimate contest, the crucial test of a culture's or an individual's strength and worth. But as Patton learns in the course of the film, there are other wars, other contests, other and more difficult versions of "winning" that underlie the grand struggle of the War itself. And these are the subtle, often petty and always intricate relationships among men who are social rather than epic creatures, the civilized transformations of war that finally and justly defeat him.

For Patton's idea of "winning" is *not* basically winning the war—at least not in the collaborative, politically and socially hygienic mode of behavior and function which made the war winnable. It is, rather, winning the war as a personal, individual triumph. Patton, in other words, is attempting to convert the European theater of operations into the theater of his own private and epic drama.

The pun on "theater" is one that both the film and the historical moment of the Second World War bear out. The war was fought and imagined—by both sides—as a moral drama or melodrama, an absolute struggle between the forces of good and the forces of evil, to a degree unusual for a modern conflict. This attitude is shared by the rhetoric of Churchill, Roosevelt, and Hitler, and it is significant that Dwight D. Eisenhower's memoir of the war is entitled *Crusade in Europe*. Even more in retrospect than actuality, from the vantage point of, first, the Korean conflict and, later, the war in Vietnam, it came to seem a real crusade, the last clearly just war of the century. It is an interesting development of taste, for example, that J. R. R. Tolkien's trilogy *Lord of the Rings* became a student enthusiasm or "underground classic" when it did. Tolkien's story is a long, self-conscious, and rather donnish coy romance, complete with wizards, elves, and magic rings, which is also an obvious allegory of the British struggle against Hitler, the Dark Lord of the west. But although published in the fifties, *Lord of the Rings* achieved wide—and, for Tolkien, somewhat disconcerting—popularity in America during the years of the Vietnam war and the height of student and intellectual resistance to it. In other words, this romance of the "last just war" was being read and valued, to a large extent, by the very students and professors who were otherwise carrying on their hopeless but brave campaign to end our involvement in the first blatantly unjust war which Americans knew to be unjust at the time of the involvement. The book was a kind of hygienic nostalgia, a battlefield memory tailor-made for conscientious objectors and pacifists too young to remember a real and moral battlefield.

But *Patton*, a product of the same years, is both tougher

and more disturbingly human in its response to the "problem" of war. Patton, as I have said, is concerned with converting the public melodrama of the war into the private drama of his own heroism. He knows everything about the art of war, in other words, except his own proper role in it. "Theatrical," of course, is a word that was often applied, disparagingly, to the historical George S. Patton, and one that is implied by his adversaries within the film. But it is important to realize how seriously theatrical Patton, in the film at any rate, really is. The opening sequence, his address to his troops, is literally theater: Patton mounts a stage, backed by a gigantic American flag, and delivers a monologue about the nature of war to his men about to go into battle. And for most of that monologue, we, the audience, are in exactly the position of the troops, watching the man on stage. But the point of the sequence is not simply to suggest to us the feel of being in a "real" audience watching the "real" Patton. It is rather, much more subtly, an overwhelming preliminary assertion that Patton exists in and for his role as soldier, as leader of men in battle—as knight. After he mounts the stage and before he begins his speech, a series of extreme closeups emphasizes the panoply, the ritual costume of the role which has become his identity: his shiny black helmet with its four stars, his famous pearl-handled revolvers, his impressive array of campaign ribbons. Everything I have said about the symbolic function of uniform or costume in romance narrative, in fact, is implicit in this series of shots, and its theatrical context. As by a maze of self-reflecting mirrors, the historical Patton is caught by George C. Scott's performance as "Patton," which itself is translated into the symbolism of uniform that *is* the legendary and historicaι image of " 'Patton.' " It is one of the subtlest transformations of history into myth that film or literature can achieve.

But the subtlety goes beyond the mere symbolic details of costume. Much as the opening invocation of Charlemagne in *The Song of Roland* establishes the theme of imperial power which constitutes Roland's heroism and against which he tragically asserts his own prowess, the image of the flag, which is the very first thing we see in *Patton,* establishes the ground and the limit of Patton's masque of heroism. The sequence is quite literally a counterpoint of symbols, and also quite literally purified out of time itself. Almost like the epigraph to a book, Patton's initial acting-out of the complexities of his role occupies precisely no time in the story of the film itself. Is he addressing his troops before his landing in North Africa, before his landing in Italy, or before his entry into the final assault on Berlin? We cannot answer that question, and we are meant not to. In fact the speech is delivered not "prior to" any of these conflicts, but in another, symbolic time altogether. Only a very canny viewer would notice what was pointed out to me by one of my students, that Patton's helmet in this sequence carries *four* stars: and not till the end of the film does Patton reach four-star rank. The film, then, goes beyond the flashback technique of Lawrence of Arabia. It is not the private story of a man who plays an important public role, but, more complicatedly, the examination of the ambiguities of that public role-playing itself.

The film pays a great deal of attention to Patton's belief in reincarnation, and his faith that he is the latest avatar of a long series of warriors stretching back into prehistory. Again, this is neither bluster nor superstition, but an essential aspect of the desperation with which he tries to live out his self-assigned function of individual greatness. For counterpointed to this faith, this vision of himself as belonging to the epic tradition itself, is his anxiety to live it, to achieve something truly great in a world—and in an army—where individual greatness is subordinated to the necessities of co-operation, subordination, of—in almost exactly Olivier's sense of the word in his speech to Roland—vassalage. If Roland has Olivier to announce this crucial idea to him,

Patton has Omar Bradley, played with brilliant com-
monplaceness by Karl Malden. Early in the film, as the generals in Berlin are examining their files on the new Allied
generals in North Africa, a German intelligence officer describes Patton as a millionaire, an amateur poet, a historian,
and a dazzlingly flamboyant figure, and then describes Bradley as the "G. I. general," the general most in touch with the
concerns and the sensibilities of the men under his command.

Malden's Bradley is dressed throughout the film in rum-
pled fatigues, contrasting with Patton's self-consciousness
about his uniform, and this too has its important effect
upon the symbolic drama. For ironically Patton's uniform,
which he has designed himself, both dramatizes his vision of
his heroic role and advertises his fatal distance from the fulfillment of that role; because a uniform that is individually,
flamboyantly designed is no longer a *uniform,* no longer the
expression of its wearer's participation in the common cause
that is a massive army. In overemphasizing the symbolic,
romantic function of costume, Patton subtly and uncon-
sciously betrays that function. At one important point in the
film, when Patton has been given a late chance to fight in the
war, and sent to Germany under the command of his own
former subordinate, Bradley, his new commander tells him,
"George, you're a friend and a good soldier, but you're a
pain in the *neck.*" It is the judgment not only of Bradley but
implicitly of the whole world of the film, the whole world of
mechanized warfare which makes Patton's personal struggle
so profoundly anachronistic and so profoundly moving.

As everything I have said about the romance world indicates, we value the figure of the knight not as we do the
epic hero, for the achievements of his creative victories, but
for the illumination of his moral quandaries and defeats. For
in those he teaches us the discipline and the acceptance of
limitation which makes life civilized. And in *Patton* this am-
biguity is raised to a nearly absolute level. Lawrence is de-

feated by his attempt to reenter the heroic past, to live as if the age of knights were still the age of founders. But Patton is defeated by something far more grim than the inaccessibility of the past: the intransigence of the present, the refusal of his own world and time to bear the weight of the symbolic role he tries to live out. Just as his first appearance exists "outside" time, so his personal agony is, finally, to be *excluded* from the present by his own sense of the posibilities of the past. Two sequences from the film catch this dilemma splendidly.

Early in the film, on the morning of his first tank battle with Rommel's army, he is awakened before dawn by his orderly, and in an explicitly ritual scene prepares himself for the fight. As he gazes at himself in a mirror his orderly—his squire, his acolyte—invests him with his campaign jacket, helmet, and revolvers. And, the investiture complete, Patton says to his reflection, "All my life I've wanted to lead a lot of men in a desperate battle. And now I'm going to do it." It is perhaps the height of Patton's personal warfare, the moment at which he is closest to achieving and grasping his own image of himself. But it is, of course, like his great opening speech, a moment out of time, a moment of mirror-time, just *before* the battle, when self-consciousness has the leisure to expand into the realm of myth. The rest of the film, after that triumphant moment, will be the long history of his struggles with the politics of the other Allied commanders, a war not against the "enemy"—indeed, he even feels a kind of fellowship with that other flamboyant and doomed soldier, Rommel—but against the logistics of modern, technologized, corporate warfare. And, as the film makes clear, his obsession with self-aggrandizement, however mythically comprehensible and admirable, seriously jeopardizes the war effort and the lives of the men under his command.

In the mirror-scene Patton becomes, for the briefest of moments, the knight he believes it is his destiny to be; and becomes that heroic figure *to himself*. As the film, and life itself, teach us, it is not enough for us to become what we hope to be, we must also *know* that we have become what we hope to be. But that second requirement, a clear and sure knowledge of our own role, is just the need of the psyche that, because it is ultimately impossible, exiles us into confusion, into doubt, into history. Counterpointing the mirror-scene, near the very end of the film, Patton once again assumes his hieratic role, but this time in a context of entrapment and limitation. The war has been won, the Germans have surrendered, and Patton is in charge of the interim military government of Berlin. In a riding arena somewhere in Berlin, he is exercising his horse while a bevy of American reporters question him about postwar conditions. Patton is once again in full and flamboyant uniform, once again the knight of his own imagination. But this time there is no mirror. There are reporters, and Patton is not seeing himself but being *seen*. It is a sequence of great visual power and in its way the melancholy summary of the whole film. The heroic rider is indoors, enclosed; horsemanship, that is, is no longer a part of the actual business of warfare but simply an exercise. And the circle of the riding arena is itself further constricted by the circle of reporters. The noble horseman, in other words, is trapped by the very world which celebrates his victory. And in the course of the interview he is fed a question—"Didn't most people join the Nazi party the way people back home join the Republican or Democratic parties?"—which he answers with an unthinking, "Yes, I guess that's about right." It is the final embarrassment to Patton's superiors. He is relieved of his position and sent home.

But Patton's final bafflement and defeat by a world whose subtleties and hidden laws he does not understand begins to anticipate another, later vision of the City. With the scene of bombed-out Berlin and the covey of reporters who distort as they transmit the news, we enter a culture, a City, where moral structures have become confused and decayed to the point where the knight can no longer attempt simply to carry out their sanctions, but must first discover and try to right their imbalance. We begin to enter, in other words, the world of the questing detective, the subtle criminal, and the struggle for dominance between them which is best called melodrama.

IV

The World of Melodrama: Pawns

We may consider a third kind of relation between the individual and the law: that of disobedience and punishment.

ROUSSEAU

The Mad Knight

Patton presents us with the spectacle, tragic in its way, of a warrior trapped, made to appear foolish by the very culture he believes he is defending; its crucial image of the noble rider on the equestrian track surrounded by the cynical, civilian-suited reporters and *paparazzi* who will, finally, pull him down, remains in the memory. But much of the power of Patton's situation is that he knows, clearly but unavailingly, that the knightly role he is trying to play is doomed from the start by the mechanization and depersonalization of the army he serves and the kind of war he is waging. In another key scene, as he is briefing his officers on the daring tank rescue of the surrounded American troops at Bastogne, he rises to a pitch of rhetorical frenzy, shouting, "And if we are not victorious, let no man come back alive!" His officers retire in stunned silence, whereupon his aide de camp says to him, "You know, general, sometimes the men can't tell when you're acting and when you're not." Patton replies, in a flat and chillingly sane voice, "It's not important that they know; it's only important that *I* know." And he does know,

although he also knows that the "acting," the fiction of warfare as the most ritualized of human acts, and of men in
battle as men transfigured by the service of a noble cause, is
the most important part of his life.

The transition from the fiction of romance to that level of
narrative we can call, generally, "melodrama" is a transition
that involves just this conflict between the knight as the
guardian, symbol, and civilizer of the City's laws and the
progressive complication, the institutionalization, of the
laws themselves. His struggle is no longer against the forces
which threaten the equity or the establishment of the law,
but with the terms under which the law has been established, their apparent departure from the vision of
human possibility in whose name he helped defend them.
The word "melodrama" is itself an invention of the nineteenth century (it was coined by the French writer Charles
Nodier), that century which more than any other saw the incipient collapse of the City's promise under the increasing
weight of its own industrialized complexity. And it means,
precisely, "mixed" drama, an affecting but confusing meld
of the ludicrous and the tragic, the comic and the pathetic.
There is, indeed, something "mixed" about the spectacle of
the knight imprisoned by the laws he has forged, driven to
play-acting, madness, and bafflement by the world whose
defender he desperately desires to be. But though the term
was invented in the nineteenth century, the type of narrative
it describes is much older.

Patton's desire to be the noble rider, the defender and
darling of a society founded upon principles of honor and
dignity, to fight real monsters in a world that has legislated
monsters out of existence, is quixotic. And there is a reason
why that adjective has become part of our common vocabu-
lary, even among people who have never read the sixteenth-
century tale from which it comes. Cervantes' Don Quixote
is a private citizen of an affluent culture—poor, mad Alonso
Quijana of the tiny village of La Mancha whose brain has

been curdled by his voracious reading of medieval romances. Deluding himself that he is the hero of one of these pernicious (i.e. outdated) books, he adopts the fictitious name "Don Quixote" and sets out on his quest. But it is a quest directed not so much toward a goal as toward the infinite extension of the act of questing itself. And this is only one of Cervantes' many brilliancies as a storyteller and, implicitly, a sociologist. For while the true knight of romance seeks nothing so much as the fulfillment and end of his task, that is just what Don Quixote cannot bear to contemplate. The quest must go on forever, the goal never be reached. For the Don in his madness and Cervantes in his sanity both know that the end of the quest is the establishment of a civilized law that will make the knight himself unnecessary, will reduce him to the dimensions of his own romanticism and foolishness. And to this degree, at least, Quixote is quite as self-conscious about his "acting" as is Patton.

I mentioned that the transition from romance to melodrama involves the battle of the knight against the "institutionalization" of his own most firmly upheld beliefs and principles. Institutionalization, of course, implies depersonalization: and though it is a necessary phase in the evolution of society, the growth of the City, it is nevertheless a melancholy one. As the law becomes more and more firmly established, it also becomes more and more complicated, less dependent upon individual effort to sustain it, but also less likely to allow for individual identity or conditions in its administration. It becomes, in other words, uniform, mechanical: not so much an open landscape for the exercise and self-realization of the individual will as a trap or a cage threatening that realization. Don Quixote wants the quest to go on forever with no end, General Patton wants the war to go on forever with no resolution, just because both of these crazed knights are sane enough to realize that their quests *cannot* end, that the return to "normality" for which they strive spells the end of their order and the beginning of one

that will not tolerate their disruptive, noble presence. It is
one of the central, cruelest ironies of *Patton* that its hero is a
general of cavalry (hence his final, magnificent and futile
scene on horseback) condemned by his century and his century's technology to lead tanks into battle. And the same
irony constitutes perhaps the most famous scene of *Don
Quixote,* when this immensely attractive madman, the sole
upholder of a code of personal honor against the encroachments of industrialism, macroeconomic class structure and
depersonalization, charges the nearest monsters he can find.
They are windmills, only windmills, as his realistic companion Sancho Panza keeps insisting. But when we remember that the windmill itself is an important development in the growth of industrialization, and therefore in the
rise of an economically self-sufficient middle class, and that
the first truly modern structural change in the windmill occurred, according to the *Encyclopaedia Britannica,* in the
fifteenth century, then we can see that the Don, from his
own point of view, is right. They are monsters, precisely the
monsters that are transforming the world around him into
one that will no longer tolerate the presence of the knight as
its emblematic hero.

"A knight without honor in a savage land" was one of the
lines from the theme song of a late-fifties television series,
Have Gun, Will Travel. It was a Western series, starring
Richard Boone as the hired gunman known only as Paladin
(itself, of course, an archaic term for "knight") who periodi-
cally leaves his wealthy, elegant life in San Francisco to ride
on "quests" for justice at a healthy fee. But what was the
"savage land" of the song? The shrinking Wild West of the
late nineteenth century, or the growing city, replete with all
the amenities with price tags on them, that was shrinking
the free landscape by filling it up with buildings? Obviously,
for our purposes, the latter.

A number of brilliant Western films reproduce the central
irony of *Have Gun, Will Travel* and develop it in much the

same way that Cervantes—perhaps in spite of his own original intent—develops the implicit irony and pathos of Don Quixote's situation. *The Gunfighter* (1949) is a remarkable examination of the decline of the West through the central figure of Gregory Peck as an outlaw, a famous gunman run to ground in a small town where his estranged wife and child live, destroyed finally not so much by the heroic and violent ethic of the "fast gun" as by the complexities, the moral uncertainties of trying to be a "good" family man, trying to reconstitute himself as a "good" citizen in a city whose terms of existence have outgrown his own simplicity and purity of motivation. He is defeated, in other words, because like the mad knight of Cervantes he tries to live his life, within the City, on terms the City itself will no longer tolerate. It is significant in this respect that Peck, whose screen persona has always been that of a man larger than the roles he is forced to play, a man trapped, with a kind of smoldering uneasiness, in situations too complex for his energy, a few years after *The Gunfighter* reproduced the same role, the same mythic situation, in a film that became in its way one of the crucial symbols of the national life of America in the fifties. In *The Man in the Grey Flannel Suit* he plays a successful businessman whose life is nearly shattered when it is revealed that during the Second World War he fathered an illegitimate child in Italy. The film counterpoints the memory of the free, adventurous life as a soldier, literally as a knight of democracy, that he previously enjoyed and the button-down, constricted suburban life he lives now, and counterpoints them in such a way as to remind us that the former life *must cede* to the latter, in the history not only of the individual but of civilization itself.

Later Western films like John Sturges' *The Magnificent Seven,* George Roy Hill's *Butch Cassidy and the Sundance Kid,* and Sam Peckinpah's *The Wild Bunch* carry on the process. In each of them, the traditional figure of the gunfighter appears finally as "quixotic," just because he tries to

sustain the personal ethics of his professional knight-er-
rantry in a landscape which increasingly appears to be that
of the modern, contemporary urban world. *Butch Cassidy*
and *The Wild Bunch* are particularly interesting in this respect since, though very different, they are both based upon
an actual historical event: in the early years of the twentieth
century the gang led by "Butch Cassidy" (LeRoy Parker),
the last gang of old-fashioned desperadoes left, was murdered by South American police in a bloody shoot-out.
Peckinpah's and Hill's films in their different ways focus
upon the historical, cultural unsuitability of Wild-West
manners in an increasingly industrialized, urbanized world.
In *The Wild Bunch* there is the appearance, in a crucial
scene, of the motorcar, which eventually spelled the end of
the heroic figure of the knight on horseback. And in *Butch
Cassidy,* perhaps more subtly, not only the motorcar but the
bicycle makes an important appearance: the bicycle, that all-
but-invisible, omnipresent toy of our age that, nevertheless,
caused such a sensation and such a radical change in the
traveling and leisure habits of the middle class when it was
perfected, just before the beginning of the twentieth century.

I suggested, discussing the world of romance, that the figures of the knight-errant and the outlaw enjoy a kind of
twinship, a complementarity that can sometimes merge into
identity. Melodramatic narrative, the next phase of the cycle
I am describing, takes this twinship to a logical conclusion—but in doing so annihilates romance. When the laws
of a culture have become complex enough to be institutionalized—that is, depersonalized—they have become too
complex for a personal agent who can represent their symbolic reality. They have become complex enough, that is,
that they need no longer be incarnated, but investigated;
their complexity, and possible malignity, needs to be explored and threaded by an individual, a private citizen who
is at once their subject and their potential rehumanizer. The
figure of the crazed knight is transformed into the "novelis-

tic" hero, the man who *understands* that his world is too confused, too threatening for the simple solutions of nobility, but nevertheless tries to find chances for nobility even in the world he does inhabit. The noble rider, in other words, becomes that most distinctive of melodramatic figures, the detective.

Detectives—professional, unglamorous private agents of the law—figure importantly in *The Wild Bunch* and *Butch Cassidy,* as the relentless avatars of a new urban age who eventually track down and destroy the aging outlaws of the age just passed. But of course the detective is not only the killer of the knight, he is also, on the positive side, his creative reincarnation. And nowhere is the essential relationship of romance to melodrama better caught than in the following, famous passage:

> "It's a question of professional pride. You know— professional pride. I'm working for your father. He's a sick man, very frail, very helpless. He sort of trusts me not to pull any stunts. Won't you please get dressed, Carmen?"
>
> "Your name isn't Doghouse Reilly," she said. "It's Philip Marlowe. You can't fool me."
>
> I looked down at the chessboard. The move with the knight was wrong. I put it back where I had moved it from. Knights had no meaning in this game. It wasn't a game for knights.

The scene is from Raymond Chandler's masterful novel *The Big Sleep.* It is as self-conscious and efficient a characterization as one could wish for of the special world of the detective story—which is largely to say the world of the modern, post-eighteenth-century novel. Carmen Sternwood is one of the clients Chandler's archetypal detective, Philip Marlowe, has been hired to protect. But she is also a nymphomaniac, an alcoholic, and possibly a drug addict: a far cry, in other words, from the courtly love mistresses served by the knights of romance. And in the scene I have quoted from, Marlowe returns to his apartment to find Carmen naked on his bed, trying to seduce him. His refusal is wonderfully ironic. "It wasn't a game for knights": the morally cancerous world of Marlowe's Los Angeles is too murky for the clear goals and clear chances of the knightly test. And a man's only protection against the corruption around him is to adopt a cynical attitude toward the very ideas of honor and justice he might be trying to act out. But, of course, it *is* a game for knights, and Marlowe behaves quite deliberately as a knight, here rufusing the offer of the seductive but morally imbecile Carmen, and throughout the book pursuing a tangled track of guilt and murder, all of it for the sake of the man who hired him, the crippled, dying millionaire General Sternwood. At the end Marlowe even conceals the discovery that Carmen, the general's daughter, is a murderess:

> Me, I was part of that nastiness now. . . . But the old man didn't have to be. He could lie quiet in his canopied bed, with his bloodless hands folded on the sheet, waiting. His heart was a brief, uncertain murmur. His thoughts were as gray as ashes. And in a little while he too . . . would be sleeping the big sleep.

Why this loyalty to an employer Marlowe has met only once before, and that briefly, at the beginning of the story? We can explain it on the naturalistic, psychological level of the narrative, for this is precisely the core of tenderness, compassion, bitter charity that makes Marlowe Marlowe, and impels him to defend a code of honor in a deeply dishonorable world. But we can also explain it on the level of mythography, and this explanation only reinforces the power of the passage and of the book in which it occurs. I have traced the figure of the king through two successive manifestations, the vibrant creator and culture-founder of the epic order of things and the withdrawn, passively imperial shadow behind the civilizing activity of the knights of romance. General Sternwood assimilates to those figures, but as something else, as a bequeather of corruption and moral debility to the world he has established, a king whose legacy is, at least partly through his own fault, deformed. And the servant of *that* king is inevitably the doubtful knight of melodrama, stripped of his allegorical armor (for how can we believe allegories in a world of uncertain meanings?) and even of his "official" role as the legate of order (for the official guardians of the law are, here, part of the corruption of the law).

Of all the writers in the private-detective genre, Raymond Chandler is certainly the most consummately aware of the mythic overtones of his stories. His seven Marlowe novels, from *The Big Sleep* to the posthumously published *Playback,* are a saga of the disenfranchised moral imagination in quest of values. And it is as such that Chandler's books have exercised such a profound influence on the myth of the private eye in American and European books and films. But it would be a mistake to assume that only in Chandler does the detective carry the special cultural weight Chandler so eloquently assigns him. From Conan Doyle to Mickey Spillane and John D. MacDonald his role is remarkably consistent, though perhaps never defined as lyrically or as self-consciously as in the Marlowe books. As John G. Cawelti's study of popular fiction, *Adventure, Mystery, and Romance,* makes clear, the private detective from his origins performs a function which is intimately related to society's vision of its own possibilities. As Cawelti paraphrases the classic movement of the Poe- or Doyle-style detective tale:

> The norm of middle-class society [is] suddenly disrupted by the abnormality of crime. The special drama of crime in the classical detective story lies in the way it threatens the serene domestic circles of bourgeois life with anarchy and chaos. The official guardians of

this order, the police, turn out to be inefficient bunglers, and the finger of suspicion points to everybody. The ordered rationality of society momentarily seems a flimsy surface over a seething pit of guilt and disorder. Then the detective intervenes and proves that the general suspicion is false. He proves the social order is not responsible for the crime because it was the act of a particular individual with his own private motives.

A novel like Agatha Christie's *Murder on the Orient Express* epitomizes many of these concerns in an especially graphic way. On its route through Europe, the Orient Express is temporarily stalled in a snowdrift, whereupon it is discovered that one of the passengers, a loud and offensive American, has been brutally murdered in his compartment. Hercule Poirot, who happens to be traveling on the Express, undertakes to investigate the murder and, for the main body of the book, interviews one by one the other passengers, who constitute a remarkably broad spectrum of national and social types. He discovers that the murdered man has been the mastermind of an infamous kidnapping and murder in America (the obvious allusion is to the Lindbergh case) but escaped trial and conviction. After his interviews with the suspects are completed, Poirot offers two alternative solutions to the crime, and agrees to let the director of the Orient Express Company—who also happens to be a passenger—decide which answer suffices. (At this point I suggest that the reader who has not yet read the novel or seen the film, and who takes such things seriously, skip the next paragraph.)

The first solution is that an anonymous assailant entered the train, killed the American, and managed to make his escape just before the snowdrift would have revealed his tracks: that is, that the crime was perpetrated by someone outside the microcosm of the train's society. The second and obviously true explanation is that the murder was committed by *all* the passengers, save only Poirot himself and the director. Poirot suggests that all twelve of the other passengers were in one way or another allied with the family of the kidnap victim and that they all undertook, as an unofficial jury, to execute the hateful cause of that family's tragedy. It is the first explanation which is accepted, of course, and the train proceeds on its way, justice of a peculiar sort having been done.

Murder on the Orient Express shares with many classic English detective stories what Raymond Chandler and other American writers objected to as the "country house" atmosphere: that is, the murder and its solution occur in an enclosed, isolated place, away from but symbolically related to the central city. But, Chandler notwithstanding, Agatha Christie's novel helps us see the possible richness of this enclosed space. It is a microcosm. The passengers on the train are a sample not just of London life but of the international society, ranging from wealthy to poor and from civilized to barbaric, whose delicate balance is endangered by the eruption of crime. And, more subtle than simply exonerating that society from implication in the crime, *Orient Express* makes the point that society as a whole is implicated in the responsibility for the chaos it harbors, and needs to be not exonerated but forgiven. And that is Poirot's function. The murder of the kidnapper was both just and horrifying; what Poirot does is to render the horror explicable, to give it an official name, and thus to exorcise it.

This special, almost magical function is caught, really, better in the film than in the original novel. For a number of splendidly lyrical shots in the film emphasize what the novel can only allude to, the overwhelmingly physical reality and power of the train itself. The train is both an enclosed microcosm of society and the mechanized, technological expression of the force and complexity, annihilating distance and foreshortening time, of urban industrial culture. Even more than the airplane, it is for the imagination of the West the prime symbol of a society whose life is motion. There is something eerie, something disturbing at a deep level, about a train immobilized in snow: and the film manages to make that special detail of the plot more fully, magically convincing than does the book. Society is paralyzed by the introduction of crime into its midst, and when Poirot solves the case, the film's cut to the pistons of the train once more beginning to churn is an assertion—and the kind of assertion only film, perhaps, can give us—that the human power of making explanations can suffice to keep the literal wheels of society moving.

If there is a major difference between the classic detective story as described by Cawelti and exemplified by Agatha Christie and the so-called hard-boiled American school of Raymond Chandler, Dashiell Hammett, Mickey Spillane, et al., it is that in the American novels the implied threat to the social order which crime presents is more serious, more potentially corrosive of the polity. And correspondingly, the "ordered rationality" of the detective is less triumphantly a *cure* of the potential chaos of crime and more a holding action, a delicate and still endangered peace between the claims of society and the dark reality of the beast within. The ending of *The Big Sleep,* where Marlowe discovers and decides to suppress the identity of the killer, can be taken as either symbolic or symptomatic of this development. For Marlowe, unlike Poirot, makes that decision *privately,* without the satisfaction of society. As society's own sense of the extent and depth of its criminal impulses grows, the detective does not so much solve as resolve the "problem" of the crime, mediating among the claims of public order, private decency, and the inescapably fallen nature of both spheres of existence.

But it is the mediating role of the detective, as heir to the civilizing role of the knight, that I wish to emphasize, even in the "classic," which is to say early-twentieth-century, English detective story. The detective, unlike the knight, is a private individual. His assumption of the role of social savior is more a matter of choice than of an inherited, hieratic role. And he is thus more deeply implicated in the very disorder he attempts to right.

Any number of commentators (Cawelti, again, most fully and perceptively) have noted the curious eccentricity which seems to be part and parcel of the private investigator's personality as established in both popular literature and popular film: Poe's Dupin, probably the first full-fledged figure of this sort, is a night-loving aesthete; Holmes's vanity, cocaine addiction, and other personal tics are probably better remembered than the details of his investigations; Agatha Christie's Hercule Poirot is conceited, orotund, and comically, explosively Gallic; and, shifting to the most popular television incarnations of the same figure, Columbo is an idiot-savant who dresses (as a character once observed to him) like an unmade bed, Kojak is a defiantly bald three-piece-suited incarnation of ethnic macho, and Ironside is a massively heavy cripple.

Indeed, in two of the most fascinating private-eye films, the "deformity" of the detective is a crucial element in the presentation of the plot, the suggestion of the kind of world these films deal with. Our first sight of Philip Marlowe (Dick Powell) in Edward Dmytryk's 1944 *Murder, My Sweet* (based on Chandler's *Farewell, My Lovely*) is in a police station, unshaven, with a bandage over his eyes. He has been blinded by the gunshot which concludes the main action of the film, and which he recounts in flashback narrative to the police who are questioning him. But the initial image of the "private eye," the sole examining consciousness and conscience of his culture, as a blind eye is one that broods over our experience of the story that follows. It is partly, of course, a visual pun on the traditional figure of blind justice outside courthouses and police stations; but it is more than simply that, since Marlowe is not justice in any

allegorical sense, but a man—claiming only to be doing a
job of work—trapped *into* behaving justly. In the same way,
Roman Polanski's *Chinatown* features, for most of its duration, its detective hero J. J. Gitties (Jack Nicholson) in an
absurd nose-bandage. In the course of his investigation, he
has had his nose slashed by a gangster (played, significantly,
by director Polanski himself). Even more than the implicit
pun in Marlowe's bandaged eyes, this deformity of the professional "snooper" signals how much the investigator's role
involves a certain necessary wounding: something implicit,
somehow, in the job itself.

Why these various deformities, internal and external? One
convincing explanation is that the oddity of the detective
serves at once to isolate him from the official standard of
"normality" of the society he serves, and to unite him, however tenuously, with the outcast, the different, among whom
are the criminals he exorcises. The detective, then, incarnates the middle position between the daylight world of the
City and the underground, between the promise and the
threat of city life. As Browning's Bishop Blougram says in
what is almost a catalogue of the typical characters of melodrama:

> Our interest's on the dangerous edge of things:
> The honest thief, the tender murderer,
> The superstitious atheist, demirep
> Who loves and saves her soul in new French books.
> We watch while these with equilibrium keep
> The giddy line midway. . . .

But there is a further explanation of the dangerous edge on
which the detective lives and which he incarnates. If his
oddity, his eccentricity, establishes him on the giddy middle
line between rectitude and criminality, it is also his badge as
unofficial mediator between those contradictory forces, the

appropriate and inevitable transformation of the heraldry
that identifies the knight of romance, since in the world of
melodrama the hero's armor *is* his vulnerability.

The Unwalled City

Rousseau's third kind of law helps us understand the peculiar ambiguities of the narrative world I am now describing:
"We may consider a third kind of relation between the individual and the law: that of disobedience and punishment. It
gives rise to criminal laws, which are actually less a specific
type of law than the sanction of all the others."

Unlike the "law" of epic foundation or the later "law" of
courtly, civil behavior, this third relation between the individual and the state is less a positive command or set of
commands than an acknowledgment on the part of society
that the laws fail, that men will not obey them, and that
punishments must be instituted and carried out so that the
life of culture, however flawed, can continue. Crime here is
imagined as more than the perennial threat to human order
posed by human nature. It is human nature itself. In the
human universe it is parallel to the principle of entropy, the
tendency to decay and disorganization against which the
cosmos must struggle. At one extreme, this variety of law
(actually, this myth of civilization) is summarized in a chilling dictum like that of Robespierre: "Virtue without Terror
is powerless." But there are more generous and humane
formulations: indeed, they comprise most of what is ordi-
narily thought of as the "realistic" tradition of nineteenth-
and twentieth-century fiction and many of the most popular
narrative films.

If "virtue without terror is powerless," our desire to be
good and our desire to be *ourselves* are in a kind of constant
struggle. It is a struggle the law—especially the criminal
law—arbitrates, but one whose solution, whose final outcome, is neither assured nor, necessarily, justified by "the

law" in abstraction. The investigatory role in this universe is just to discover what will suffice, what path through the thickets of the law will bring us to the truly human City whence we began.

In this respect, one of the epoch-making assertions of *The Social Contract* is that the central political problem is to develop a theory of government which can guarantee to each of its members *both* a maximum freedom to participate in the ongoing commerce and business of social responsibility *and* a maximum freedom for self-realization and self-expression. The two freedoms, of functioning in the polity and of becoming an "authentic" self, suddenly cease to be congruent with each other: and at this moment of thought the modern City comes into existence in its full problematic. Gunnar Myrdal, in his massive study *An American Dilemma,* paraphrases Rousseau's observation in direct application to the traditions of American government and sociology when he calls attention to the implicit conflict, throughout our history, between the revolutionary promise of the Declaration of Independence and the conservative, private-property oriented strictures of the Constitution which, written as a rein and corrective to the much more libertarian Articles of Confederation, is in fact in constant tension with the original revolutionary promise.

This conflict of laws and freedoms is, I suggest, of direct and crucial importance for understanding the novels and films which seem to speak most intimately and most "naturally" to our sense of our present condition. In a recent study, *Violence and the Sacred,* René Girard comes very close to summarizing all I have been saying about the evolution of melodrama out of epic and romance, and about the complicated nature of Rousseau's third kind of law. Girard's concern is with the relationship, in primitive societies and in our own, between the idea of the holy and the perennially violent ideas of society and of human nature itself. These ideas, Girard insists, are not really in opposition to each other but are in fact *versions of the same fundamental self-perception.*

Specifically, in his opening chapter, Girard addresses the question of sacrifice in early religion, the astonishing and appalling presence of human and animal murder in almost every religious mythology we have discovered. The function of sacrifice, he suggests, is only "officially" an expiatory act performed for the sake of a putative deity. Its real function is precisely, by a prophylactic release of the violent impulses we all nurture from the caves, to avert the threat of that violence, vengeance, murderous joy breaking out in the everyday life of the tribe or the culture. Our own society, however, really has no sacrificial rituals. Our religious experience, such as it is, seems to survive without the necessity of this prophylactic bloodletting. Why? asks Girard. His answer is that the judicial system, the institution of a public law of "vengeance" for crime which takes the necessity of personal vengeance away from the wounded or violated individual, incarnates, generalizes, and *abstracts* that primitive compulsion to sacrifice.

This formulation of the symbolic importance of the judiciary is not only very close to Rousseau's idea of a law which is a "sanction"—that is, a reinforcement *and a control*—on the earlier laws of culture, but it also explains the simultaneous attraction and repulsiveness of criminality in melodramatic narrative. If the detective is part criminal, or allied to the very underworld he explores; if the lover is part adulterer, or allied to the violation of the same "grand passion" which informs his life, this is simply another way of observing that we understand the sanctions that allow us to live peacefully together most fully, most dazzlingly, at the very moment we betray them. All of us, heirs to a polity which has formed us and which we do not completely understand, seek for the accurate, efficient rules for the conduct of our own lives. But—in melodrama if not in theol-

Bataille

ogy—we never understand those laws as well as we do when
we transgress them: we glorify God by sinning.

To say this is to suggest that the world of melodrama is,
in a real sense, a "Protestant," even a "Calvinist" world as
opposed to the simpler, more clarified, but also less intricate
world of "Catholic" romance. Protestantism, and especially
Calvinist theories of predestination, managed to collapse the
externalized, sacramentally based moral schematism of
Catholic piety into a personal drama, a day-by-day confrontation of the believer with the fate of his immortal soul. In
its most extreme predestinarian form, this theology turned
the act of faith itself into a kind of cosmic detective work:
the believer must discover, from the "evidence" of his daily
life, how he stands in relation to an eternal law that has,
whether he knows it or not, classed him among the saved or
the damned from the beginning of time.

This transformation of thought implies some important
transformations in the sorts of stories we tell ourselves
about our condition. The great sociologist Max Weber, in
one of his most penetrating analyses traced the economic
"fiction" of capitalism—our belief that making money is a
kind of secular salvation and a sign of spiritual power—to
the rise of Calvinism. If good fortune in this life is a promis-
sory note of God's favor in the next, then it becomes a positive moral sanction to try and "succeed" as much as you
can, since your success or lack of it will give you the surest
of clues about your eternal fate. But that, of course, is a relatively primitive derivation from the Protestant, melodramatic mode of thought and storytelling. At a more sophisticated level, these concerns imply some serious alterations
in our idea of the City itself.

The "law" of predestination, the "law" of the abstract judiciary, the criminal code of Rousseau's formulation: all
these varieties of law suggest at least one common thing, a
law that has become so massive and so universalized that it

Violence + Melodrama

allows very little to exist *outside* it. The City of laws which
was originally founded and civilized against the encroachments of circumambient chaos has grown large enough to
possess the entire landscape. It has become a truly technological city, one where we may go from end to end and see
only the work of man. And is this not the City we inhabit?

Norton Long, in his book *The Unwalled City,* suggests
that the crucial problem of modern urban society is locating
a principle of social cohesion, a myth of identity, in a city
whose traditional "walls"—both its physical and ritual, liturgical structures of independence and autonomy—have
largely disappeared. Long is an economist and political
theorist, with only the most attenuated interest in the matters of storytelling and mythmaking I am discussing here, so
I am especially pleased to record his insight, since it tallies
so well with the specifically literary and filmic structures I
have examined. The city ceased to exist, said Weber, when
its walls were torn down. After it lost that fundamentally
epic principle of containment and continuity with its own
past, it diffused into a loose amalgam of suburbs, industrial
and trade centers, and pockets of poverty and crime, none
of which have any real hope of reforging connections with
the traditions of cultural creativity or solidarity of which
they are the shattered remnants. Long's concern is to deny
Weber's thesis, and to argue for ways in which the modern
commercial city, with all its suburban sprawl and multina-
tional, multiracial, sometimes multilingual complexity, can
continue to satisfy the deep needs for order and identity
which are the traditional psychic rewards of the idea of the
City.

Now this world, the world of the unwalled City, is in a
very real sense the world which the hero of melodrama attempts to thread, the world for which he attempts to locate
the clue, the fact, the essential bit of information which will
resolve the seeming contradictions and chaos of its life into
a fundamental continuity with the epic and romance past,

the past of its own best ideas of nobility, dignity, and decency. It is also the world of the criminal and the wage
slave, and of all those characters who discover—sometimes
to their cost—how complex the law really *is* that allows us
to be human.

Let us begin with *Citizen Kane.* The film is, whatever else,
melodramatic. The history of Charles Foster Kane's publish-
ing empire, and of his gradual isolation from the people
around him until finally he is self-strangled by his own in-
ability to love, is of course an exemplary tale—but exemplary of what? The welter of interpretation and analysis to
which *Kane* has been submitted—it is probably the most
written-about film in the history of the art—can blunt our
response to it, can convince us that we understand its mystery when, in fact, to "understand" the mystery is to lose
much of the power of the film. Is wealth bad for you? Does
pride make it impossible for us to love each other? Is capitalism a soul-destroying force in the modern world? All
these morals, and others equally vapid, may be drawn from
the film, and none approaches its rich, Gothic resonance. Its
first reviewers, even those most sympathetic and enthusiastic, were confused by it; and their confusion may be a better response than the more elegant and academic discourses
that have come to surround *Kane* since.

For the confusion of the film is not simply due to an in-
ability of the naive to put together the multiple flashbacks in
which Kane's story is told. It is a confusion at the heart of
the film's own power. The flashbacks *are* confusing, not
because they give us contradictory information about Kane
or Kane's life, but precisely because they take the idea of a
"life" and convert it to the stuff of a mystery, a pilgrim's
progress through a world where the landmarks and the
monsters are indistinct, through a city without walls. And in
this respect the frame-story of *Kane* is not, as some commentators have argued, an excrescence on the main business
of the film, but central to our "reading" of it. We begin with

a film within a film. After the initial sequence showing
Kane's death and the gigantic, empty collection of world-
cultural bric-a-brac which was his mansion, we see the
March of Time–style newsreel documentary which provides,
in brief and telegraphic fashion, all the details of the life
whose mysteries the body of the film will plumb. Except, of
course, for the meaning of Kane's last word, "Rosebud."
Reporter Thompson (William Alland, whose face is never
clearly seen) is sent by his bosses to interview Kane's friends
and associates and discover who or what "Rosebud" was.
As one of the bosses says to him at the end of this framing
sequence, "It will probably turn out to be a very simple
thing."

And so it does, though neither Thompson nor anyone else
in the film ever discovers its meaning. Only we witness, in
the last scene of the film, the burning of Kane's childhood
sled, "Rosebud," among the other debris of his lifetime as a
collector of things and people. Thompson's quest for
"human interest" (that most ironic and debased of journal-
istic terms) is a failure. Or is it? We can object to the last
scene of *Kane,* where the secret of "Rosebud" is revealed, as
a sentimental excess in an otherwise stunning film, or as a
trivialization of Kane's own agonizing loneliness. "Rosebud," the viewer will remember, is the sled the young Charlie Kane is playing with in the earliest scene from his life we
are shown: when banker Thatcher comes to his parents'
cabin to announce that the boy has come into a large inheritance and, as befits his new position, should be taken east to
go to the best schools. It is the sled with which young Charlie, who does not want to go, tearfully strikes Thatcher. It is
Kane's lost innocence, etc. All of these meanings, again, are
there in the film, just as are all the bromidic morals I have
suggested we could extrapolate from *Kane.* But none of
them really explains why "Rosebud" *works,* why, in spite of
all the critical objections that can be raised against it as a

plot device, it is such a central and unforgettable feature of the film's continuing power to fascinate us.

Leo Braudy, in his excellent book *The World in a Frame*, makes a point about *Kane* that goes far toward clarifying things. The important thing about "Rosebud," Braudy observes, is that it is evidence. That is, it is an object that implicates rather than symbolizes something about Kane's personality and past: a clue rather than a metaphor.

In fact, it is with clues such as Rosebud that *Citizen Kane* abounds, almost to the exclusion of metaphors, symbols, or the more conventional varieties of meaning. The profound modernity of *Kane* is its articulation of a world of things that surround and threaten to strangle its characters, to none of which we can assign a specific "meaning." Indeed, the newsreel documentary that is our first exposure to Kane's career is itself a thing, a clue, an object that points toward Kane's meaning but does not itself participate in or include that meaning. *Kane* is one of the most crucial and influential films ever made, that is, because its elementary story line—Thompson's quest for evidences of Kane's salvation or damnation—is so closely allied to the nature of film narrative itself.

Reading the film as melodrama, in the special sense I have tried to assign to that term, we can say in fact that one of the "mysteries" of *Kane* is that it is not Kane's story at all but Thompson's. The reporter, the faceless citizen on a quest for the truth, the reasonably prudent man (that hallowed fiction of tort litigations) is culturally and spiritually the heir to Kane's ramshackle estate, to the world of moral confusion he leaves behind him. And his search—which is, after all, on one level a search to make a film about Charles Foster Kane which will have "human interest"—is also the search we, as viewers of *Citizen Kane,* are embarked upon. The difference is that we are allowed to fulfill the quest, we see what Thompson never gets to see, Rosebud. I have said that *Kane* is a film without "symbols." But there is one object in the film which, on re-viewings, becomes almost a symbol of the special—and archetypal—epistemological world of the film. Kane and his second wife Susan are sitting in the gigantic, funereal salon of Xanadu, Kane's mansion. The marriage, like all Kane's attempts at love, is failing, and as they sit separated by what seem to be the acres of the room they have to shout at each other even to be heard. "You never give me anything I really care about," whines Susan to her husband as she crouches before the immense fireplace, playing with an equally oversize jigsaw puzzle. It is the puzzle that fascinates, a shattered whole to be put back together, not a meaning but, like puzzles of every sort, a *possibility* of a meaning; a set of clues whose assembly will fill in the absence of love.

After the "recollection" of the newsreel, the first recollection, the first flashback, in *Citizen Kane* is by a dead man. Walter Parks Thatcher, a financier and political gray eminence to whom Kane's parents entrusted the education and supervision of their newly rich son, has left some reminiscences of his young ward among his papers, and Thompson begins his search by reading these in the crypt-like gloom of the Thatcher Memorial Library: a dead man's reminiscences of another dead man. Kane and Thatcher despise each other throughout their lives, and at the low point of Kane's fortunes, when his newspaper empire is failing and he is retreating more and more into the privacy that finally destroys him, he is forced to sign over control of most of his holdings to the cold and unloving capitalist who has been his surrogate father and whom he loathes. As he signs the papers, Kane ruefully observes that, had he not been rich, he might have been able to become something or somebody really important. Thatcher asks him, "What would you like to have been?" And Kane's response is unhesitating: "Everything you hate." It is one of the most powerful moments in the film, as Thompson (always the implied spectator of the ac-

tion) witnesses Kane's obsessive, central motivation, his
hatred and rejection of all that Thatcher, the remote and
flawed patriarch of his world, stands for.

In this scene, in other words, we can see the three generations of heroes, the three generations of story, we have discussed so far. The reporter examines the patriarch's evidence about the intermediate figure, the young agent of
civilization upon whom both depend for their final meaning:
king, knight, and detective are all there. But something has
gone wrong. Something always goes wrong in melodrama—
otherwise, it would not be melodrama; the puzzle becomes
confused, the terms of the game are obscured, the inheritance of order is covered over and distorted by its own
growing web of complications.

This line of inheritance characterizes not only *Citizen
Kane,* but a great number of stories at this level of narrative.
It is no accident that the nineteenth-century novel—English,
American, or European—is as concerned as it is with problems arising from inheritances, legacies, and wills. Whether
in *Citizen Kane* or *Bleak House, The Red and the Black* or
Before the Revolution, we are dealing to some extent with
the problems of inheritance, and the more dangerous problems of the quest by the detective, the single intelligence, to
discover and define his inheritance in a City which seems
organized so as to conceal that crucial information. Things
have gone wrong, or the puzzle is missing a few of its central pieces: in either case, in the world of the melodramatic
film and of the classic novel the crucial and unspoken problem of the hero is precisely to uncover his own heritage, his
own relationship to that central law that is the sanction of
all the other laws which surround him and define his world.

The figure of the knight becomes the figure of the detective—or, more generally, the quester for information. And
the City, the principle of cultural continuity, becomes epit-
omized in the problems of inheritance, of the transmission
of money, of the making of Wills, of Legacies.

There is of course a pun implicit in the word "Will," one which resonates through a number of novels and films of the sort I am now examining. In an urban, economically complex society, my Will is something like the fullest expression and most crucial test of my ability to control and order my own financial universe, to preserve and perpetuate the state of affairs I have imposed upon, or managed to construct from, my world: my Will, that is, is ideally the final and fullest expression of my *will*.

But inheritances in this world go notoriously wrong. The heirs begin to quarrel over their portions; new or putative heirs, if the inheritance is large enough, are mysteriously forthcoming; and the law courts themselves tend to obscure instead of clarify the mechanics of transmission. These are immediately recognizable as the details of any number of melodramatic plots, ranging from monumental novels like Dickens' *Bleak House* and Henry James' *The Wings of the Dove* to the most tawdry and cliche-ridden of Victorian stage entertainments. We may also remember that the central pathos of *Citizen Kane,* the detail that makes Thompson's quest for and loss of Rosebud possible, is the fact that Kane leaves no heir—that his Will, in other words, is self-strangulated and sterile.

At a more general level, the problem of inheritance is simply the problem of money, of jobs. How does one make money, and what measures may one legitimately take to ensure the making of enough money to survive—and how much is enough? Henry James, who knew as much about the moral problems of those matters as anyone, once observed that to be truly rich is to be able to satisfy every requirement of the imagination. And the poet Howard Nemerov* once wittily defined the novel as a story about an ordinary man who would never lie, cheat, steal, or murder—except once in his life, when it really mattered. Be-

* In conversation.

tween those two epigrams lies the territory of melodrama, of the nineteenth- and twentieth-century novel and of the most popular narrative films. For money is, in the urban world I am now examining, not simply the means to an end but an almost sacramental element, a concretion of power itself.

The poetic power of money has not been generally discussed by literary or film critics. But its pressure is felt and manifested in numerous and complicated ways. F. W. Murnau's *The Last Laugh*—one of the most influential and richest films of Weimar Germany—is among other things an extended fantasia of the themes of money, the City, and the victim/detective hero. And the often-discussed "happy ending" of the film makes a kind of elegant and oddly bitter sense in this context of ideas.

The film's German title, *Der Letzte Mann,* is more immediately appropriate for this dark story than the optimistic, even flippant English one. For the central character, the hotel porter who is demoted from his officious, uniformed role to the demeaning job of lavatory attendant, *is* the "last man." He is man at the end of his tether, man at the end of his world and his self-respect and, by implication, the last man alive in a world grown intolerant of individuals. But he is also a man out of a job—or, rather, a man shunted from a satisfying, fulfilling job to a lower, personally revolting one.

Emil Jannings' portrayal of the Doorman is one of the most triumphant, compelling performances in the history of film. And among the specific triumphs of that performance, perhaps the most striking is the combination of pomposity, vanity, stilliness, and deep human vulnerability that Jannings manages to mime. His Doorman convinces us of his humanity, a humanity he shares with us, precisely by being nonallegorical in a story which has much of the simplicity and abstraction of allegory: his is a very real toad in a brilliantly imaginary garden.

More to the point, though, *The Last Laugh* is a commentary on money and the function of money that incarnates

the transition from the world of romance to that of melodrama. Marshall McLuhan, in *The Gutenberg Galaxy,*
suggests that one of the crucial transformations from the
medieval to the early Renaissance or early modern sensibility is the shift in imagination from a world of *roles* to a
world of *jobs.* The inhabitant of a role is a man whose work
is an expression not only of his distinctive powers or gifts
but of his place in a global conception of the universe, of the
"right" way for him to be. The artisan, the cleric, and the
knight are all—at least in the official fictions of the romance
vision—men who feel the pressure of this particular kind of
indentity. But a job is something else again, and here McLuhan and Karl Marx are in fundamental agreement. A job is,
has to be, "alienated" labor, since it is an arbitrary direction
for the employment of one's talents rather than a vocation
that inserts those talents, means and ends, into a total sense
of existence.

The Doorman in *The Last Laugh* is trapped in a job that
he thinks is a role. Our first view of him is at his post at the
expensive, glamorous hotel he works for, in the full, absurdly overdone uniform, acting out the role of his own
pomposity, blowing his whistle at cab drivers and struggling
(he is an old man) to handle the immense trunks of the hotel's wealthy guests. He is a king, or at least a knight, in his
own little world. But the film cruelly reminds us, from the
beginning, what a little and hallucinatory world it is. And it
is a world in which he is already at the mercy of forces over
which he has no control, a pawn in knight's clothing,
though he does not yet know it. When the hotel manager
gives him notice that he is to be demoted from Doorman to
washroom attendant, he is humiliated. Returning home to
his squalid apartment, he gets drunk and, unable to tell his
daughter and neighbors of his demotion, dons his cap and
wildly, desperately blows his treasured whistle while neighbors and daughter roar with laughter. Like Lear, in other
words, he has the made the shuddering transition from lord

of his own world to fool. But while Lear crosses that gap of his own volition, sacrificing the robes and symbology of power that separate him from the choas of supply and demand, the Doorman is simply and terrifyingly awakened to the fact that he already lives in, and has always lived in, that later world. When, next day, he begins his new job, clothed in the demeaning white jacket of his post and trapped in the lavatory, he has shrunk. But he has shrunk to the dimensions of his own "real" size, the dimensions of a world without hieratic roles, where one's job is not the key but the challenge and perhaps the enemy of one's identity. Rousseau describes the third kind of law, which I am calling the law of melodrama, as the "sanction" of the earlier laws of the polity. But it is a sanction which demands its own reality, which is also to say its own power to reform and reduce the broader, more expansive possibilities of epic and romance. And the "crime" which the *letzte Mann* of Murnau's film commits is precisely the crime of ignorance: he does not know, he must be painfully taught, the parameters of his own selfhood.

Innocence and Experience

Kane does not learn that he has wasted his life on a system that offers him no real human salvation until the very end— until it is too late. And the Doorman in *The Last Laugh* learns the same lesson at the beginning of the main action of the film, and spends the rest of the story trying to assimilate that bitter wisdom. The world of melodrama, in other words, can tolerate and celebrate two kinds of heroes, the deluded optimists who are defeated in the end by the innocence of their own trust in "things as they are," and the pessimists who, out of some primary and shocking realization of the deformity of contemporary social life, try to construct and sometimes succeed in constructing a *modus vivendi* with the system. The first kind of hero is the man who is reassured about his life until some great and ineluctable catastrophe changes its whole shape; the second is the man who, after that catastrophe has occurred, manages to reconstruct from it a new innocence, a new basis for believing in the efficacy of the law.

These alternatives—a bitter experience and a perhaps even subtler innocence—run through the course of the nineteenth-century novel and the narrative film. In the English novel at the end of the nineteenth century, two masters appear who dramatize the complementarity in an especially striking way. Henry James and Joseph Conrad were close friends and warm admirers of each other's work. And between the two of them fiction attains a watershed of self-consciousness, undergoes a self-discovery unlike anything previous in the English tradition. In James, the tradition of Victorian "innocence," the belief in the ultimate benevolence of the urban universe, achieves a kind of final expression. And in Conrad, a more hard-bitten and pessimistic "experience," a conviction that all human culture and all human art are unavailing against the chaos which lies around us, finds its first and perhaps its definitive modern expression. These writers define, between them, the alternatives for the kind of urban, melodramatic narrative I am discussing.

Generalizations like this, of course, are useful only when we realize that they are half lies, half realities. Neither Henry James nor Joseph Conrad, nor any other novelist worth reading, probably, ever thought of himself as "continuing" an older tradition of "innovating" a new one. It is critics, not creators, who transform the history of literature into a kind of massive corporate enterprise complete with changes in the board of directors and redefinitions of company policy. Nevertheless, it is true that James and Conrad show a fascinating and crucial relationship to each other, in terms of the modalities of violence their respective worlds contain, in terms of the openness or closure of the social games they invent.

The novels of Henry James, with their tightly defined social world and almost mandarin concentration upon the details of behavior, have often been called the vision of a "closed" world. It is a correct description—although usually invoked for the wrong reasons. Any careful reader of James, especially of the novels of his late years, soon discovers that beneath the surface calm of the action, and implicit within the difficult, torturous prose in which that action is narrated, is an obsessive concern with moral choice and the possibilities of good and evil as profound as any attained or envisioned in the tradition of the novel. Indeed, we can say that James's imagination of evil, and of the moral chaos introduced by crime into society, is stronger than that of many of his more overtly violent colleagues in fiction, precisely because he is able to imagine the very real effects of criminality even *within* the bounds of the criminal law. We need not be murderers, thieves, or betrayers to violate the sanctions that hold us together: we need only dissemble, raise a skeptical eyebrow at the right place in a conversation, treat another human being as an object rather than a soul, and we have encountered the void that lies on the other side of civilized law. But James's world *is* closed: it is a world where one assumes that chaos, the void, the apocalyptic eruption of violence (which is most often, of course, the subtle and quiet violence of the betrayal of love) comes from *without,* comes as the intrusion of bestiality into a closed game which otherwise could maintain its own balance, and which can still—if everyone involved is intelligent enough— regain that balance, however precariously. No one who has read him can really suspect James of "simple" answers to any problem: Whistler's famous observation about James's involved prose style is that he chewed more than he bit off. But at the heart of his fiction—and at the heart of one variety of this kind of fiction—lies a fundamental assumption that society is a good, that it offers human beings real options for positive moral action, and that its ethical confusions or deflections can be, somehow, solved.

This attitude is not innocence. In fact, as James's fiction develops and grows in power, it becomes a more and more difficult, grim meditation on the vulnerability and even the dangers of innocence. But the possibility of innocence remains, and the further possibility that past innocence and past the end of innocence lies the hope of reconstitution—of society, of the self, of whatever has been damaged or destroyed by the eruption of chaos.

In *The Golden Bowl* these themes and attitudes achieve a power both of articulation and orchestration unlike almost anything else in English fiction. The basic situation of the novel is simple and even, as James himself confessed in his notebooks, somewhat tawdry. Adam Verver, a widowed American millionaire, and his daughter Maggie have come to England on a grand tour of Europe during which Adam is buying the art treasures he loves. In England, they encounter Charlotte Stant, a brilliant and attractive indigent young lady, and Prince Amerigo, an impoverished but deeply cultured and sensitive nobleman. Charlotte and the Prince have been lovers, but their financial circumstances make it impossible for them to marry. So Charlotte arranges a grotesque scheme whereby she marries Adam Verver, the Prince marries Maggie Verver, and they continue their adulterous affair—after some understandable hesitation—under the very eyes of their spouses, benefactors, and trusting friends. Both Adam and Maggie are American innocents of the type that fascinates James. Both have intelligence, wit, even canniness—but also a boundless faith in the good intentions of others and in the fundamental clarity of moral choice. And it is Maggie, not her father, who at the novel's turning point discovers the terrible consequences of that innocence. It is she who learns—without the thing itself ever being expressed—of Charlotte's and the Prince's betrayal. And it is she who, carrying the burden of that all but unbearable knowledge, attempts to salvage her own marriage and her father's, preserving at the same time her father's innocence (or ignorance) of the abyss on which all four characters are perched. In this she succeeds, though at a cost to all involved that almost makes us doubt the *goodness* of such goodness. At the end, a defeated Charlotte is about to return to America with Adam—who himself is distraught and saddened by the separation from his beloved daughter—while the Prince and Maggie remain in London. Maggie, or the vision of good for which Maggie stands, is triumphant; the order of things, even after a deep and violent fissure, has been righted. But few writers show us the painfulness and the terror of this ultimately optimistic vision as fully as does James.

It is not difficult, indeed, to see in James's vision of the chances for social survival a rather close resemblance to the most characteristic films of Alfred Hitchcock. Hitchcock has been, by now, moralized over and interpreted in terms of his "metaphysics" probably as much as any director in film history; often with great intelligence, more often with great silliness. But whatever we may think about lengthy and ingenious discussions of the doctrine of the Fall in *Vertigo* or Catholic theories of penance in *Notorious,* it is undeniable that Hitchcock throughout his long career has managed to transmute the elements of the thriller, his chosen genre, into structures of often dazzling and frequently disturbing moral implication. The process is very like what James managed to do with his own inherited tradition, the tradition of the novel of manners and social comedy: by penetrating to the underlying implications of their respective narrative forms, both men achieve a kind of artistic finality, an understanding of the potentially apocalyptic nature of their universes which is all the more convincing because it avoids, at the last moment, the full shock of apocalypse. (*Vertigo* and

Psycho are, perhaps, exceptions.) For Hitchcock as for James, that is, society is ultimately salvageable; the chaos of violence erupts from outside into an essentially balanced and benign culture. Again, this is not to say that Hitchcock's worlds are comfortable; but they are, in a deep sense, at least habitable. Indeed, in many of his films this ultimate habitability of the world is very close to being the explicit plot.

From *The Thirty-Nine Steps* (1935) through *North by Northwest* (1959) to *Frenzy* (1972) and *Family Plot* (1975), one of his most permanent and famous situations has been that of the "wrong man," the ordinary individual who finds himself thrust into a situation of nightmarish complexity and danger through a case of mistaken identities, or who finds himself accused of a crime he did not commit. But, of course, the "wrong man" theme involves also a sense of the basic innocence of the accused individual. Like the heros and heroines of James, the heros and heroines of Hitchcock's films exist in a condition of unthinking, uncaring normality until they are pulled out of that somnolent state by the absurd accident of circumstance. But the idea of innocence remains. However brutalized or tarnished by the circumstances that imprison them, Hitchcock's characters always try to fight back toward the "normal" state of society, the "normal" state of their own lives in which they can continue to function as citizens, husbands, wives, etc. For Hitchcock, in other words, the ordinary is also the optimal.

In *North by Northwest* this thesis is established as completely as it ever is in Hitchcock's films. Róger Thornhill (Cary Grant) is a successful Chicago businessman and bachelor who, through a ridiculous accident, is mistaken for a spy and nearly killed by the ring of foreign agents the supposed spy is working against. In the course of his attempts to avoid the spies, furthermore, Thornhill meets and falls in love with a beautiful woman, Eve Kendall (Eva Marie Saint) who is herself a spy, a double agent in fact, working with the foreign agents who are out to kill Thornhill but really employed by the American intelligence agency which is also carefully watching Thornhill's persecution by the foreigners. It is, on the surface, an absurd plot; and *North by Northwest*, like most of Hitchcock, is as enjoyable as a comedy as it is as a melodrama. But the absurdity of the plot is part of the content, part of the point. Thornhill has crossed a boundary: a boundary which it can be death to cross. Like a James hero, Thornhill must both lose and rediscover his innocence. But the value of that innocence is itself never questioned.

Without overschematizing or overpsychoanalyzing the film—two options which have too often been taken with Hitchcock—we can observe that Thornhill, at the beginning of the action, is innocent but flawed, a bachelor still tied to his mother, a case of arrested sexual development. All this is hinted at in the most delicate, lightest of ways, but is nevertheless important. Thornhill is the kind of middle-aged boy who does not need to be reminded to buy his mother a birthday present. All of that changes as he is mistaken for an American secret agent and thrust into the complicated plot of the film. But it changes in an interesting way; Thornhill does not so much lose his innocence (like the Doorman, say, of *The Last Laugh*) as he preserves it, but on a higher level of responsiveness to the real complexity of life. Part of this sense in *North by Northwest* is the result not so much of the explicit action or dialogue as of the casting of Cary Grant in the role of Thornhill. Grant, perhaps the most accomplished comic *actor* (as opposed to comedian) in American film, brings to *North by Northwest* an irrepressible sense that nothing, after all, can really go too wrong in the world. Even when he is being strafed, in the film's best-remembered scene, by an airplane on an Indiana road, even when he and Eva Marie Saint, in the climax of the film, are being pursued by killers along the massive slopes of the Mount Rushmore statuary, his very presence carries with it a kind of reassurance; not so much that, as with all melodrama, we never really expect the hero to die, but rather that this much physical and personal grace will be adequate to survive the void, will be enough to free Thornhill—and us—from the nightmare of menace and violence that has momentarily surrounded him.

And, in fact, it is because of the nightmare opening up before him that Thornhill meets and falls in love with the beautiful Eve Kendall, winning what at least implicitly is the first fully mature and fully responsive sexual experience in his life. Through his fall from innocence, that is, Thornhill is introduced to another, better version of innocence through a lady named Eve. It is not exactly good theology, but eloquent and humanizing mythmaking. That Eve has been, for the sake of her undercover work for American intelligence, the mistress of foreign spymaster Philip Vandamm, only underscores the quality of the gift she gives Thornhill. For an innocence not based on a thorough recognition of the fallen nature of all of us is a poisonous, claustrophobic innocence; and that is not only good theology, but excellent Hitchcock. A rather more grim version of the same situation occurred in Hitchcock's *Notorious* (1946) with Ingrid Bergman being urged by secret agent Cary Grant to become the mistress of Claude Rains. But there as here the outcome of this grisly and seedy event is a rediscovery and reassertion of the things that can bring us together and ennoble rather than destroy us.

The general movement of *North by Northwest,* as has often enough been remarked, is defined by the film's title. In their search to discover and destroy the spy network of Vandamm, Thornhill and Eve are led from Chicago north by northwest to Mount Rushmore, South Dakota. But in terms of the City-myth I have been describing it is also important to notice that the movement of the film is out of the City, from closed to open landscapes. Of course, since the City of melodramatic narrative is "unwalled," one never really leaves it; and Thornhill and Eve Kendall carry with them into South Dakota the full complexity and danger which first grasped Thornhill in the middle of Chicago. But the movement from enclosure to openness, like the parallel movement from sexual immaturity to satisfying sexual love, from innocence to mature innocence, is essential to the rhythm of the film. The tension between claustrophobia and vertigo is central to the plots of a number of Hitchcock films. What I have already described as the counterpoint between closed rooms and the unwalled city is part of the central situation of *Lifeboat, Rear Window, Vertigo,* and *Psycho.* But in *North by Northwest* it achieves one of its fullest, most graphically beautiful and most eminently reassuring forms. The pilgrimage of Thornhill and Eve is, after all, not simply into open space, into the myth of unspoiled landscape as a refutation and cancellation of the enclosure of the City. It is a journey to a landscape which is also a human artifact. The monumental sculpture of the presidents on Mount Rushmore is a metaphor, simultaneously comic and immensely serious, for the extent of man's dominion over the land itself; antiromantic if you wish, for it insists that there is no escape from the human scale into sublime vistas, that our fate and our responsibility is precisely to face the degree to which we have made the world our own, infinitely extensive dwelling place.

In Hitchcock at his most assertive, in other words, as in James at his most hopeful, there exists the chance for reconciling the closed room of the psyche and the open, agoraphobic hell which is other people. This wedding of inhospitable alternatives is graphically caught in one of the most lyrical sequences Hitchcock has ever filmed, just before the final pursuit and climax. In a birch forest near Mount Rushmore, Thornhill says goodbye to Eve, who is about to leave the country with Vandamm. One is quite certain by this point in the film that this will not really be goodbye. And in fact their leavetaking subtly underscores the fact that—in

terms of the surface plot and the psychic rhythms of the
film—they are literally each other's destiny. They approach
and converse, in full profile, amid the austere, at once classically ordered and "naturally' spontaneous vertical lines of
the birch trunks. Openness and enclosure, landscape and the
organizing hand of man are caught for a moment reconciled
to each other, just as Thornhill's naivety and Eve's experience are creating a mutual and mutually supportive *modus
vivendi*—although they do not know it yet.

The benign good humor of *North by Northwest*, though,
is less easy to find in Hitchcock's later films. Not that it
ever fully disappears: the often criticized *dénouement* of
Psycho, in which a psychiatrist explains away the true, harrowing terror of the action in bogus, Sunday-supplement
Freudian terms, is—whether satisfying or not—a reassertion
of the normality, the rationality of events much like the
conclusion of a classic detective story. The world is a terrify-
ing place, but we can name the terror and thereby, to some
extent at least, control and contain it. This, though, is not
an easy balance of terror to maintain. As the landscape of
the City, and our own understanding of the vulnerability of
its culture deepens, the chaos can appear more and more to
come not from without, but from within: to be not a random eruption into human affairs, but the very condition of
life. This is, on one level, the process of evolution I noted at
the beginning of this chapter from the classic English detective story to the Chandleresque, American mode. But it is
also the point of division between the fiction of James and
that of his friend Conrad, the moment in the history of
storytelling when the closed game of melodrama becomes
terrifyingly, vertiginously open, when the rules of survival
themselves are imagined as subject to instantaneous and
inexplicable change. One attractive definition of civilization
is that it is a mutual agreement to leave the abyss alone. But
the corollary to that definition is that once the abyss has

been recognized, leaving it alone becomes harder and harder.

At that moment of transition, we also begin to move from the world of melodrama to the world of satire, where the life of the City is not merely threatening but intolerable. The novels of Conrad and the films of Fritz Lang between them suggest the dimensions of the transition. For in Conrad and Lang, as opposed to James and Hitchcock, society is no longer assumed to be naturally benevolent. And that change in vision, however slight or subtle, implies a massive shift in the moral weight of the universe described. In novels like *Lord Jim, The Secret Agent,* and *Heart of Darkness* Conrad explores the implications of a view of society probably as unrelenting and dark as any in the last two centuries. In *The Secret Agent* especially, London is a city grown almost intolerably threatened by the forces which, deep within men, are on the verge of erupting and reclaiming their domain over society. That "law" which is the sanction of all other laws of culture, and which is the crucial law of melodrama, is here revealed to be a legal fiction. Our order, our structures of civilization, even our imagination of time and space, are for Conrad a set of screens we throw up around ourselves to stave off our enforced recognition of the horror of bestiality and vacuity, the heart of darkness that lies not outside, but within.

Verloc, the secret agent of the book's title, is in fact a double agent, ostensibly a member of a terrorist organization but really working for the British government as an *agent provocateur* to bring disgrace upon the anarchists. He is a shabby little man, a dealer in vaguely pornographic novels whose secret agent work is simply added income. In other words, he is the figure of the private detective as knight reduced to laborer, as hieratic role reduced to job at its most tawdry. His superiors hatch the plan—which Verloc passes on to his revolutionary cadre—of blowing up the

Greenwich Observatory as the ultimate terrorist act. It is a plot not only against culture but against space and time themselves: destroy the instruments with which we perceive and order our civilized "reality," Conrad suggests, and you thereby destroy that "reality" itself, returning man to the primal chaos over which we construct the rickety bridges of our rationality. But the plot fails. Verloc sends his wife's idiot brother Stevie to set the bomb, and Stevie blows himself up. In the investigation that follows, Verloc's wife eventually learns that her husband is responsible for her cherished brother's death and in one of the most striking scenes in all Conrad's fiction, kills Verloc. She herself attempts to escape with one of Verloc's anarchist companions, but is abandoned by him and kills herself. Finally, at the end of this grim book, all that is left in the world are the anarchists, the government anti-anarchists, and the unthinking hordes of the city of London who do not understand the deadly and chaotic games being played in their midst.

The City has been progressively emptied, throughout *The Secret Agent,* of all but the flimsiest of its claims to offer human beings a productive, creative, significant life on earth. And with a kind of inverse mysticism—a mysticism directed away from, not toward, transcendence—Conrad makes the predictions of the anarchists come true. The plot to blow up Greenwich Observatory fails; but its implied threat, a threat to all the pretensions of civilization to civilize, comes terrifyingly true in the climax of the book when good, simple, drab Winnie Verloc gives in to the beast of vengeance within her and kills her husband. We see the murder from Verloc's own point of view. He is lying on his sofa: he has just confessed to Winnie his culpability in Stevie's death:

> He waited. Mrs. Verloc was coming. As if the home-
> less soul of Stevie had flown for shelter straight to the

breast of his sister, guardian, and protector, the resemblance of her face with that of her brother grew at every
step, even to the droop of the lower lip, even to the slight
divergence of the eyes. But Mr. Verloc did not see that.
He was lying on his back and staring upwards. He saw
partly on the ceiling and partly on the wall the moving
shadow of an arm with a clenched hand holding a carving knife. It flickered up and down. Its movements were
leisurely. They were leisurely enough for Mr. Verloc to
recognize the limb and the weapon.

When Hitchcock made his film based on *The Secret
Agent, Sabotage,* in 1936, he altered the ending to a happy
one in which Winnie (Sylvia Sidney) after the death of Verloc (Oscar Homolka) is united with the heroic and dashing
young detective who finally "solves" the case. More importantly, though, he altered this unforgettable scene. In *Sabotage,* after Homolka has crassly confessed his involvement in
Stevie's death at the dinner table, Sylvia Sidney—for a moment—glances at the carving knife between them on the
table. Homolka follows her glance and advances upon his
wife, whereupon she grabs the knife in self-defense. But
Homolka continues to rush at her and literally impales himself upon the knife. Audiences, especially student audiences
who have read the novel, never fail to laugh at this scene as
a moment of bad faith or sentimentality on the director's
part. It may be that, but it is also a natural and, in its way,
profound substantiation of the fundamental benevolence—however complex—of Hitchcock's vision of society.
For, as Conrad says of Winnie's murder of her husband:

> Into that plunging blow, delivered over the side of the
> couch, Mrs. Verloc had put all the inheritance of her im-
> memorial and obscure descent, the simple ferocity of the
> age of caverns and the unbalanced nervous fury of the
> age of bar-rooms.

Not only a reversion to the terrifyingly aboriginal, in other words, but a moment in which she—and we—perceive that the distance between the sterile, disinterested rapine of our animal past and the sterile, disinterested rapine of the "age of bar-rooms," *our* age, is actually nil. The "game" of civilized life is laid open to the total ferocity around and beneath it: it is a myth of civilization Hitchcock, in his most characteristic films, avoids. But not always. Twenty-four years after *Sabotage,* Hitchcock did film this scene. It is, visually and emotionally, the shower-murder sequence from *Psycho* (1960). But even there the bias toward a preserved innocence, some kind of marginal salvage, is implied. For the murder victim in *Psycho* is Marion Crane (Janet Leigh), who has just decided to return the money she has stolen— who has reentered, in other words, the structures of civilized, decent social behavior—while the killer, "Mrs. Bates," is mad (is not even "Mrs. Bates"). And while we may be terrified by madness, we are not as terrified by that as we can be by the spectacle of ordinary men and women reverting to the primitive modalities of violence which make mockery of our very concepts of "sanity" and "madness."

However the vision of Fritz Lang, Hitchcock's equal in genius and like Hitchcock primarily identified with the thriller film, seems quite close to that of Conrad, and to the all but despairing myth of the City which underlies Conrad's fiction. Near the middle of *The Secret Agent* there is an interview between the Assistant Commissioner of Police and a "great Personage," Sir Ethelred, who is urging the Assistant Commissioner to investigate the explosion near Greenwich with the greatest dispatch. Sir Ethelred, like all "great Personages" in the modern bureaucracy, is continually pressed for time, continually insisting that he is not at liberty for any but the most important questions of state, any but the most presifted information: although he is also of course condescendingly gracious with his time in interviews with underlings. At the end of the interview, Sir Ethelred dismisses the Assistant Commissioner. And as he does, Conrad gives us a privileged, inhuman viewpoint on the human action that has been played out before us:

> He turned his big head slowly, and over his shoulder gave a haughty, oblique stare to the ponderous marble timepiece with the sly, feeble tick. The gilt hands had taken the opportunity to steal through no less than five and twenty minutes behind his back.

This passage resonates throughout *The Secret Agent,* for it is the most ironic and most disturbing articulation of the book's theme. Time—the time in which our lives are measured, and which we think we control because we have named it, partitioned it into minutes, seconds, and hours—that same time is in fact the devourer of life, is, whatever minimal control or order we think we have imposed upon it, not really human time at all but cosmic time, the time of the biological clock each one of us carries within and the cosmological clock the universe itself carries. And its scale is not a human scale. The clock has "stolen" twenty-five minutes while Sir Ethelred has been speaking. But that means, simply, the twenty-five "minutes"—and what are minutes but artificial divisions of the great moment of universal creation and demise, of entropy itself?—have been lost to the "great Personage" while he spoke about his comparatively petty plans for his comparatively petty investigation. Conrad, perhaps as much as any English novelist of his time, forces us to see that on the cosmic scale—the only scale we can, finally, call real—human activity is simply a mockery. Man is crucified, as he is crucified nowhere else, upon his own clocks.

And although the last image is presented somewhat disingenuously, it *is* finally difficult not to think of Conrad in connection with the films of Fritz Lang. Lang, more consistently and more brilliantly than any other American director, is the father of the *film noir,* about which I will have more to say. But, more important, he remained throughout his long and creative career one of the most intelligent and acidulous explorers of film's potential to describe not the advance but the decline and self-strangulation of Western culture. Partly this is the result of his origins: for he was one of that select and dazzlingly intelligent group of German directors who came to prominence during the troubled years of the Weimar Republic, and whose films—whose world— was precisely the world of the City gone manic, the City as social and psychic disease. But Lang went beyond even the nightmare world of Murnau's *The Last Laugh.*

In *Metropolis* (1926) Lang created if not the first at least the most permanently durable of science fiction anti-utopias. And here the City manifests itself as a machine made not for men to live in but rather to devour them. Jon Frederson, the young hero who is the son of the Master of the futuristic, capitalist city of Metropolis, has a vision early in the film. He has descended to the lower levels of the city, where the workers live and tend the massive machines that feed energy to the leisure classes of the upper levels. And when one of the machines has a momentary breakdown, causing the death of a handful of workers, Frederson hallucinates the machine as a steel-and-iron, technologized image of the bloody god Moloch of the Babylonians, of all those mentioned in the Old Testament the god most closely associated with the demand for human sacrifice. Later in the film, Frederson visits the lowers working area of the city, where—in one of the most famous and arresting moments in all of film—he sees a worker literally crucified upon a massive clock, the chief coordinator (if we can extrapolate from the rather vague and fanciful technology of the story) of all the machines of Metropolis. The man is a technological Atlas: he bears, if not on his shoulders, at least between the span of his arms, the responsibility for the whole life of the giant city which the planet has become. And, since he is only an ordinary man, he is exhausted by his task. Frederson volunteers to relieve him for the rest of his shift, donning the drab uniform and cap of a Metropolis worker. And later, crucified himself, agonized and drained by the necessity of continually shifting the massive hands of the giant power clock, he cries out, "Father! I never realized till now that nine hours could be an eternity!" It is an obvious, but deeply moving, parody of the last words of Christ from the Cross: more so since we realize that Frederson literally *is* the son of the General Manager of all things, voluntarily undergoing his expiatory crucifixion to alleviate the sufferings of men who, as he discovers, are after all his brothers.

But it is not the hopeful, Christian aspect of *Metropolis* one remembers first of all; it is rather the image of the city as nightmare, the city a great and vulnerable artifact cast up against the permanent possibility of apocalypse. The apocalypse indeed comes in this early film of Lang's, and though it is averted at the last moment by a sentimental (and unbelievable) alliance of workers and managers for the common good (reminiscent of the Nazi slogan of ten years later, *Arbeit macht frei*), we believe as we do not in the case of the happy or peaceful endings of Hitchcock that Lang himself has no faith in such possibilities. In his later films, particularly the American films he made during the forties, he explores with increasing darkness of imagination the idea of the city as trap, as jungle, as nightmare. In *The Big Heat* (1953), Lang describes the chaos underlying so-called normal life in terms as disturbing as any yet developed by the film or the novel. It is the story of Dave Bannion (Glenn Ford), an unprepossessing and happily married police officer, who finds himself at war with a representative of the mob, of that great sub- and antilegal organization whose mere presence is a scandal in the contemporary life of America. In his just passion to investigate and uncover the illegality of the syndicate, Bannion first causes the death of his wife (in a mined car meant for him to drive), and then the maiming of a syndicate gun moll (Gloria Grahame) who sympathizes with him and tries to help him in his fight against the mob.

All the characteristic Lang elements are present in *The Big Heat,* including the uncomfortable sense that the masters of illegality, the managers of the mob, might be more powerful ultimately than the forces of so-called legality. And the investigator's innocence is maintained at a cost. Glenn Ford, that paragon of fifties-style normality, becomes increasingly manic, increasingly obsessed with vengeance, as the story develops. So that by the end, stripped of his badge and gun, stripped of his insignia as official representative of the "law," he has become really nothing or little more than the forces of chaos he opposes, the only difference being that *he* stands, at the breaking-point of culture and civilization, on the side of right. But what is right, after all the bitter wisdom Bannion has had to imbibe? The whore and syndicate collaborator who befriends him, and who in fact loves him, has been irreparably scarred, in a shockingly violent scene, by her lover (Lee Marvin); she helps Ford defeat the gangsters in the final shoot-out scene of the film, but only to die herself. And Bannion's quest for vengeance, whatever its violence or excitement, has not really served to make up for the loss of the normal life with wife and children which, the film makes clear, he will never enjoy again. Nothing has been really won, in other words, and almost everything has been lost: including, chief of all, the innocence that led us to believe that we *could* win.

Winners and Losers

Roger Thornhill and Dave Bannion have this much in common: they are both "winners" who find out that they are really "losers," and have to learn to live with that knowledge. One of the characteristics of melodrama, and of the dangerous criminal code that is a "sanction" on the other laws of society, is that you can never be quite sure whether you *are* a winner or a loser until the drama has been played all the way to the end. Graham Greene, whose novels are among the most compelling metaphysical thrillers of the twentieth century, has spent much of his career exploring the dimensions of winning and losing in the modern, unwalled, capitalist city. And, having been a film critic during the thirties, he is also especially attuned to the relation between this kind of story and the art of the film. In *The Confidential Agent,* one of his best "entertainments," he describes a scene where his hero, a Loyalist agent during the Spanish Civil War, goes into a London movie theater to hide out from the counteragents who are trying to kill him. The film being shown is a cheap Hollywood musical. But the confidential agent—and Greene—discovers a significance in it quite beyond that:

> It was curious and pathetic; everybody behaved nobly and made a lot of money. It was as if some code of faith and morality had been lost for centuries, and the world was trying to reconstruct it from the unreliable evidence of folk memories and subconscious desires—and perhaps some hieroglyphics upon stone.

"Everybody behaved nobly and made a lot of money." That, of course, is the optimal situation, to win both ways. But, as Greene's thrillers make clear and as the melodramatic film makes even clearer, you can't do it. Our quest— and it is important that Greene uses the word—is for "evidence" of a code of honor that has been lost or obscured: evidence both in the Calvinist sense and in that of the private investigator.

But in place of sure evidence the city gives us only clues of ambiguous nature that may point to our winning, and may point to our losing, and most terrifyingly may change their meaning in the middle of the game. The American gangster film of the thirties and its curious heir in the forties, the *film noir,* are perhaps the most crucial and most mythically absolute formulations of this uncertainty. (And it is significant that while writers like Greene and Chandler draw a good part of their inspiration from the gangster genre, their own powerful novels contribute much, in turn, to the consolidation of the *noir* tradition.)

One of the earliest and in many ways purest gangster films is *Little Caesar* (1930). Caesar Enrico Bandello (Edward G. Robinson) is a winner. He rises to the summit of his profession, that of underworld boss, but only to realize that he is, as the title of the film suggests, a *little* Caesar, a man whose energies are exercised in a sphere—organized crime as big business—that inevitably undercuts and trivializes his longing for power, authority, absolute control. Little Rico begins his career as a petty crook in partnership with the "soft" Joe Massara (Douglas Fairbanks, Jr.) robbing Depression-era diners and roadside cafes. But when they get to the big city they part company. Joe goes straight, becoming a ballroom dancer, while Rico joins a major gang, rapidly rising to the top. He is hard, an obsessive winner, although the film makes clear that he does not really know what it is he wants to win. As he says to the gang's former boss, Diamond Pete Montana (Ralph Ince), as he takes over leadership, "Ya know, Pete, you're gettin' so ya can dish it out, but ya can't take it no more." Rico can take it. But winning and getting, taking it, become less and less meaningful for him. And when, at the end of the film, he dies ignominiously in a gang war, the message is blatant (but not, therefore, banal) that this sort of winning is a defeat.

Any number of sociological analyses of *Little Caesar* have appeared by now, perhaps the best of them in Stuart Kaminsky's book *American Film Genres.* But what most of these commentaries, for all their perceptiveness and intelligence, miss is the degree to which the pathos of the film is implicit in its title. The gangster, or, to use a common and revealing phrase for him, the "underworld czar," is in his way the lord of his world, the figure of maximum power and maximum authority in a society dominated by its own medium of exchange and obsessed with establishing its own hallmarks of legitimacy. He is the man who, by daring to cross the border between legality and crime, tests the claims of his culture to an efficient organization of life—who tests, in fact, that law which is the "sanction" for the earlier laws of society's founding. We demand that such a man be defeated, of course: and from *Little Caesar* to *The Public Enemy* to *The Godfather*, the price exacted by society from its criminal experimenters with power is their own death, their own defeat by precisely the risks we are fascinated to see them take. But this, too, is nothing more or less than self-definition by society at a certain level of mythmaking. Caesar Bandello's last words, as he is gunned down at the end of *Little Caesar*, are, "Mother of Mercy, is this the end of little Rico?" It is a justly famous closing line, since it is spoken by Robinson in his role as "little Rico," but uttered in fact by the whole culture which makes a film like *Little Caesar* possible. At the moment of his death, in other words, Rico becomes *objective* to himself, becomes the witness to his own life and its judge. And the judgment he utters is the judgment of the capitalist, success-oriented, post-*Lear* world in which he has tried to live as a king without legitimacy. He is dying, he is little, he is not even anymore a parody of Caesar, but—in a reduction which is the reduction of all our lives, and the reason we value him so much—only Rico.

It is important in this respect that *Little Caesar* is the story not only of the archetypal gangster Caesar Bandello, but of his friend and sometime partner in crime Joe Massara, who abandons the criminal life to become a ballroom dancer. Kaminsky suggests that this counterpoint between Bandello and Massara is an opposition between the "manly" though misdirected energies of the tough guy and the less masculine, vaguely epicene behavior of the "artistic" type. This is surely true, and important to the whole range of American (and European) crime films, but there is another and perhaps richer point to the contrast. The dancer Joe, in choosing his harmless, comparatively impotent escape from the world of his friend Caesar, also underscores the disorganization and danger of Caesar's world. Like those of the Fool in *Lear* or the (misnamed) "comic relief" characters in Dickens' grimmest novels, the world of the dancer—of intricate, musical, and fundamentally powerless patterns—is a world that not only contrasts to, but is made necessary by, the world of urban panic and potential disaster. This helps explain the almost constant presence, in gangster and detective films of the thirties and forties, of singers, nightclubs, even of full-scale musical numbers. The song, the dance, the moment of respite granted by music are as much responses to the melodramatic city as the crime, the mystery, and the lost inheritance which needs to be found again. There is even a kind of appropriateness in the color-contrast and complementarity between the Italian name for thirties musicals and the more celebrated French name for thirties and forties crime films: the periods of *i telefoni bianchi* and of *le film noir* are, in an intimate way, the same period.

The *film noir,* an inevitable derivation from the gangster film of the preceding decade, was anticipated by a social protest film like *I Am a Fugitive from a Chain Gang,* which Mervyn LeRoy directed two years after he made *Little Caesar.* James Allen (Paul Muni) is another man who tries, in Greene's phrase, to behave nobly and make a lot of money. But the difference between him and Caesar Bandello (or Scarface, or Tom Powers in *The Public Enemy*) is that he really does behave nobly; he is innocent of the crime he is charged with and condemned for. Having stumbled onto the scene of a killing in an all-night diner (the same locale, significantly, where *Little Caesar* began) he is sent to a Florida chain gang for murder and armed robbery. Revolted and dehumanized by the appalling conditions of the chain gang, he manages to escape and to begin a new, creative, successful life as an architect—a planner and builder of cities, that is. He falls in love, and is about to enter that most middle-class of paradises, marriage, when his true identity is revealed. In the ensuing scandal, rather than try to escape again he volunteers to trust the judicial system, returning to the chain gang for what he is assured will be a brief term before his full pardon comes through. But something—again—goes wrong in the functioning of the machine. His pardon is delayed, postponed, and his treatment at the hands of the chain gang bosses is more brutal than ever. He escapes once more—this time not to try the "straight" life of the system, but rather to live hand-to-mouth as a fugitive and thief.

It is a very grim parable indeed of the dysfunctions of justice. The term *film noir* was originally designed to describe not only the moral darkness of certain forties melodramas, but the very real physical darkness of their *mise-en-scène;* and the great last line of this film, in its visual context, is almost an epigraph for the *film noir* of the next decade. When Allen returns to see his beloved one last time before continuing what is now his lifelong vocation of escape, she asks him, "But how do you live?" The answer, in a dying wail, comes out of an almost totally black screen: "I steal."

Of course, the *film noir* is not a genre in the way that the Western and the detective film are established, self-conscious genres; *film noir* is a term invented by French film critics to describe a phenomenon in American film at least ten years after the phenomenon itself was prominent. Nevertheless, it makes elegant sense of a number of melodramatic films which are, in their way, the terminal extension, into a near nightmare of crisis, of the terms I have been discussing. What they have in common is, first of all, a visual tone. Classic examples like *Laura* (1941), *The Maltese Falcon*

(1941), *The Woman in the Window* (1944), *Double Indemnity* (1944), *The Lost Weekend* (1945), and *Out of the Past* (1947) involve largely urban, constricted landscapes and a preponderance of richly chiaroscuro nighttime scenes. But the visual darkness is a running metaphor for a deeper, spiritual darkness. Expanding upon the world of *Chain Gang* and of Fritz Lang's 1936 *Fury,* these films and their numerous cousins all, in one way or another, rehearse the theme of the uncertainty and the potential nihilism of life under a complex, confusing criminal code that seems to have lost touch with human reality. One false step, they seem to be saying, and anyone—anyone—can find himself on the wrong side of the law, banished within the heart of the city, the victim of a paranoid universe which is the dark underside of our official legality.

Don Birnam, the alcoholic brilliantly portrayed by Ray Milland in Billy Wilder's *The Lost Weekend,* may stand as a type of the *noir* hero. A "normal" young man, even a charming one, he is nevertheless driven by his savage appetite for drink to violate family loyalties and romantic love, then to become a petty thief, and finally to madness and near-suicide (and it is important to remember what the film makes eloquently clear: that alcoholism is not only a spiritual and social but also an economic disease—you are forced to buy the very drug that is killing you). In a very real sense, Birnam is the investigator and reporter of his own fate (he wants to be a novelist, and at the end of the film he begins a story called *The Lost Weekend).* But, characteristically, the *noir* detective learns nothing more damning than his own complicity in the crimes he explores.

The Lost Weekend has a happy ending, in which at the moment of suicide Don Birnam is saved by the love of his fiancée (Jane Wyman) and resolves to stop drinking and start writing. Many *films noirs,* as well as *Fury* and *The Last Laugh* and a great number of the darkest Victorian novels, have such willful, adventitious conclusions where the hero

or heroine seems to win back everything that has, terrifyingly, been taken away. But we would be wrong to
dismiss these endings as merely sentimental, or as capitula-
tions to corrupt popular taste. The winners learn that they
are really losers; and then, at the eleventh hour, the last possible moment, they become winners again. The extreme use
of this mechanism is probably Otto Preminger's *Laura*
(1941—the year of *Kane*). Detective Dana Andrews is inves-
tigating the murder of the beautiful Laura (Gene Tierney)
and falls in love with the dead girl—only to discover that
she is not dead after all. They win through to happiness and
to the "solution" of the film's crime, but it is all a kind of
melodramatic inversion and parody of that most romantic
version of "losing," the love-death or *Liebestod*. (It is also
worth noting that, just as with the first flashback in *Kane*,
the whole of *Laura* is the narrative of a dead man: the
voiceover we hear at the beginning of the film turns out to
be that of the killer who dies at the end.)

But what does winning mean when you have learned how
terrible it is to lose—really to lose? The happy endings of
these tales satisfy us for a moment, pacify us and reassure us
that everything is, after all, all right. But, perhaps more convincingly than could unrelievedly tragic, nihilistic conclusions, they also bring home to us how fragile and capricious
is the mechanism of "success" or of respectability, which
means so much to us and has so little to do with what and
who we really are. The system, these films and stories argue
at their best, is not "about" winning or losing: it is about
winning-and-losing as an endless, self-motivating whirligig
which we are forced to board, which we must try to understand, but which we will never, probably, be able to control.

To say this much is to take the idea of the "law" a far
way, indeed, from its manifestations in epic and romance.
And while the classic gangster film, or the classic *film noir*,
may be a period-bound, historically and socially conditioned
variety of the basic situation of melodramatic narrative, nev-

ertheless it retains a perennial point and relevance to later exercises in the same mode. Is Francis Ford Coppola's *The Godfather* (Part One, 1972; Part Two, 1974) a resurrection of the gangster-movie genre, a late but exceptionally brilliant (and exceptionally dark) *film noir,* or something beyond either of those categories? It is obviously the last, but it would not be possible without those two traditions from which it arises and to which it gives new depth and impetus.

I have said that Coppola, who wrote the screenplay for *Patton,* has been concerned throughout his career with the mechanics and metaphysics of success. And *The Godfather* carries on the exploration begun in *Patton,* but in a more confusing, richer moral universe. Patton may try to be a knight in a world that will no longer tolerate knighthood. But Michael Corleone (Al Pacino), the son of a Mafia Don who comes unwillingly to inherit his father's mantle, experiences a more disheartening thing: he becomes the reincarnation of his noble father (the "Don"—that most appropriate of knightly names!), but only at the cost of discovering how empty of any once-admirable meaning that role has become.

Indeed, we can think of the story of *The Godfather* in a curious analogy with the situation of *Don Quixote.* The term "Don" (like the secondary term "Godfather") is a dynastic one, signifying continuity with the traditions and values of the past. But it is a past whose traditions and values are those not only of family loyalty and an intense code of personal honor, but also of bloodshed, vengeance, and cold cruelty to outsiders. Don Vito Corleone (Marlon Brando), the patriarch of the family, carries these values with assurance and a kind of ceremonial grace. Partly because of the nature of the role itself, and partly through Brando's marvelous performance, the aging Don seems literally a character from another age, from the "old world." And his plans for Michael—college-educated, a hero in World War II—are that he should succeed, should "make something of himself," in legitimate business, in law, or in politics. The Don, in other words, wants his favorite son to make the transition from his own world of blood feuds and archaic codes of honor to the daylit, commercial, melodramatic universe of industrialized, postwar America. And that is precisely what Michael also wants, at least at the beginning of the film. He is in love with a young woman, a beautiful WASP named Kay (Diane Keaton). At the wedding celebration that opens *The Godfather,* he points out to her the various members of his family and their entourage, detailing some of the outrageous things they have done. As her eyes grow wide with shock, he says to her, "Kay, this is my family; it's not me."

It is one of the most crucial lines in the film. In parallel with and in contrast to the dynastic implications of the names "Don" and "Godfather," Michael's ambition is to enter the economic mainstream, the great commercial archetype of American success: in other words, to be able to behave nobly and make a lot of money.

The rest of the film not only shatters Michael's hopes but, more subtly and more frighteningly, indicates how much those hopes were based upon an initial delusion. Like the hero of a classic gangster film, Michael in Part One of *The Godfather* rises, like a good entrepreneur, to the top of his profession. But like the hero of a *film noir,* he resists that transformation, is taken by it almost unawares. Any number of commentators have remarked upon the liturgical rhythm of Part One: it begins with a marriage ceremony, features another marriage in its central section, and climaxes with a baptism. But at each of these events, each of these ceremonies which, like all liturgy, bind us to a recurrent, cyclic, orderly sense of time, there is an intrusion from history, from the linear, shabby, violent history which undercuts our desire for continuity, which reminds us that our sense of orderliness is a sham. At the first marriage, the wedding feast of Michael's sister, this element is muted: in an almost comic shot, we see F.B.I. agents assiduously checking the license plates of the guests at the Don's party. The second wedding is Michael's to a lovely Sicilian girl. It is celebrated, a truly archaic and pastoral ceremony, in the midst of the Sicilian hills where Michael has had to escape after avenging the shooting of his father. But for all the pastoral splendor of this marriage feast, the intrusions of violence are more marked and ominous. We, and Michael, know that he is in danger from rival families; his men of honor carry carbines on the wedding procession; and he is still handicapped by the embarrassing aftereffects of a broken nose he received from a New York policeman.

The last ceremony in the film completes the archetypal cycle of life begun in the initial marriage celebration: it is the christening of the baby born to Michael's sister and brother-in-law. But the marriage has turned into a hateful shambles; so much so that the brother-in-law, Carlo, has used his wife to set up the assassination of Michael's brother Santino, the son originally intended to become the new Godfather, the new head of the family. And it is during this ceremony also that Michael—who is standing godfather for the baby—engineers his own massive revenge against the rival families of New York.

The baptism scene itself is one of the most overwhelming bravura sequences in American film, cutting rapidly and dizzyingly from the ritual in the church to the bloodletting, spanning half a continent from New York to Las Vegas, which the new Godfather has carefully planned. It is, of course, a double baptism, and one where the twin worlds of the film coalesce grimly, even satanically. The infant (whose father Michael will soon have murdered) is baptized with water and the spirit into the ritual family of Christ—using lines from the Roman Catholic ceremony itself—while the new head is baptized with blood and a very different spirit into the family of his dead father, a father whose malign influence has only been increasingly brutalized, increasingly turned into something less than human, by the new, industrialized efficiency and coldness Michael brings to the family business.

Part Two of *The Godfather* continues and elaborates on the grim ironies of that last scene from Part One. If the world of the kings and the knights, the world of the old Don, has died into the world of the hero as criminal/corrupt investigator, Part Two is in its way a long fantasia on the distance between those worlds. The first of its main plots recounts how the young Vito Corleone (Robert DeNiro) became a Don, forced into his nefarious trade out of love for his young wife and child, and out of despair at the false promises of American affluence. The second plot continues the story of Michael, who, having accepted the baptism by blood, sinks deeper and deeper into the soullessness that surrounds him, losing his wife, losing his oldest friends, finally becoming a fratricide.

The contrast between the two plots deepens and increasingly ironizes the distance between the two worlds the characters inhabit, to the point that *The Godfather* as a whole almost becomes a deliberate and disturbingly obscene pun upon whatever originally may have accrued of nobility or respectability to the role the old Don played. But this is to say that, in the profoundest of ways, *The Godfather* is a mock-epic, a parody of the order and the human meaning that has been lost or betrayed in the way we live now, and a plangent argument that such order must be restored if civilization is to survive. Everything from *Godfather I* is present in *Godfather II* except the idea, itself, of continuity, of transmission. And in the unstated, massively implied gap between the innocent world of the early twentieth century and the complex, damnedly self-conscious world of midcentury, we glimpse the possibility of a return to judgment, or at least of an implicit judgment on the present terrible situation. We glimpse, in other words, the possibility of satire.

But what are the limits of melodrama and satire? When

does the pain of the world, in other words, become so intense that we can no longer even moan about it, but only laugh with the laughter of despair and rage? Franz Kafka's story *The Metamorphosis* is a disturbing parable about a life so private, so manipulated, that it is transformed from tragedy to absurdity. Indeed, the German title of the tale, *Die Verwandlung,* is much better rendered as "the change" or "the transformation" than as the classical-sounding "metamorphosis."

Gregor Samsa, as the famous opening sentence of the tale declares, awakes one morning from a night of troubled dreams to find himself transformed into a gigantic vermin. The rest of the tale is simply an extension and elaboration of the implications of this opening proposition. As a large cockroach (or dung-beetle) Gregor, who has been the sole support of his ne'er-do-well father and mother and adored sister, is suddenly cast into absolute dependence upon them for his sustenance—and, more importantly, for his sense of a humanity surviving his grotesque change. He is trapped in his tiny bedroom, and in each of the three sections of the story he makes an attempt to escape from that room, to rejoin the minimal, elemental human community of his family, and in each attempt is defeated. As Gregor grows weaker and more stupefied—which is to say, more used to his insect state—his family grows stronger: the mother takes in lodgers, the father takes a job, the sister promises to accomplish great things on the violin. And at last Gregor dies, of a wound inflicted by his own father in his second attempt at escape; and nobody cares.

It is one of the grimmest, most legitimately depressing tales ever written. But what does it mean? Is it a science-fiction tale of a horrible but physically explicable change? Is it all a bad dream? Is it a chronicle of mere delusion or psychosis?

It is none of those things, I suggest, but something much more serious and much more frightening. It is a story of what it *feels like* to be so dependent upon other people, so brooded over by their demands and their sheer presence, that you have no "self" left at all: what it feels like, in other words, to be human. As the first sentence of the story tells us, Gregor discovers that he is a vermin—that is, an object of scorn and disgust—when he awakens from troubled dreams. But are not those troubled dreams simply the unconscious, self-assured, comfortable sense each of us has that life is all right, manageable, meaningful—until one morning, at three o'clock, we awake to realize its full horror? What Gregor awakes to is, as the existentialist philosophers Jean-Paul Sartre and Albert Camus later realized, the human condition itself. He awakes to a consciousness, which the rest of his family never achieves, of the full horror of living in *this* body, at *this* time, with this absurd vulnerability to the whole universe of chance, change, and other people.

There is something horrifying about the story of *The Metamorphosis,* and something funny. For the human condition itself, past a certain pitch of agony, becomes laughable: not because the agony lessens, but because it increases beyond the scale of our comprehension.

The Metamorphosis is as powerful as it is, among other reasons, because of the brilliance of Kafka's narrative technique. We begin the story from Gregor's point of view and, until the very end of his life, we remain trapped—as Gregor is trapped within the physical form of a loathsome insect—within his own vision of things, his own perception of space. (One reason, for example, that students always have trouble imagining how *big* a cockroach Gregor is, is that we, depending on how we feel about ourselves at the moment, have constant trouble deciding how big our own bodies are.) And when Gregor dies—imperceptibly, the way people do die—the story continues for some pages, telling us what happens to his parents and sister, in a horrifying manifestation of the *absence* that is all we know of death.

Martin Scorsese's film *Taxi Driver* achieves the same shattering, violent transition from one narrative world to the other, from a tragic to an even more bitter, comic vision of the human universe. But it does so through the special powers of film, as opposed to literary, narrative.

Travis Bickle (Robert DeNiro) is a Vietnam veteran who is already deeply, if inarticulately, disturbed as the film opens. An insomniac, he decides to take a job driving a taxi in New York on the late night-to-dawn shift. The city during those hours, as the film powerfully suggests, is the city gone rancid—literally and hopelessly a hellish place, the prowling ground of the corrupt, the violent, the spiritually maimed, acting out their sad fate in the hours when the official, daylight certainties of culture are suspended. And it drives Travis mad. For these psychic wrecks are not only the population of his nighttime life, they are his passengers. They keep invading the private space of his taxi, as they keep invading, in their full horror, his consciousness.

The first thing we see in *Taxi Driver* is the taxi itself, emerging in garishly overlit color from infernal clouds of steam. It is, in the richest metaphorical sense, the room where Travis lives for the duration of his story, which is to say also the "room" of his braincase, of his awareness. But unlike Gregor Samsa's room, it is on wheels and vulnerable to the intrusions of other people: not claustrophobically closed to human connections, but *too open* to those connections at their most violent. And as the main titles appear on the screen, we see them superimposed over a series of distorted, slow-motion shots of people stepping onto curbs, walking along the streets of New York: the monsters of his world, seen from the point of view of Travis inside the taxi. Like Gregor Samsa, Travis Bickle will be driven down to madness, down to a perception of his own awful loneliness, by other people. But for Gregor, Hell is other people because he can't escape the closure of his own room to reforge a union of love in charity with them. For Travis, Hell is

other people because he can't keep them out. Gregor becomes a monster because he awakes to find himself different
from other people. Trevis becomes a monster because he
can't sleep, can't deny that others in their monstrosity are
also part of himself.

Travis tries to escape, tries to forge relationships with
three people: a pretty young girl working as a volunteer for
a political candidate (Cybill Shepherd), an older cabbie on
the same shift (Peter Boyle) and a hapless runaway, a
twelve-year-old prostitute (Jodie Foster). Like Gregor's three
attempts to leave his room, these are Travis' three attempts
to escape the horror of his isolation—but by letting people
in, people he hopes can enter the space of his mind bringing
love and not a distorted reflection of his own worst fears
about himself.

All three attempts fail, and Travis undergoes the central
transformation of the film: he becomes a killer. Surrounding
himself with high-powered handguns, he shaves his head (as
did some soldiers during the Vietnam war) to resemble that
of a Mohawk warrior, dons a set of dark glasses, and sets
out to kill the world he cannot love. At a rally for the candidate Shepherd is supporting, Travis edges his way to the
front of the crowd, but is noticed by some Secret Service
men and has to flee. He then visits the pimp (Harvey Keitel)
who manages Jodie Foster and, in the literally explosive
climax of the film, shoots his way into her shabby apartment,
killing Keitel and getting seriously wounded himself. The
police break in to find him, apparently dying, smiling at
them and putting his bloody hand to his head in the traditional gesture of suicide.

It is a powerful ending to an overwhelming film. But it is
not the ending. In the controversial last few minutes of *Taxi
Driver*, we first watch the camera pan over the news clip-
pings, sloppily tacked to a wall, of Travis' escapade while an
offscreen voice reads a banal, cliche-ridden letter from the
prostitute's father to Travis thanking him for saving his

little girl from a life of degradation. Is Travis alive? Has he, in the most absurd of ways, become a hero? He has. The next shot shows us Travis—his hair regrown, his face smiling for the first time in the film—being congratulated by his fellow cabbies on his first night back at the job. He leaves to go to work, and his first fare is none other than Cybill Shepherd, the girl who rejected him. But she, too, has read the newspapers, and makes a mild, diffident overture to him. Travis, now confident and happy in his new role, politely turns her down and drives away—and the last freeze-frame of the film catches his smiling (still mad?) face in his own rear-view mirror.

This ending may be, as some opponents of the film have suggested, the disastrous collapse of a harrowing vision of insanity into a relatively cheap kind of social satire: the killer becomes a hero because he had the luck to kill the right person (a pimp) instead of the wrong person (a political candidate). Or it may be, though there is no evidence in the film itself for it, something subtler: Travis' internal fantasy, at the moment of his death (when he makes that suicide gesture to the police), of the kind of heroism he would like to achieve by his act of violence—even to that last pitch of male fantasy, being able to turn down the girl who once turned him down.

But I think it is something better than either of those readings. Throughout the film Travis has been trying to maintain some sense of individual decency, some personal identity, against the influence of the monstrosities with whom he is surrounded. But that struggle is foredoomed (as is Gregor Samsa's struggle to retain a sense of his own humanity) because Travis, as much as the monsters who surround him, is the product and the victim of an artificialized life-style, a city gone manic, that predetermines and cheapens even his attempts to revolt against it. He is a victim of junk food, physically and psychically. He takes to drinking from a bottle of peach brandy he keeps constantly in his pocket, his meals are peach brandy poured over bread crumbs, he becomes an ardent watcher of afternoon television, that most unredeemed of American junk meals for the mind. In the single most frightening scene of the film, he is sitting in his apartment, eating his favorite meal, cradling a .44 Magnum pistol in his lap, watching an inane afternoon TV game show, his foot resting against the TV table. He begins slowly to rock the table back and forth with his foot. His face, in profile, is completely expressionless. And he finally rocks the TV all the way over, where it explodes in a sizzling display of shorted circuits.

It is the central scene of the film, the moment when his violent response to the intrusion of other people into his mind (including the intrusion of TV–junk food into his body and head) becomes finally mad, finally murderous: he *kills* the television. But it is also the moment of his defeat. The product of a junk, throwaway society, a culture that throws away people as easily as it does beer cans, he is foredoomed in his attempt at rebellion. He can become either a universally loathed assassin (if his victim is political) or a popularly praised hero (if it is a pimp); but in either case he will, finally, be assimilated into the very structure of dehumanization and processing of human beings that has driven him to madness (or to a terrible kind of sanity) in the first place. So that the last sequence of *Taxi Driver,* like the last pages of *The Metamorphosis,* is a chilling narrative of death. He may have survived the gunshot wounds of his attack upon the whorehouse. But in becoming that most American of personalities, a "personality," Travis—the Travis we knew and with whose descent into the maelstrom we sympathized—has disappeared. He has become a mock hero, and a mockery of the heroism he himself at his best might have hoped for.

V

The World of Satire: Fool's Mate

*In addition to these three kinds of law,
there is a fourth, the most important of all.
It is engraved in neither marble nor brass,
but in the hearts of the citizens.*

ROUSSEAU

Thersites' Revenge

One of the most curious characters in the *Iliad* is a man named Thersites. He engages Homer's attention for less than a hundred lines in the second book of the poem; but at a crucial moment, and a moment he helps to shape. Thersites is a common and—according to Homer—a particularly ugly, cowardly, and insubordinate foot soldier in the Greek army around Troy: not a king, not a warrior, not even a good citizen. But, as Book Two of the *Iliad* opens, the kings, warriors, and citizens besieging Troy have themselves hit a low point of demoralization. The war is in its tenth indecisive and wasteful year; a bitter and petty feud has simultaneously undermined the authority of the expedition's leader, Agamemnon, and lost the Greeks the services of their greatest warrior, Achilles; unrest and confusion are rampant, and the once-glorious venture of the war seems on the thin edge of failure. Enter Thersites.

Agamemnon decides to call an assembly of all the Greek troops, at which he will propose that they give up the struggle and sail back home. His plan is that the assembly—

prompted, to be sure, by a few carefully placed co-conspira-
tors—will indignantly reject his suggestion and return to the
battle for Troy with a renewed sense of purpose. And the
plan works. But it works because of something Agamemnon
has *not* planned, a moment when his advice is almost taken.
As soon as the king finishes his address to the troops, Thersites—ignoble, eminently unrespectable Thersites—begins to
rail at Agamemnon. Homer's single epithet for Thersites is
ametroepes, "of unmeasured (both endless and disordered)
speech"; and his ranting oration earns the epithet. Agamemnon is a grasping cheat, he says. He just wants to keep all
the spoils from the war for himself; he is not half the man
Achilles is; the Greeks are all fools for following his lead at
all; so let us, indeed, sail home and leave him here to see
how he does without us.

The speech is one long, spluttering insult, and it plays
right into the king's hands. After Thersites finishes, Odysseus, that sublest and most persuasive of orators, replies that
since Thersites is well known as a coward and a misshapen
scoundrel, his counsel is obviously also cowardly and misshapen, and finally refutes him with that most ancient and
convincing of rhetorical devices, beating him about the head
and shoulders. While Thersites howls in pain, the Greek
host laughs uproariously at him and rejects both his advice
and the suggestion by Agamemnon that prompted it. Agamemnon is enthusiastically reaffirmed as field marshal, his
disruptive and damaging quarrel with Achilles forgotten.
The war will go on.

We never hear of Thersites again, nor in the rest of the
Iliad is there another moment like this one, where the aus-
terity of the poem descends to slapstick, low comedy. But
the sequence of events is crucial. The king has failed; a
clown attacks, mocks the king; the clown goes so far that he
makes himself look foolish, and is *laughed* at; the king is
reinstated. By attacking Agamemnon Thersites in effect defends Agamemnon, diverting the unrest of the crowd onto

his own head, saving the order of his society by being as outrageously disorderly and antisocial as he can be. The episode is not only unique in tone for the *Iliad*, and a canny bit of political drama: it is also one of the earliest, most perceptive examples we have of the role of the satirist and his strange, at once destructive and creative role in the ongoing life of culture.

Thersites is a clown in both the original sense of the word (a commoner, an inconsequential person) and its ordinary current sense. There is even speculation that in the original episodes of which the *Iliad* is a collection and epic transformation, he might have been a kept fool, a court jester to Agamemnon. Certainly there is a rich appropriateness to finding so "late" a form as satire embedded in so "primary" a narrative as the *Iliad*. As splendid studies like Enid Wellsford's *The Fool* and William Willeford's *The Fool and His Scepter* establish, the presence of a fool, jester, or very often a certified madman in a royal court is not only picturesque but very ancient and very widespread. And the function of this strange character is precisely to rail at, mock, and lampoon the royalty of the court itself. It is as if civilization is somehow reassured by making room within itself for a representative of that chaos, that mad disorder which lies just beyond its frontiers. We make much the same place in our culture for comedians, publicly sanctioned zanies with a license to mock.

But it is not just that the fool represents a domesticated, reassuringly tame form of disorder. Our ancient and perennial fascination with madness, eccentricity, and the perverse is also founded on a nagging suspicion that the fool in his lunacy might somehow be saner than we in our sanity. Satire depends upon this archaic fear and veneration of madness, and elevates it to the level of high art.

Thersites, as I have said, appears for only the briefest of moments in the *Iliad*. Immediately after his explosion of ridicule and *lèse-majesté*, he is put back in his place and his society and king are put back in *their* proper places. But, for the moment he is speaking, the "natural" order of society is in abeyance, between dissolution and a hoped-for rebirth. This is the moment of satire, a moment of lunacy, panic— and judgment—literally outside time.

One of the most "Thersitean" of films, the Marx Brothers' *Duck Soup* (1933), realizes this moment of abeyance in an especially graphic way. As the film opens, a splendid social gathering is in progress to welcome the newly innaugurated president of the Republic of Fredonia, Rufus T. Firefly (Groucho). From the top of the central, monumental staircase a herald announces "The Honorable Rufus T. Firefly," and everyone, as they only do in Marx Brothers movies, bursts instantly into a choral arrangement of the Fredonian national anthem as all eyes turn to the staircase. No Firefly. The herald announces, the crowd intones again. No Firefly. At the third repetition, Groucho slouches in at the bottom of the screen, complete with cigar and greasepaint moustache, peering up the staircase with everyone else to see what all the singing is about.

Eleven years later the most solemnly nationalistic of epics, *Ivan the Terrible,* opens with the ritual, liturgical coronation and inauguration of the king who will institute a new age of law and order for his people. But the inauguration that begins *Duck Soup* occupies a point in time which is at once before and after the moment of *Ivan.* Fredonia is not only wealthy and resplendent but, as the rest of the film will make clear, riddled with all the vices of advanced civilization: hypocrisy, snobbery, venality, and above all an insane chauvinism. The king, the central authority who is also symbolically the continued authority of the law, is absent, has disappeared from the civilization he has instituted. The top of the stair is empty. But a new king (or president) *is* there. He enters, physically and symbolically, from the bottom, a wise-cracking conman innocent, as far as one can tell, of any ideals except his own comfort (he even eats crackers in bed) and the pursuit of women (even the monolithic Margaret Dumont). He finally manages to wise-crack his country into a pointless war which all but demolishes the landscape, and which he wins—with the aid of Harpo, Chico, and Zeppo—only by blundering into capturing the enemy general. But the victory is as wonderfully silly as everything that has gone before it.

If, indeed, warfare is the central theme of epic narrative, it is inevitable that most great satire should in one way or another reduce this theme to absurdity. But by reducing the pomposities of nationalism to psychic rubble, *Duck Soup* not only maniacally celebrates the decay and collapse of a social order gone rancid, but—in true Thersitean fashion— at least implies the possibility of a new, better order, founded on the bedrock of common sense, of the humbling and liberating perception of sham, that underlies all the Marxes' clowning.

The ancient superstition about the truth of madness, in other words, is not really a superstition at all but a permanent and saving possibility of civilization. Not long ago, British psychoanalyst R. D. Laing (in books like *The Divided Self, The Politics of Experience,* and *Knots*) established himself as a "radical" Freudian by arguing that, in an insane world, the schizophrenic may be the sanest man of all. But though this may be news to psychoanalysts, it is not to satirists. From Thersites to Groucho and beyond—to James Joyce, Mel Brooks, Woody Allen, and Thomas Pynchon—it has been their metaphysics, their technique, and their funniest joke. Satire is the mad, funny truth because the satirist himself, he insists, is *driven* to be mad and truthful. Groucho, Thersites, and their colleagues are carriers and caricatures of all the vices of their societies but one: they do not lie.

When war is declared in *Duck Soup,* once again the whole Fredonian court bursts into happy song—"To War!

To War! We're going to go to War!"—led by Groucho, a truly crazy song and dance to celebrate a major disaster. At an analogous moment in Robert Altman's *M.A.S.H.* there is a football game in the middle of the Korean War. It has been organized by the insubordinate, disruptive army surgeons Hawkeye and Trapper John (Elliot Gould and Donald Sutherland) and is complete with army nurse–cheerleaders, dirty tricks, and plentiful marijuana for all the participants. As the climax of this particularly explicit, gory representation of the horrors of war, it is a mock conflict (as all games are) whose silliness and disorderliness parody and trivialize the swagger-stick earnestness of the officers conducting the war.

What both these episodes share is just the atmosphere of abeyance, a sudden suspension of order and reason, which I have described as the moment of satire. They are both moments of *carnival*, and as such indicate further the position of satire in the history of civilization—or rather, civilization's myth of its own history.

I have been tracing the evolution (or devolution) of civilization in terms of its developing fictions of authority and order, in terms of the way a culture's archetypal stories incarnate the functions of its archetypal varieties of law. After the essential founding narrative of epic, the law of kings, and the secondary, civilizing narrative of romance, the law of knights, a dissonance enters culture's image of itself. In melodramatic narrative, we have seen, the law is envisioned as somehow more confusing, less human than in earlier levels of story. It has become criminal law, a necessary "sanction" (as Rousseau says) on the other laws of society. The very need for such a sanction is an admission that society is endangered from within, that the City has become as much a threat to freedom and self-realization as it is their essential arena. Thus the hero of melodrama, the detective/investigator, does not, like his predecessors, institute or incarnate the laws of his culture. He tries to understand them and to apply them creatively in a society that seems half inclined to pervert their original promise.

Satire is the phase of narrative that lies beyond melodrama. If the melodramatic hero is concerned to salvage his culture, the satirist sets out to savage his, since its order has cankered, its once-humanizing authority disappeared in a welter of sinfulness.

Thus the "carnival" atmosphere of satire is both frivolous and deeply serious. In those societies we like to call "primitive," the death, departure, or failure of the king is a time fraught with peril, with the dangers of reversion to primal chaos and dissolution until the new king is inaugurated. This sense, for example, lies behind the medieval myth of the Waste Land and the Holy Grail. The Grail King is sick, wounded, and therefore his land is sick, unfruitful, until the predestined Knight of the Grail—in fact the reincarnation and successor of the wounded king—comes to cure him and the land. And it is highly significant that in this romance translation of the theme of civilization's death and rebirth, we once again find the figure of the fool. For in the original versions of the story the Grail Knight is not—as in the Cistercian legends—the Christ-like Galahad, but the curious, deeply engaging figure, Parzival (*Peredur* in the stories of the Welsh *Mabinogion,* probably our most archaic version of the original tale). And Parzival, in all the tales in which he appears, is not only a pure and noble knight, but a pure fool, *der reine Tor.* Raised in the woods by a mother who does not wish him to become a knight, he is innocent of the ways of the court and the subtleties of social behavior. When he rides into Arthur's court, on a broken-down horse and armed with crude wooden javelins, he is laughed at. And yet he is the knight who will bring the greatest honor to Camelot, will win the Grail and cure the sick king of the Waste Land. The fool—the "natural," as he was also called

in the Elizabethan era—comes from nature, or from the out-
skirts of the City, the border between its orderliness and the
circumambient disorganization: and he comes bringing
traces of that chaos with him, precisely to restrengthen the
order that has failed.

As in the Grail story, civilizations tend to institutionalize,
ritualize, the dangerous but regenerative moment of the
king's failure. As Mircea Eliade tells us in *Cosmos and History: The Myth of the Eternal Return,* every New Year's celebration is, at least symbolically and usually in outrageous
fact, a liturgical riot, a descent to the aboriginal lawlessness
from which the world is supposed to have been created (and
is annually re-created) by a lawgiving god. On December 31
in America, we put on funny hats and try to convince one
another to be as uninhibited as we can before midnight. At
the Roman feast of Saturnalia (Saturn being the eldest of the
gods, the Titan from whom all later divinities spring), slaves
were jokingly given the rights of masters and masters assumed the license they thought appropriate to slaves. And
Mardi Gras in the Middle Ages, in a scene bound to remind
us of the opening of *Duck Soup,* featured the selection and
mock veneration of a Lord of Misrule, usually the most
misshapen or hopelessly retarded member of the community; a crazy king for a day (a day literally out of time)
before the return to sobriety, the penitential season of Lent,
and the preparations for the Feast of the Resurrection.

As the Feast of Misrule generalizes and institutionalizes
the dangerous moment of the king's failure, so satire as a
narrative mode generalizes and intellectualizes the atmosphere of carnival. But it is important to remember that,
however elegant, complex, or "classical" it becomes, the
mode of satire retains its roots in the strange, archaic, and
arcane images of the fool and his feast. I have noted how
Parzival amid the splendor of Arthur's Camelot "acts the
natural" and thereby both ruptures and reestablishes the no-

bility of the court itself. The same process is at work in one
of the most brilliant and bitterest satirical films of recent
years, Milos Forman's *One Flew Over the Cuckoo's Nest.*

Into a state mental asylum from a prison farm comes
Randall Patrick McMurphy (Jack Nicholson), a rowdy, outrageous, monumentally insubordinate hobo in a state of per-
petual sexual heat. (In his first interview with the unctuous,
self-satisfied head doctor, he is asked: "This report, Patrick,
describes you as 'antisocial.' What do you think that
means?" McMurphy ponders a moment and then, breaking
into the Nicholson killer smile, says, "Well, I guess it means
I fight and fuck too much.") He expects his stay at the institution to be a welcome, lazy relief from the work farm. But
he soon finds himself locked in a struggle, at first light-heart-
edly nasty but soon deadly serious, with the repressive, de-
humanizing regime of the hospital, headed by the chilling
head nurse, Miss Ratched (Louise Fletcher). McMurphy discovers that most of the other patients in the ward are volun-
tary: they have had themselves committed and remain will-
ingly under Nurse Ratched's totalitarian control because
they fear life outside, fear making choices, fear their own
bodies. McMurphy in his splendidly disruptive individ-
ualism, his frank acceptance of the life of the senses, becomes the hero of the other inmates, inspiring them by simply *being there* to recognize Nurse Ratched's tyranny for
what it is and to imitate his own resistance to it: in other
words, he becomes a very real Lord of Misrule, generating
around himself a reign of disorder against the cruelty and
sterility of the official order.

Nicholson's performance catches beautifully McMurphy's
growing sense of the urgency of his struggle, the solemnity
of his role as a messiah for the misfits of a thuddingly nor-
malized culture. In the climactic scene of the film, he arranges for his escape from the asylum. It is to be a liberation
not only for McMurphy, but for the other inmates who
gleefully collaborate in his escape plan. As a gesture against

the head nurse, it will be their "escape," however limited, also. The night before the breakout, McMurphy smuggles into the ward two dazzlingly unselfconscious girlfriends and a case of assorted liquor. It is a real carnival, a feast of fools and madmen in defiance and parody of the daytime order that saps their lives. But McMurphy gets drunk and sleeps through dawn, when Nurse Ratched and her minions return to find the ward a shambles. Nurse Ratched terrorizes the weakest of the inmates, young Billy Bibbitt (whom Mc-Murphy has just "made a man" by bedding him with one of the whores) into blaming McMurphy for the whole riot. Billy, agonized and humiliated, kills himself. And Mc-Murphy, finally driven to the full rage against this institutionalized torture that has been building in him throughout the film, throws himself on Nurse Ratched and tries to strangle her.

He is taken away and, as an "excessively violent" patient, is subjected to a full frontal lobotomy: turned into a vegetable. When he is returned to the ward at night, his—quite real—crucifixion is discovered by the giant Indian Chief Broom, whose autism McMurphy has "cured" by bringing the Chief back to a passionate participation in his world and his own body. "I feel big as a damn mountain now, Mac," Broom whispers just before he sees the telltale marks of lobotomy on McMurphy's forehead. For the sake of what McMurphy was, Broom smothers him and, in the triumphant last scene of the film, breaks out of the asylum in a gargantuan act of strength and runs toward the free, welcoming mountains on the horizon.

But McMurphy's sublime criminality, his hieratic performance as fool, Thersitean rebel, and prophet of the passionate self, has not just liberated Broom to return to the natural world; it has also reconstituted the society of the ward into a *human* society of fallible, wounded, but self-trusting men against the false, rancid order imposed upon them by the head nurse. Ken Kesey's original novel told the

tale in the first-person narrative of Broom, gradually emerging from the self-imposed fog of his terror through Mc-
Murphy's influence. The inevitable loss of this first-person
intimacy—brilliantly realized in Kesey's novel—has its com-
pensations in the objectivity of the filmed *Cuckoo's Nest*.
Kesey's story is a mock-Gospel (and, of course, also a highly
serious one), a narrative by one of the redeemed about the
career of the redeemer, a gloriously raunchy translation of
the Gospel declaration "We have seen his glory." Forman's
film keeps much of this flavor—for example, the great moment of confrontation begins when McMurphy takes twelve
inmates out of the asylum in a daring escape, and teaches
them, literally, to become fishermen. But also, by necessarily
displacing the emphasis of the tale from McMurphy-seen-
by-Broom to McMurphy himself as radical, challenging
presence, the film reaches an even more archaic, more
graphic level of satire, of the reinstitution of the saving feast
of fools, than does the novel. The final Saturnalia in the hospital ward is a New Year's feast. It will cost McMurphy his
life, but not before it has reestablished the creative self-
realization that can enable his society to govern, forgive,
and respect itself. The final revenge of Thersites for the beating he takes is simply that the beating makes the *Iliad* possible.

Hephaestus' Stratagem

Everything I have said so far about the role of the satirist
implies an innate contradiction. The satirist is two-faced, at
once apocalyptic and re-creative, a king and not a king, a
fool whose foolishness fills the vacuum left by the departure
of order, and an agent of order whose clowning holds up a
funhouse glass to our own distortions of humanity. He
teaches—more earnestly, more deliberately than do the
other types of narrator I have discussed. But he teaches, at
least half the time, by giving us a bad example.

In his book *Discipline and Punish: The Birth of the Prison*, Michel Foucault writes of the odd, paradoxical "carnival" atmosphere that frequently surrounded public executions or chain gangs before the institution, at the end of the eighteenth century, of the modern, "humane" discipline of incarceration. The criminal to be tortured, the convict yoked to a chain gang, appears as the object at once of loathing and of admiration, even of encouragement and applause, to the populace. The condemned man, the man on the bottom, is the projection, by the official society and the folk community, of their own sinfulness or criminality into a symbolic figure to be reviled, mocked, and excluded. At this level the public torture or execution has obvious analogies to the habit, in "primitive" societies, of "driving out winter," of exiling a symbolic scapegoat to preserve the health and fecundity of the culture. But he is also a real person, and most likely one of the masses before whom his punishment is carried out: capable of serving, that is, not simply as scapegoat but as a sympathetic representative of the life of the community itself, an exemplary victim of a repressive regime, even (and this often happened at public executions) a rallying-point for the community's own, instantaneous, and revolutionary unification against the official powers of torture and repression. Foucault even suggests that one reason for the disappearance of such public exhibitions—at the very time of the emergence of the modern, industrialized state—may be that the privacy of incarceration offers less risk than the open spectacle of "justice" for such revolutionary counter-demonstrations.

In any case, Foucault observes, the body of the condemned in these situations is a dark double to the mythic image of the body of the king, an inversion of that overplus of power assumed to surround the royal body and to emanate from it. Just as the touch of the king was anciently believed to cure disease, I might add, so the touch of the condemned is frequently thought to be a contamination. He, too, is a Lord of Misrule. But his "kingship" is now explicitly a kingship of the lower depths. Whatever carnival atmosphere accrues to the public execution, it is a carnival not of the mock exaltation of the fool as braggart, but of the ritual debasement of the fool as victim.

These observations of Foucault help us see how the satirist, or the perfect and wise fool, educates us. He does it in one of two ways, by excess over the human norm (the mock king, the braggart conman, Groucho) or by deficiency from that norm. The satirist's art, in other words, is the art of the funhouse mirror, giving us images of ourselves either larger or smaller than we know we are, and thereby reminding us of what we should be.

This is implicit in the fourth and last variety of law Rousseau discusses in *The Social Contract*:

> In addition to these three kinds of law, there is a fourth, the most important of all. It is engraved in neither marble nor brass, but in the hearts of the citizens; it forms the true constitution of the state; it renews its vigor every day, and when other laws become obsolete and ineffective, it restores or replaces them. . . . I am referring to morals, customs, and above all, public opinion.

This is a full but classically abstracted definition of the function of satire. When the officially promulgated, visible laws of a culture fall into mis- or disuse and, as in the world of melodramatic narrative, the criminal code has to be invoked as a sanction to ensure their observance, the life-cycle of culture is nearing an end, a long and grim descent into social entropy. The satirist, by reestablishing the urgency of those primal laws, not as they are engraved on brass but as they are registered in the hearts of the citizens, promises the chance at least of a return to the world of the founding. But it is a founding on a new basis, an internalized, subjectivized basis whereby we all become kings, all become custodians, founders, civilizers, and enforcers of order. Near the origins of satire lie the figures of the king of fools and the publicly exiled criminal. Rousseau helps us see how, just beyond the limit of satire, rise the figures of the prophet and the saint.

But before that limit is reached, before the re-founding can take place, comes the teaching. I have examined the teaching of the mock king, the man who gives us a disorderly but humanizing reflection of the true grandeur of kingship, the man at the bottom claiming to be the man at the top. The counter-possibility is that of the exile and the scapegoat, the man at the bottom claiming to be below any "bottom" we would like to imagine for human possibility. And just as Homer's Thersites is a convenient archaic version of the first possibility, so Homer's Hephaestus is a startling realization of the second.

At the very end of the first book of the *Iliad,* just before the Thersites episode and as an obvious structural parallel to that episode, a quarrel breaks out among the gods on Olympus. Father Zeus sympathizes with the Trojans, though he knows that Fate has decreed final victory for the Greek host. But till that inevitable time, he is quite willing to see as many Greeks die as possible. Mother Hera, though, a passionate Greek partisan, wants them to win *now.* They argue, enlisting all the gods on one side or the other, until Zeus, enraged, is about to loose his thunderbolt against his fractious children. And at this point Hephaestus intervenes— Hephaestus the lame god, the cuckold of Aphrodite and Ares (that is, the mockery of passionate love and heroic warfare), the most clownish of the Olympians. He begs his mother Hera not to oppose the will of Zeus and recounts in painful detail how Zeus once punished *him,* casting him to earth and laming him. The gods smile at Hephaestus' self-ridicule, and the explosive tension is relieved. And as the first book ends the lame god hobbles from one Olympian to another pouring nectar, while they indulge in what Homer calls "inextinguishable laughter" at his grotesque, servile shape.

Here as with Thersites we see the saving action of a fool diverting violence onto himself when it threatens to break out against the stability of his society. Hephaestus in fact is much more obviously a court fool than Thersites, kept on mainly for the jokes his superiors can have at his expense.

But Thersites, the unruly (how appropriate that word is for the royal vacuum, the legal chaos of the satirist's world), attacks the king and does not know how much he is helping to reestablish the king's rule. Hephaestus attacks *himself;* and he knows exactly what he is doing. Instead of a madly excessive, curative monster, he is a nascent social engineer: instead of *ametroepes,* Homer's epithet for Hephaestus is *klutotechnes,* "crafty"—and obviously not just because he is the patron of craftsmen.

There is, of course, a Hephaestian figure in *Duck Soup* doubling and complementing the Thersitean outrageousness of Groucho. It is Harpo, blissfully and eternally silent while his brother seems incapable of shutting up, scurrying crazily through the film in a jungle of hair, telescoping scissors, and bicycle horns. Groucho's overreaching caricatures the chauvinism of Fredonia while Harpo's single-minded, ithyphallic innocence does not overextend but undercuts the same absurd array of pretensions. There is even a marvelous scene, one of the Marx Brothers' most famous, where they meet in what I can only call a mythic confrontation. Harpo sneaks into Groucho's home at night, to steal some important state papers; and no one, of course, sneaks more noisily than Harpo. Groucho, in nightcap, nightshirt, glasses, and cigar comes downstairs to investigate and finds, on the other side of a doorway, Harpo—miraculously clothed in the same nightshirt, with cigar, glasses, and greasepaint moustache. And for the next two or three minutes, Groucho tries to convince himself that Harpo is not his reflection in a mirror, cavorting from one side of the doorway to the other in insane postures, each of which Harpo imitates exactly and instantaneously. The most vulgarly reductive question we can ask about this great scene is, why doesn't Groucho just *reach across* the "mirror"? It is also the best question we can ask: he doesn't reach across because, for for some deep reason, he *can't*. The "mirror" is real, more real than the doorway that is "really" there, because across its imagined surface we see two archetypal varieties of the clown meet as the twins they are at the profoundest level of their cultural heritage. Even the exchange of qualities in this confrontation is complete, for if Groucho "imposes" his face on Harpo, Harpo imposes on Groucho his own most salient characteristic: the scene is absolutely silent.

The apostle of noise and the avatar of silence are—symbolically as well as, in this case, really—brothers. But there is an important difference. Harpo's eternal silence, in some of the funniest and loudest movies ever made, is a kind of ultimate, primal example of that peculiar habit of mind we call *irony*. Not just "understatement," as the dictionary usually describes irony, it is a constant and triumphant anti-statement, a positive absence of speech that challenges the pretension and falsehood of official language, of "declaration" as lie. Once again thinking of the satirist's role as exemplary victim, we may remember that in public tortures of the Middle Ages the custom was to advertise the victim's crime by a placard affixed to his clothing or hung around his neck, and that the victim was allowed to speak before the torture began only in order to confess his crime—just as Hephaestus in the *Iliad* says only enough to unite the gods in ridicule of himself, to drown out his self-accusing voice in deathless laughter.

This idea that the satirist as "little fellow" as opposed to braggart mock monarch is at his most powerful when he speaks least runs through some of the greatest satirical works of the Western tradition. We may think of Socrates

himself, the master of irony and the great destructive and
reconstructive satirist of the windy philosophical pretensions
of the Sophists, who (in Plato's dialogs at least) demolishes
self-important opponents by his diffident, humble questioning. Or of William Langland's fourteenth-century allegory,
Piers Plowman, in which the central humble and Christlike
figure of Piers turns the pomp and hypocrisy of "official"
theologians to scorn through the very simplicity of his discourse. And in Byron's *Don Juan,* that massive attack upon
all human wisdom, including language itself, there is only
one, richly suggestive moment in which the hero achieves a
satisfying, fulfilling relation with a woman and with his own
life. At the opening of Canto III, cast ashore after a ship-
wreck on one of the Greek islands, Don Juan is discovered
by Haidee, the beautiful daughter of a pirate leader. She
nurses him back to health and they fall in love for a brief
idyllic moment before her father returns. But they fall truly
in love, Byron is at pains to tell us, precisely because they
cannot speak to each other. Haidee knows no Spanish, Juan
no Greek; they cannot articulate, generalize, falsify their
passion for each other and so are driven to the primal,
aboriginally silent language of the eyes and the body.

The Haidee episode, and the whole tradition of the silent
or near-silent ironic clown, must remind us of the accomplishments of silent film comedy: especially, perhaps, of
the final scene of Charlie Chaplin's *City Lights,* a scene that
Andrew Sarris has rightly called one of the greatest moments of acting in all film. Chaplin, as the nameless, faintly
absurd Tramp, has fallen in love with a beautiful blind girl
who sells flowers on the street corner. She believes him a
wealthy, handsome man, and he spends much of the film
taking demeaning or painful jobs to afford the food and
gifts he regularly brings her. At last, in a complicated encounter with a Jekyll-and-Hyde millionaire who only recognizes Charlie when he (the millionaire) is drunk, Chaplin
"steals" enough money to pay for an operation to restore

the girl's sight. After he gives her the money he is appre-
hended and imprisoned—coming very close indeed to the
archetype of public, exemplary victim. When he enters the
prison door, escorted by a policeman on either side, he is
jaunty; as the door opens he takes a last puff from his cigarette, throws it over his shoulder and kicks it away with his
heel. The next shot shows the same door opening to let him
out after serving his term, and the transformation is as grim
and shocking as any in film. His tramp's clothes, formerly
baggy and comically disarrayed, are now torn, a mockery of
the very mockery of his former ironic unconcern. His celebrated gait, flat-footed but dancing, has become an aimless
shamble. And his face is ashen. He wanders into the city
where he is taunted by two newsboys, directly outside the
shop window of the blind girl, now sighted, prosperous, no
longer beautiful but abjectly *cute*. She laughs at him, he sees
her and is rapturously transfixed. She, still laughing, leaves
the shop to offer him a coin and a flower. But as their hands
touch she recognizes him—the language of the body, again,
speaking more truly than any other. And as she recognizes
him her face is miraculously retransformed to the beauty it
had when she was blind. "So you can see now?" he asks her
(in caption, of course). "Yes, I can see now," she replies.
And the very last shot of the film is the famous, stunning
closeup of Chaplin's face, a rose between his teeth, smiling
in a state beyond either tragedy or joy at the transformation
he has wrought, at the romance he has forever lost by being
seen.

An image like this is inexhaustible in the same way as the
most resonant symbols of literary narrative. But here we can
at least observe that the "little fellow" (Chaplin's habitual
term for his Tramp character), by accepting fully, and des-
cending fully into his own exclusion from the self-confident
world of the city around him redeems its best chances for
humanity. The blind girl may be less ethereally, spiritually
beautiful at the end of the film than at its beginning; but at

least she can now *see,* and Chaplin is tough-minded enough
to insist that the cure is worth whatever sacrifice in "ethe-
real" quality it may necessitate. But, just as we have seen
that the clown is important as ironist whose silence exposes
and ridicules the loud self-importance of his world, so it is
essential to realize that the clown in this phase of his existence is a teacher, a savior through his defenseless visibility.
Hephaestus, remember, is grotesquely lame; Socrates is constantly described as being a very ugly man; and Piers the
Plowman is an obviously rustic tatterdemalion. Chaplin's
great discovery as filmmaker and metaphysician was that
the cruelest, and therefore potentially funniest, pressure we
exercise upon one another is that of seeing each other.

Indeed, in Chaplin we can see with particular clarity how
the vulnerable visibility of the fool, his ironic silence, and his
social function as satirist are all facets of a single vision.
City Lights and *Modern Times* (1936), both made after the
invention of the sound track, are still silent films—with
music and incidental sound effects, but without speech ("A
Bittersweet Romance in Pantomime" is Chaplin's subtitle
for *City Lights*). They are also the last two films in which
Chaplin portrays the "little fellow," since he knew that the
little fellow's special power would dissipate if he ever began
to talk. And Chaplin's lifelong passionate sympathy for the
poor and the oppressed, his Dickensian understanding of the
special terrors of living at the bottom of things, were never
again to achieve the purity and point of expression that they
did in the silent Tramp films. In his talking films, even *Mon-
sieur Verdoux* and the marvelous *The Great Dictator,* the
satirical edge becomes too sharp, too deliberately propagan-
distic—and thereby ceases to be true satire and becomes instead rhetoric.

Even more graphically than in *City Lights,* though less
movingly, a happy conjunction of elements appears in the
two-reeler *The Idle Class* (1921). There Chaplin plays a
dual role, his tramp character and an alcoholic socialite

whose wife is about to leave him because of his drinking. The plot of the film, predictably, is a case of mistaken identities. Charlie the tramp falls in love with the wife (Edna Purviance) while Charles the husband is placidly drinking in his room. But the climax occurs at a fancy dress ball. The husband has been invited to meet his wife there for a reconciliation, and dresses in a suit of armor whose visor, once he shuts it, he can't open again. Charlie the tramp wanders accidentally into the ball, where the wife immediately mistakes him for her husband *made up* as a tramp, and begins to make love to him. The husband, completely and unwillingly disguised in his knightly armor, sees them and indignantly attacks the tramp. The action continues into the lady's bedroom, where finally the husband manages to pry off his helmet, husband and wife are tearfully reconciled and the tramp is indignantly driven away. The "idle classes," for whom Chaplin's distaste is barely concealed, have been humanized and cured. But by what? Precisely by the carnival atmosphere of the fancy dress ball, where people assume masks that ironically reveal rather than conceal their truth, and by the struggle, both low comedy and highly serious, between a millionaire pretending to be more than human (the knightly armor is the *necessary* disguise) and an outcast, silent and clownish, who claims to be nothing—except a lover.

This is not to say that the invention of sound makes it impossible for the fool-as-little-fellow to continue his special role in the self-definition and continuity of civilization. From Stan Laurel through Jacques Tati to Woody Allen he continues his function more successfully, if anything, once his special gift of irony begins to speak. Allen's *Annie Hall,* in fact, is in its way an extension and completion of *City Lights.* Playing a comedian whose manner and career are almost undistinguishable from those of Woody Allen, Woody Allen narrates how he meets, falls in love with, and furthers the show business career of Annie Hall (Diane Keaton), a neurotic but charming and immensely talented girl from the Midwest. Like Chaplin and the blind girl, Woody—or Alvy in the film—and Annie complement each other's deficiencies and humanize each other against the giant, unsympathetic landscapes of New York and Los Angeles, until finally Alvy, a humble pygmalion, loses the woman he has "cured" of her uncertainty—first to a high-powered Hollywood entrepreneur (Paul Simon) and then to the momentum of her own career.

The ironic "little fellow" I have been discussing is, in Yiddish, the *schlemozzl*—the fellow who always gets the soup spilled on him in a restaurant—and Allen has made a brilliant career in film playing the *schlemozzl* as an almost mythic character. But in *Annie Hall* he makes the character truly mythic: Allen as comedian/neurotic/schlemozzl is the narrator of the film, the first face we see, talking directly to the camera and trying to encompass his experience in a series of outworn, self-deprecating one-liners. The story of his love affair with Annie develops not sequentially, but in flashbacks, each of which is an occasion for the comedian once again to address us with a joke about his own inadequacy, until finally we realize that this sort of inadequacy is, in a world deprived of values, the best substitute for or the best *version* we have of what demands to be called charity. In the final meeting of Woody/Alvy with Diane/Annie, after their love affair has been long dead, he is still nervously, funnily concerned with her welfare and generously willing to let her welfare predominate over his own desire for her: a humanization, less sentimental if anything, of the final scene in *City Lights*. And in the very last scene of the film, instead of Chaplin's comic, tragic face, we *hear* Woody Allen (the camera shows an empty street) telling a very old joke about his uncle who thought he was a chicken. Why didn't the family take him to a psychiatrist? Because they needed the eggs. And that's why I continue to believe in true love, says this archetypal child of the century of the hangup: I need the eggs.

In that speech Allen invokes the code of decency and faith engraved "in the hearts of men" as well as any satirist or comedian ever does. For he calls on us to remember that we are, after all, doomed to believe in human chances for nobility and fidelity even if we have lost the power to convince ourselves that these chances are somehow guaranteed by the mere fact of our being human. It is a civilizing, deeply civilizing, speech. And not the least part of its civilization is that it is a speech that admits—as, in a way, does Chaplin's face at the end of *City Lights*—that the film we are seeing *is* a film we are seeing, that it is a construction by a single intelligence to control the chaos of a broken love affair simply by describing it and claiming no more than the human debt for its loss. If Chaplin subtitled *City Lights* "a bittersweet romance," it is significant that Allen subtitles *Annie Hall* (in its advertising copy) " a neurotic romance." The difference in adjectives may mark the distance in self-consciousness (which is the same as self-distrust) we have traveled since 1931, but the effect is the same. Both comedians, like Hephaestus and like Piers the Plowman, remind us of how human we should be by the strategem of enacting for us how less than human the world often wants to make us.

The Braggart and the Ironist

The duality I have been describing as central to the satiric mode, between the overreacher and the underreacher, the braggart and the ironist, is a very ancient one indeed. Aristotle in the *Poetics* does not have much to say about the art of comedy; or rather the students upon whose notes the *Poetics* is based seem not to have been paying attention when he did talk about it. But between what there is in the *Poetics,* and a later, curious pseudo-Aristotelian fragment called the *Tractatus Coislinianus,* we can reconstruct what looks like a fairly accurate, and richly suggestive, Greek idea of the comic (or the satiric, since the two genres tend to merge both in their innate structure and in their deepest cultural implications).

The essential comic conflict, Aristotle says, is a battle of either words or blows or both between a character he calls the *aladzon* and one he calls the *eiron;* between the boastful man, who exceeds the human scale to his own cost, and the ironic man, who falls below that scale, purposefully, to our education. Comedy for Aristotle, in other words, is a quite self-conscious exercise in defining the *norm,* the common— whereas tragedy is a definition of that which makes the common possible, the noble or the normative. And in the conflict of the *aladzon* and the *eiron,* itself a parody of the conflict (or *agon*) of the tragic hero with the gods and fate, we can see the obvious traces of that most brilliant and most lasting manifestation of the Greek comic genius, the comedy of Aristophanes. An arch-conservative, concerned above all else with recalling the citizens of Athens to a recognition of their lost glory of rational balance and responsible democracy, Aristophanes in comedy after comedy dramatizes the human norm by pitting against each other a grandiose *aladzon* and a humble but wise *eiron.* Perhaps the most famous case of this, *The Frogs,* is especially interesting since the braggart and the ironic man are themselves tragedians, the "new" tragedian Euripides, full of blustering atheism and irreverence for the hallowed traditions of Athenian life, and the older, pious, self-effacing Aeschylus, whose works, though he claims less for them than does Euripides for his, outweigh those of his younger adversary. Satire, in other words, reexamines and recreates the "epic" world of high tragedy, but with a view to internalizing its grandeur, teaching us that though the age of the heroes (and of the heroic writers) may be over, our responsibility to the ideal of the heroic is not.

Of course, any watcher of American comedy will recognize in the battle of *aladzon* and *eiron* the fundamental principle of that curious syzygy, the "comedy team." We remember the films of Laurel and Hardy, Bing Crosby and Bob Hope, Abbott and Costello, Dean Martin and Jerry Lewis not because of their plots or elegant cinematography, but because these "teams" act out for us a comic warfare we never, apparently, tire of seeing. It is the same conflict acted out, in Roman comedy, between the *miles gloriosus* or braggart soldier and his canny *servus* or slave or, in one of the greatest of comic novels, between the insanely self-glorying mad knight Don Quixote and his "squire" Sancho Panza, who only half believes the Don's megalomaniac promises of romance and adventure and more than half redeems his master's grandiose failures by keeping his eye on the everyday, homely aspect of things that the Don ignores. In the same way, we know that Hardy's corpulent egocentrism will always be balanced and undercut by Laurel's underfed placidity, that Bob Hope's self-interested scheming will be both defeated and disarmed by Crosby's unflappable disengagement, or that Bud Abbott's street-smart, racetrack conmanship will be less than a match for Lou Costello's childlike, even infantile guilelessness.

In each of these instances it is difficult to think of the "team" as other than a curious unity; even Hope and Crosby, who both enjoyed legendary careers separately, both before and after the *Road* pictures, are permanently associated one with the other because of that happy partnership. And in the case of Martin and Lewis, the idea of the "comedy team" reaches both a kind of terminal point of tension and a graphic level of interdependence. It would have warmed Aristophanes', if not Aristotle's, heart that neither Dean Martin nor Jerry Lewis has managed to generate the same sort of energy in his films since their celebrated split as they did during their partnership. Martin is an almost absurdly hyperthyroid sexual *aladzon,* handsome beyond the stage of caricature, gifted with a baritone that communicates nothing so much as a narcissistic eroticism. And Jerry Lewis as *eiron* goes beyond even the infantile innocence of Lou Costello: he is, quite simply, an idiot, a loud, unruly, hopelessly retarded and incurably innocent child as incapable of guile as he is of recognizing the world for what it is. These are both, it should be pointed out, immensely distasteful varieties of personality: they go so far beyond and below the human norm that the "norm" itself disappears as a center point balancing their extremes. But, in the films that Martin and Lewis made together, they do balance, remarkably and constantly at the point of flying off either end of the human scale into chaos. Instead of the friendly-enemies, mutually but benevolently mistrustful relationship that characterizes Hope and Crosby (or Laurel and Hardy, or Abbott and Costello), Martin and Lewis operate on a very thinly veiled principle of total hostility, the potentially violent finale of the "team" in an explosion of absurdity that would cancel the humanity they are supposed to define between their excesses.

In *Living It Up* (1954), one of their best and strangest films, this perennial possibility of disaster and nihilism is especially clear. Directed by Norman Taurog and based on a screenplay by Ben Hecht, *Living It Up* is the story of how Lewis, playing a boy from Desert Hole, Arizona, who longs for the glories of New York, is accidentally exposed to radioactivity from a nuclear test. Martin, playing the local doctor (who graduated, he is proud to say, at the bottom of his class) incorrectly diagnoses that Lewis has only three weeks to live. At this point Janet Leigh, a reporter for a New York newspaper, gets the idea of giving Lewis an all-expenses-paid trip to New York for the last days of his life: a grisly publicity stunt warmly encouraged by her venal and skinflint boss, played by the reptilian Fred Clark. The boys get their trip to New York, but Martin has discovered his error, so they spend the rest of the film "living it up" while

Lewis, with his friend's careful coaching, masquerades as a
dying man.

The deception is inevitably revealed and—also inevitably—the boys are saved, Janet Leigh falls in love with
Martin, and all ends (sort of) well. But what kind of comedy
is this? Mel Brooks, who should know, once told an inter-
viewer, "Listen: art has nothing to do with good taste." And
Living It Up, far from being in any taste at all, is a very ugly
movie. It is also a very good one. Yeats' great line "Man has
invented death" makes special sense as an epigraph for this
film. Martin and Lewis literally do invent a death: Martin as
an ultimate conman, a braggart surgeon concerned only to
prolong the illusion of disease, Lewis as the most abject of
"little fellows," the man under sentence of death. But as
they dance their deceptions on either side of the abyss, they
do humanize: not one another, not even Janet Leigh or the
city of New York, but us. By making death (and that most
distinctively fifties image of death, radiation poisoning) a
joke and a "routine," in the vaudevillian's sense, they exorcise momentarily its fearfulness, and satirize cruelly the public relations sentimentality with which we surround it.
Against the standard of the lugubrious prose with which the
newspaper treats Lewis' impending death, the antics of these
two hypocrites return us to a basic, even if dishonest,
human gusto.

I have said that the figures of *aladzon* and *eiron* form a
symbiosis. The braggart and the ironist—or rather the men
who *claim* to be those things, when they are really just our
size—are, like Groucho and Harpo in the scene from *Duck
Soup,* mirror twins. In many of the richest and most compelling satires, though, that twinship collapses into a more
complicated unity. The braggart and the ironist, the fool as
loudmouth and the fool as victim can become a single,
heroic and antiheroic, figure. It is not surprising that the
greatest examples of this figure in literature appear after the
age of classical Rome. For the first important character to

combine the two roles was himself an enemy, and often a satirist, of the rigid imagination that separated the braggart lord from his ironic slave, a character who alternately behaved in the humblest of ways, consorting by preference with the lowest of the low, and claimed for himself the most outrageous, absurdly gigantic kind of importance. And he came from neither Athens nor Rome, but from Bethlehem by way of Jerusalem.

To return again to the ceremonies of carnival, Saturnalia, and public riot I have been invoking as parallels to the satirist's function, it is impossible not to see in the drama of Christ's crucifixion a startling transformation of these elements. He is given, by popular demand, the most disgraceful of criminal executions, the cross. And yet complementing this lowness is the legend Pilate has affixed to his cross, "This is Jesus of Nazareth, King of the Jews." Like his mock coronation with thorns during his trial, it is an irony by his tormenters that turns back on itself. He is the most abject of victims (early Christian apologists were quick to associate him with the "suffering servant" of the prophecies of Isaiah), but his victimhood is precisely the form of his triumphant godhead. And he is braggart (he breaks his silence at the trial only to assent to the one thing—that he is the Son of God—certain to get him executed), but his braggadocio is ironically borne out through his descent to victimhood.

In his book *Mimesis: The Representation of Reality in Western Literature,* Erich Auerbach argues that the fact and the doctrine of the Incarnation, the interpenetration of the highest and the lowest ranges of existence in the person of Christ, is the single determinative event for the nature and development of European literature. And we may also wish to remember that two of the greatest theorists of film, Sergei Eisenstein and André Bazin, speak frequently of the representational power of cinema in terms that are all but explicitly "incarnational" (as does Siegfried Kracauer in the subtitle of his *Theory of Film: The Redemption of Physical Reality*). Throughout this book, I have argued that the special quality of film as opposed to literary narrative is just that it begins, unlike written story, with a perception and totally convincing representation of the world of things that lies all around us, and builds from that initial image of the mute, material universe to the articulation of consciousness, self-consciousness, the "I" who is really the hero of all mythologies. But Auerbach's study reminds us that this interpenetration of matter and mind, of the lowest and the highest, is initially, as early Christian writers never tire of saying about the Incarnation itself, a *scandal:* a shocking and challenging inversion of our "normal" expectations about the order of things, a reestablishment of that order on new and more generous grounds.

"Scandal" in this sense is the satirist's, the comedian's, most valuable weapon as well as his greatest gift. We can be shocked back into a recognition of our civilized responsibilities by the scandalous excess or deficiency of the antihero; and never more efficiently than when that excess and deficiency are combined in a single image—a real "incarnation" of the limits of humanity, whose function is precisely to save us, above all from ourselves.

The ideal, almost graphically crude combination of the big man and little man, *aladzon* and *eiron,* in a single self would be, perhaps, to imagine a gigantic infant, a monstrous baby. And that is just what Rabelais imagines in *Gargantua* and the four books of *Pantagruel,* that most scandalous, outrageous, and supremely intelligent of Renaissance attacks upon the benightedness and pettiness of medieval scholasticism. Gargantua and his son Pantagruel are an epoch-making vision of the vitality of the new humanism, with all its adventurous intellectuality and frank sensuality. They are giants; giants immense enough that the narrator, in one famous episode from *Pantagruel,* can get lost inside his master's mouth, wandering here and there over the mountains of his teeth, visiting the quaint villagers who live there. And their gigantism insists upon being recognized as the gross, physical humanity it is: defecation, urination, eructation and flatulence account for a significant portion of the dramatic action of the Rabelisian books, all on the same massive scale as their producers. It is a serious philosophical argument: by overreaching, by outrageously enlarging the presence, the odors, the *bodiliness* of the body, Rabelais reconciles us through laughter to forgive ourselves for our own physicality, initiates us into that acceptance of the senses which is such a fundamental aspect of humanism at its most brilliant.

But at the same time that Gargantua and Pantagruel are giants, they are also childlike, possessed of an intelligent naivety that is also one of the salient virtues of Renaissance rationalism. Surrounded by superstitious priests, hair-splitting theologians, and hypocritical enemy kings, they triumph over these reactionary forces simply by their clear-eyed, unprejudiced acceptance of things as they are. One of the funniest and most significant instances of this activity is the war conducted against Gargantua's kingdom by the vain and ignorant ruler Picrochole. Gargantua, peaceful *eiron* that he is, is baffled by Picrochole's enmity, and perfectly willing to make peace on decent human terms. But when things become too unbearable to tolerate, Gargantua single-handedly defeats the armies of Picrochole and imposes upon the beaten soldiers a punishment both humane and dazzlingly appropriate to the theme of the whole book. He sets them to work in his printing presses, forcing them to operate those machines that more than any other single invention spurred and disseminated the new learning throughout Europe.

In a somewhat different fashion, near the end of the age which Rabelais helped initiate, the image of the simultaneously big and little man reappears, in what is probably the most celebrated and most inexhaustible of all satires in English. Swift's *Gulliver's Travels* is, among much else, a bitter, almost cosmic attack upon the dishonest, self-serving, often inhumanly cruel uses to which men put that gift of "reason" so celebrated by Rabelais. The great promise of humanism has, by the early eighteenth century, become tarnished, clotted with mankind's innate corruptibility (Swift unlike Rabelais takes the doctrine of the Fall as a prime datum); and Swift writes to recall men to a decent recognition not so much of their gigantic possibilities but of the limits, the elementary laws of decency that can still make them human. In the first two books of the *Travels* he introduces Lemuel Gulliver, his not particularly bright everyman, first into a world where he is a giant—among the tiny people of Lilliput—and then into a world where he is a miniature—among the giants of Brobdingnag. He becomes a "big," then a "little" man; and what he sees, and what Swift wants us to see, is first the absurdly grandiose pretension of the human race as midgets challenging the universe, and then the awful ugliness of the race as vile bodies unaware of their own coarseness. The Lilliputians, those short people with dreams of grandeur, parody and demolish the European pretensions to civilized discourse and rational organization; they are a nest of *aladzons* who do not know, or will not admit, that they inhabit an anthill. And while in the first book Gulliver looks at humanity through the wrong end of a telescope, in the second book he examines the human body itself on the specimen slide, as it were, of the microscope. The Brobdingnagians have few of the political perversions of their tiny twins, but in them Gulliver is forced to regard humanity, in all its smells, noises, and physical crudity, writ large and ugly. They are not *eirons* only because they can never know, as Gulliver cannot but know, how gross, disgusting, and naturally savage they are, for all their civilization.

There is no real point in arguing that Gulliver's twin roles as big man and little man make him especially "Christlike";

though he does share, with the heroes of Rabelais, a combination of innocence and intelligence, an openness to the
more unpleasant aspects of experience and a nostalgic, even
tortured sense of the possibilities of human greatness, that
would probably not be there at all if it were not for the
vistas of nobility—and of failure—opened by the idea of the
Incarnation.

One of the most remarkable of American films, a masterpiece of *kitsch* that transforms itself into a legitimate masterpiece, catches many of the elements we have been discussing as classically satiric and comic. I am referring to *King
Kong.*

"He was a king in his world. But we'll teach him the
meaning of fear." That is what filmmaker and showman
Carl Denham (Robert Armstrong) says as his crew prepares
to transport the drugged giant ape from Skull Island to New
York, where he will be exhibited as the "Eighth Wonder of
the World." It is perhaps a more crucial and more poignant
line than Denham's famous observation at the end, as Kong
lies dead, having been shot off the Empire State Building:
"It wasn't the planes. It was beauty killed the beast." For
Kong is not really about giant apes or jungle adventures, it
is about cities, and the ways cities teach *us* the meaning of
fear—which is to say the ways they distance us from our
most elementary impulses, and punish rather than support
and civilize our attempts to integrate those impulses into our
lives. Kong is driven by his passion for the blonde, beautiful,
infinitely vulnerable Ann Redman (Fay Wray); but that is a
passion we can all understand. And in finding Fay Wray
quite as desirable as does the giant ape, we are complicit
with him. None of us is Kong—he is too gigantic and too innocent for the human scale. But, really, we all recognize that
his monster's body and baby's brain are in some important
way the parent, the body of our desire.

I have said that the moment of satire takes place between
the moment of the king's death and that of his hoped-for

resurrection or reincarnation. In this respect *King Kong* is an especially extreme, post-Darwinian version of that moment. His "kingship" is the kingship, the primacy, of racial memory; and the "law" he institutes or incarnates is not so much that pop-Darwinian cliche, the "law of the jungle," but rather the frank celebration of those sexual urges that we can see—even without Freud's or Darwin's guidance—to be the generative, crucial, and most problematic forces behind the institution and continuance of civilization. He was a king in his world: and this is the only time in the film *King Kong* that Kong is *called* a king. But the big man, or big preman, from Skull Island becomes a very little individual indeed in New York, especially in the self-confidently industrialized, art deco, chromium and steel New York of 1932, whose triumphant architectural expression, the Empire State Building, is precisely the instrument of Kong's public crucifixion.

It is not just beauty that kills the beast; it is showmanship, particularly the showmanship of filmmaker Denham, who goes to Skull Island to make a documentary and winds up participating in an improbable tragedy—which he does not film, but which is the film, *King Kong*, we see. There is something inescapably voyeuristic about the film experience; this has been pointed out by numerous critics and theorists of the art. We are all, in the theater, peeping toms, seeing without being seen. But *Kong*, as subtly as the films of Antonioni or Godard, confronts and comments upon this phenomenon. Kong becomes "King" Kong only at the moment he is displayed on stage in New York: only at the moment, that is, when his power and danger have been (everyone thinks) converted into sheer visibility, into mere showbiz. And his subsequent escape and brief rampage only underscore and bear out the implications of that initial humiliation. The city, the complicated web of passions, appetites, and responsibilities engendered, symbolically, somewhere in the dawn-time out of Kong's loins, has grown too big—or too small—to tolerate his presence: the king must die. And he must die in a public ceremony, a controlled riot, that announces not only his own exclusion from society— that he is a monster—but also that he is an exemplary victim—his implicit, unspoken, unselfconsciously ironic criticism of the society that exiles him.

Rabelais, Swift, and *King Kong* not only indicate the importance of the big man–little man twinship for satire of this sort; they also remind us of the importance of the elementary form behind the differentiation of "big" and "little" men: the flesh, the body. Flesh, indeed—the reality, the attraction, the potential grossness of the bodies we have—is one of the most powerful themes of satire in all its forms. I have been tracing throughout this study, among other things, the different functions of clothing, of the symbolic adornment of the body, in different forms of narrative. In satire, not surprisingly, clothing approaches one of two complementary and terminal limits: it becomes either the motley of the clown or nothing at all, i.e. nudity. Both varieties of clowning are, really, the emptying-out of the idea of clothing of all possible symbolic significance. As William Willeford, whom I have already cited, argues in *The Fool and His Scepter,* the ill-fitting, absurdly uncoordinated, sloppy motley of the court jester is an expression of the reign of disorder, a sartorial chaos that precisely symbolizes and supports his social function as destroyer and reaffirmer of the reign of law. The clown's ill-fitting costume (Chaplin's baggy pants, Groucho's painted-on moustache, Woody Allen's owlish hornrim glasses) calls to mind the fact that it *is* a costume. By fitting ill, that is, the costume reminds us that there is a body to be fitted ill, that there is a "poor bare forked animal" (as King Lear observes of the false madman Edgar) beneath the robes of state and the uniforms of civility. But that is to say that the fool's motley itself is a kind of nudity. The famous couplet

When Adam delved and Eve span,
Who was then the gentleman?

is clear enough that we need not even gloss, for twentieth-century readers, the meanings of words like "delved" and "span." And it retains its clarity after half a millennium just because it comes so close to the archetypal satiric imagination of the body and of nobility. The father and mother, king and queen, of the human race are at once reduced to mere nakedness and exalted to a real humanity by the intercourse of "span" and "gentleman"—a rhyme that perfectly reduces the petty pretensions of "gentleman" to the insufficiency and secondariness that the writer wants them to have, and that they deserve.

A joke of Woody Allen's is particularly appropriate here. Asked some years ago, on a television talk show, what his next film project would be, he said that he planned to make the first pornographic monster movie: Godzilla rises out of the Bay of Tokyo and exposes himself. Satire is never really very far from pornography. Rabelais and Swift are quite straightforward about what I have to call, for acceptability's sake, the full implications of their characters' gigantism. *Kong*, however, is not. That massive, questing penis which *has to be* the motivator for Kong's attraction to Fay Wray, his dowsing rod for the sublime, is never, of course, shown.

It is not even shown in Dino de Laurentiis' 1975 remake of *King Kong*, although it is much more strongly intimated as a moving force in that much maligned, quite misunderstood film. *Kong* I, for all its satiric point, is a good-natured film: no one really wants to do evil, though that is the inevitable final outcome of everyone's behavior. In *Kong* II, however, everything has gone sour: especially the motivations of the characters. Instead of Denham, the dedicated filmmaker, the expedition to Skull Island in *Kong* II is led by an oil speculator, played with appropriate corporate creepiness by Charles Grodin. And instead of the innocent and vulnerable Fay Wray, the girl in *Kong* II (Jessica Lange) is a burned-out, jet-set performer in pornographic movies named Dwan ("I picked it out because it sounds like Dawn, sort of—don't you like it?" she daffily asks in her first scene). The second *Kong* is, in its way, a science fiction film. For it describes a world entirely like ours, in every respect of venality, ambition, cruelty, and hypocrisy, with one essential and determinative difference: no one in the world of this film has ever seen the first *King Kong*.

Twice-Told Tales

Marx remarks somewhere that every event occurs twice: first as tragedy, then as farce. Whether or not this is a good philosophy of history, it is a splendidly appropriate philosophy of storytelling. With a crude, rough-hewn urgency, it precisely catches the relationship of satire to epic, of comedy to tragedy, of the "latest" to the "earliest" stories civilizations tell themselves about their growth and decline and growth again. That relationship—as we imagine it, though not necessarily as it happens, in every case—is one of circularity, replication, parody, and rediscovery.

What a farce it all is: or what a tragedy. The second *King Kong* parodies and reduces the first *King Kong*, and the first *Kong* itself was already a reduction, a satire, of our urban, cosmopolitan pretensions.

As the biggest of big men, the giant ape acts out a tragedy (or a romance, or a melodrama) that is inevitably reduced, parodied by the fairy-tale archetype against which he is pitted: Beauty and the Beast. And as the little man, the man defeated and mocked by his culture, he is equally undercut, equally reduced to caricature by the story in which he finds himself. How, after all, can the little man make it in the big city? There are an infinite number of answers to that question, but the one answer *not possible* is to attack the city itself: that is what Kong does, in both versions, and what he is killed for.

Kong, in other words, loses two ways. He loses as an outrageous, failed tragic hero, and he loses as an exiled, reviled comic clown. But the distance between *Kong* I and *Kong* II, and the difference between their modes of presentation, allow us to recognize another, richer difference between types of satire: one that goes beyond the image of the satirist as fool, and approaches the specific foolishness of his performance as *story*.

The kind of comedy or satire I have been describing arises upon the disappearance of the king. Thersites attacks the ruler, Hephaestus attacks himself for the sake of the ruler, Kong is destroyed—not entirely without his own complicity—in the absence of a definite, recognizable ruler. What conclusion can we draw from these cases, what common bond can we find among them? None, perhaps, except that the satiric mode, the moment of the fool, is somehow always the moment of mockery, of *imitation* of the nobility whose absence it celebrates.

The idea of replication and parody as techniques of satiric narrative takes us beyond the image of the satirist as elemental clown, and introduces a central structural principle, one we have already seen working in the narratives we have examined. *Kong* II parodies *Kong* I; *City Lights* and *Annie Hall* both refer, in subtle ways, to the myth of Pygmalion and Galatea; *Gulliver's Travels* is partly a mock–re-creation of the narratives of exploration that were so popular during the seventeenth century; and even the Gospels, particularly the Gospel of Matthew, attempt to show how the career of Christ fulfills—but with an ironic inversion of nationalistic arrogance—the ancient prophecies about a deliverer of the people. Satire, that is, is always a twice-told tale, repeating as "farce" what was once told as "tragedy" or, in our terms, epic. And the point of the repetition is, like the character of the satirist himself, twofold: both to chasten us by reminding us how far we have fallen below the epic scale we try to imitate, and to suggest to us new ways of reinstituting, even in an iron time, the laws and possibilities of the age of gold. And depending upon which of those urges predominates in a given narrative, the satire veers toward one of the alternate possibilities of mock-heroic or fantasy.

Juvenal, Rome's greatest satirist and the first writer to speak self-consciously about the business of being a satirist, establishes this proposition in the most perceptive, subtlest of ways. Why write satire at all, he asks himself in the First Satire; why not continue to produce the second-rate minor epics which are all the rage in the Empire?

> You can
> With safety match Aeneas and Turnus in war; no one's hurt
> If you tell how Achilles died or how many a search was
>   stirred
> For Hylas, who fell in a well with his jug. But when in rage,
> As though with drawn sword, Lucillius roars, the hearer,
>   whose wage
> Of sin lies cold in his conscience, burns, he sweats to hear
> Of crimes he knows are true. This brings on anger and tears.*

This is quite close to Rousseau's "law . . . engraved in the hearts of men." The true epic, the right poetry, for a corrupt age is precisely the poetry that reminds us how unworthy we are of the noble rages, the nontrivial passions, celebrated in the poetry of our origins. Again and again Juvenal shows us the pimps and prostitutes, usurers and thieves of his Rome transacting their petty deals, in plain air, beneath the very statues of the great legislators and founders of the now-dead Republic. Satire as a self-conscious art, in other words, is born at the same time the satirist discovers the possibilities

---

* Tr. Hubert Creekmore (New York: New American Library, 1963).

of the mock-heroic mode. This is nowhere clearer than in
the brilliant passage from his Second Satire, directed against
the sexual license of his day:

> The notion that there are such things as spirits of the dead,
> And kingdoms under the earth, and Stygian streams bespread
> With black frogs, and all those thousands crossing in one
>   boat,
> No boys believe except those too young to pay a groat
> For the baths. But suppose that it were true: What would
>   Curius and both
> The Scipios think; and what would Fabricius and the ghost
> Of Camillus, the legion slain at the Cremera, or the host
> Of youth that fell at Cannae, all those brave hearts, feel
> When a shade like Gracchus came among them?

It is a proposition of existentialist urgency. Though we can
no longer believe in the spirits of the dead, having long
passed that point of innocence and nobility, we are nonetheless compelled to accept the implications of such a belief:
morality, in other words, survives even its death into official
sanction and acceptance. The satirist's job is just to remind
us that, even when the law has achieved the marmoreal
repose and distance of legend, it is still the law.

The most Juvenalian of English satirists, Alexander Pope,
created what may well be the most flawlessly executed
mock-heroic poem in Western literature in *The Rape of the
Lock*. This poem, which more than almost any other one
can think of deserves the word "perfect," is the narrative of
a very trivial historical incident, indeed. On a day in 1711,
an English nobleman named Lord Petre, infatuated with the
beautiful young Arabella Fermor, made so bold as to cut a
lock of her hair for a keepsake while she was playing cards
at a tea party. It was, perhaps, a silly thing to do; but not
nearly as silly as the lady's response to the incident, which

rapidly inflamed both families involved into something like a major feud. Pope originally wrote the *Rape*, in a much less ambitious version than the one we read today, as a peace-making gesture, intended gently to tease both sides of the quarrel out of taking so trivial an act of goosey infatuation so seriously. But, finding that the family of Lady Arabella was outraged by even his poem about the incident—finding that the balm he was trying to apply to everyone's wounded feelings was in fact salt—he wisely decided to intensify and expand rather than surpress what he had already written.

The *Rape of the Lock* may not be the most suggestive, leering poem in English; but if not, it certainly isn't Pope's fault. From the title onward, he carefully loads as many lines as he can with double meanings and erotic overtones, until not even the most inattentive reader can miss the point that the events being narrated, for all their stylization, pre-meditation, and *politesse,* only disguise a sexual adventure no more complicated than that of the simplest explication of the plot of *King Kong.* Generations of schoolteachers have carefully explained to their classes that "Rape" as in *The Rape of the Lock* comes from a Latin word, *raptus,* meaning "abduction" or "theft." And the same generations have failed to mention that, while Pope is quite aware of this etymology, his age like ours understands a prior and stronger suggestion in the word. By "rape" Pope means rape.

The story, as mock-heroic, is carefully patterned on that most profound and noble of English poems, John Milton's *Paradise Lost.* Indeed, the "rape" of a lock of the beautiful Belinda's hair by the grotesquely romantic and silly Baron is a situation with obvious parallels to the seduction of Eve and man's consequent exile from Paradise into the grim world of history. But it is a *silly* parallel, as the Baron is a silly tempter and Belinda herself a vapid Eve. *Paradise Lost* opens with the mighty epic theme

> Of man's first disobedience, and the fruit
> Of that forbidden tree, whose mortal taste
> Brought death into the world, and all our woe. . . .
> Sing blissful Muse, who from the sacred top
> Of Oreb or of Sinai didst inspire
> That shepherd who first taught the chosen seed.

Pope's epic invocation reduces Milton's "Muse"—the Holy Spirit who taught Moses—to Belinda herself—who teaches nobody:

> Say what strange motive, Goddess! could compel
> A well-bred Lord t'assault a gentle Belle?
> Oh say what stranger cause, yet unexplor'd,
> Could make a gentle Belle reject a Lord?
> In tasks so bold, can little men engage,
> And in soft bosoms dwells such mighty Rage?

The last two lines especially catch the ironic brilliance of the poem and of the mode in which it is conceived. "Little men" and "soft bosoms" define, for Pope, the human world has characters inhabit. And their trivial, absurdly overblown quarrels are all the more tellingly reduced to their true shape by being described as "bold tasks" and "mighty rages." The very verse form which Pope makes preeminently his own in English poetry, the "heroic couplet," is a kind of constant model, at the level of language itself, for his activity of reduction. In place of the expansive, rolling energy of Milton's blank verse, the couplet's values of balance, wit, and precision make each single pair of lines—at least in Pope—an act of satiric miniaturization. Addressing Queen Anne as Belinda approaches her fateful moment at Hampton Court, he says:

> Here thou, great ANNA! whom three realms obey,
> Dost sometimes counsel take—and sometimes Tea.

It is a little world. But it is a world whose littleness, Pope leaves no doubt, is criminal, just because it either ignores or trivializes the reality of its own life (and its own mortality), and that of the world around it. For one powerful moment in the *Rape,* Pope lets us see what lies beyond the elegant and life-denying rules of the game in Belinda's world. And the vision is shattering:

> Mean while, declining from the noon of day,
> The sun obliquely shoots his burning ray;
> The hungry Judges soon the sentence sign,
> And wretches hang that jury-men may dine. . . .

The same combination of wit, miniaturization, stylized brilliance, and immense bitterness obtains in what must be one of the most complete mock-heroic films ever made, Jean Renoir's *The Rules of the Game.* There is, in fact, one crucial moment which is as close as anything I know to the spirit of the heroic couplet as Pope uses it in *The Rape of the Lock.* Returning from a morning's shooting on her country estate (in which dozens of rabbits have been shown being obscenely, revoltingly massacred by the laughing members of the upper-class house party), the Countess Christine de La Chesnaye (Nora Gregor) examines a small field telescope belonging to one of her guests. "With this instrument you can peer into the most private lives of the animals," he tells her. And for a moment she gazes admiringly at a squirrel in a distant tree—a cruel reminder to the viewer, perhaps, of the rabbits just pointlessly slaughtered. But then she shifts the telescope to see her husband Robert (Marcel Dalio) kissing his mistress Geneviève (Mila Parely) whom he had promised to abandon for conjugal fidelity. It is a farewell kiss, though Christine cannot know that. This is the moment at which she reaches the decision to leave her husband that precipitates the bedroom farce, culminating in a very unfarcical murder, that occupies the second half of the film. The instrument that lets you peer into the most private lives of the animals is, of course, not only the telescope but Renoir's camera, and the whole involved situation which is the story of *The Rules of the Game.* Like Pope's heroic couplet, it allows us to see into the life of things—and to learn how restrictive, how literally deadly that life has become.

The "rules" of the title are the unwritten social laws governing marriage and sexual adventurism among the upper classes: rules parodied by the "downstairs" people in the persons of the maid Lisette (Paulette Dubost), her husband the gamekeeper Schumacher (Gaston Modot), and the romantic poacher Marceau (Julien Carette). But they are also the "rules" of nineteenth-century French farce (the film is based on Alfred de Musset's 1833 *Les Caprices de Marianne*) and the "rules" that allow society to survive and continue despite the ever-threatening chaos of human passions: a mechanism, like the telescope and like the film camera, that gives us a vantage point and a minimal control, at least, over the "lives of the animals." But the central point of Renoir's great film is precisely that the rules are breaking down, the machinery is going haywire, just because it has become *too* complicated, *too* intricately designed for its own original and originating purpose: to make the world habitable.

Nowhere is this breakdown better caught than in the gala party and amateur show the Count de La Chesnaye puts on for his guests in the film's climactic sequence. The Count, who has something rabbitlike about him—if not sexually at least in his nervous, hopalong desire that everyone have a good time without getting hurt—is a collector of antique, mainly eighteenth-century music boxes and animated toys. His sense of his own role, in other words, and of the "rules" of the life he leads, is brilliantly expressed in terms of his antiquarian's obsession with relics of the age of splendor, with beautiful, intricate, and absolutely sterile mechanical artifacts. The high point of the gala so far has been a bizarre parody dance of death. With the lights turned out in the main ballroom, three of the guests in luminous white sheets dance inanely to the music of Saint-Saëns in a "visit to the underworld," a recognition of the abyss underlying our daylight civilization, that cannot fail to remind us of the underworld journeys of the heroes of epic, and cannot fail to radiate its own comparative triviality. While this dance is taking place, moreover, the various lovers, flirts, and cuckolds scattered among the halls are bringing their affairs and assignations to a series of carefully orchestrated climaxes.

And then comes, for Robert de La Chesnaye, his grand moment. Grinning uncertainly at his guests from the ballroom stage, he announces the masterpiece of his career as a collector. The curtains behind him part to reveal an immense, rococo music box which begins, to enthusiastic applause, to grind out a loud, tinnily complicated, merry tune. And as Robert beams at his masterpiece and his audience, his wife Christine agrees to run away with her suitor the handsome aviator, the gamekeeper discovers his wife with the poacher and begins chasing him through the halls, firing his pistol, the party dissolves in a series of delighted squeals and screaming faints, and the music box breaks down, grinding out not its happy tune but the skin-crawling noise of stripping gears.

It is, again, a carnival moment of the return to chaos. But this chaos, like the "Fall" in Pope, calls attention to its own rather pathetic silliness. Order is momentarily and unsteadily restored, but only as a prelude to the film's final and real tragedy. The aviator Jurieu (Roland Toutain) is sent by his friend Octave (Renoir himself) to meet Christine in the garden. There he is shot and killed by the gamekeeper, who mistakes him for the poacher Marceau going to an assignation with his wife. Again, after the disaster, Count Robert manages somehow to restore a semblance of order. Apologizing from the front steps of his estate to his guests for the disturbance, he reassures them that all is well and gracefully covers over the passions and betrayals that have led to the murder by a convenient reference to a "shooting accident." And as the guests, casting grotesque and otherworldly shadows, file back into the house, one of them remarks to his companion, "La Chesnaye has class; it's a vanishing breed." Indeed, it is. For while the "rules" of the game retain, however creakily, their ability to keep functioning, they have lost their force to do what they were designed to do, humanize us and make room for our humanity.

In the "hero" and "antihero" of the film, in fact, we recognize those two figures whose twinship and complementarity I have already discussed, here explicitly in a mock-epic setting. The aviator André Jurieu, passionately and hopelessly in love with Christine, is a true hero for our time, a daring, flagrantly unconventional young man who is literally too big for the world at ground level, and who is frustrated, infuriated, and finally destroyed by the earthbound society in which he tries to find love. And his friend, confidant, and collaborator in his suit, Octave, is also in love with Christine but is a self-confessed failure, a witty and self-loathing parasite and flatterer of the rich. His failed career as a conductor (a man, that is, who could make truly human music instead of the absurd, mechanized parody of Robert's aged toys) has fully equipped him to play the quintessential ironic role in this deadly farce. For he understands the rules more fully, more intricately than anyone else in the film, and yet also understands, with a kind of calm, even charitable despair, how terrible in its cost the observance of those rules can be.

Renoir's performance as Octave is surely one of the great pieces of acting in the history of the film. And an essential part of its power is that we realize that this ironic, kindly victim of the rules, who attempts to stage-manage events for the happiness of his friends and fails dismally, in fact is also the creator, the triumphantly intelligent and ironic author, of the film itself; the successful stage manager of this entire little world, who is not victimized by its own rules because he creates it, and sees the rich possibilities which it excludes.

Satire at the level of *The Rape of the Lock* or *The Rules of the Game* requires, of course, a culture imbued with a knowledge of the rules. It is, and can only be, the product of a very sophisticated level of culture indeed. Thus one might think that American cinema has been less rich in examples of this variety of narrative than the European cinema precisely because, though American society is fully as complicated as most cultures in its unwritten social rules, it is less explicitly, less officially willing to admit that such rules exist and are in operation. A country, after all, in which nearly seventy percent of the population claims to belong to the "middle class" hardly seems a likely field for a narrative that depends upon the perception of class differences and levels of style for its very operation.

But this turns out to be not the case. In many ways, it is just the predominance and apparent omnivorousness of the idea of the "middle class" in American culture that allows class satire, "mock heroic" in the fullest sense of the phrase, to thrive. If every one of us belongs to the great middle class, and if the *idea* of the great middle class (invoked as recently as Richard M. Nixon's public flirtation with the "silent majority" of Americans) retains something of its Jeffersonian, republican associations of a nation of honest, humble laborers tinged with the nobility of the common folk, then the possibilities of satire expand rather than contract. The "heroic" level of existence to be invoked and parodied by the narrative is not that of the lordly epic founders of civilization, but rather of the romantically noble hero of democratic revolution, the Concord farmer, the honest working man capable of becoming president—the populist hero, in other words, of a poem like that most American of romantic epics, Walt Whitman's *Leaves of Grass:*

> I celebrate myself, and sing myself
> And what I shall assume you shall assume,
> For every atom belonging to me, as good belongs to you.

From *I Am a Fugitive from a Chain Gang* (1932) through *The Grapes of Wrath* (1940) to *On the Waterfront* (1954), American films of so-called social realism have frequently explored the betrayals of this democratic promise in terms it is easy to conceive of as satirical, mock-heroic. As I have indicated, the difference between the world of melodramatic narrative, where the city is dangerous and difficult, and the world of satire, where it is intolerable, is a difference of attitude more than anything else. And in Paul Muni's unjustly condemned and criminalized character in *Chain Gang,* in Henry Fonda's impassioned, sensitive sharecropper in *Grapes,* and Marlon Brando's failed, self-betrayed prize-fighter-turned-petty-hood in *Waterfront* we can see figures who cross the borderline between the two modes: "little" men whose faith in the system, in the benevolence of the rules of the game, turns sour and horrifying as they learn that they are not the unsung potential heroes of their economic, industrialized world, but its victims.

One of the most complex satires of the last few years, though, and one that carries the activity of the mock-hero, the parodistic knight, to a kind of outrageous, existential limit is Mike Nichols' *The Graduate* (1967). The plot is relatively simple, with more than a little of the atmosphere of bedroom farce about it (it is based on Charles Webb's splendidly funny novel of the same name). Ben Braddock (Dustin Hoffman) has just graduated from college and is ready to begin a career as a businessman of some yet unspecified nature. Returning to his comfortable Los Angeles home for the summer, he is seduced into an afair with Mrs. Robinson (Anne Bancroft), the cynical, alcoholic wife of a blustering neighbor; an affair heavily laced with the boredom and barely concealed mutual distaste of most such suburban passions. But soon after the affair has begun, Mrs. Robinson's lovely daughter Elaine (Katharine Ross) returns home. She and Ben meet, see each other frequently, and fall in love; but Mrs. Robinson, in a desperate and hateful attempt both to keep Ben for herself and punish him for loving a younger woman, reveals to Elaine that they are lovers. In disgust and panic Elaine returns to Berkeley to begin her fall classes, where Ben pursues her, doggedly but hopelessly trying to win her back. Finally she agrees to marry a dull nonentity who has been courting her all along. Learning of it, Ben in the famous last sequence frantically races to Santa Barbara, getting to the church just as the ceremony is ending. After the final vows have been taken and exchanged, he appears, beating against the glass partition at the back of the church like an imprisoned bird, shouting Elaine's name. She turns, sees him, and at the last possible moment—after the last possible moment, actually—shouts "Ben!' and runs to join him. Ben and Elaine make their escape from the outraged crowd—Ben fighting off their attackers with a large cross he has pulled from the church wall—and they run to the nearest bus stop, boarding the next bus to an unknown destination, he in jacket and slacks, she in bridal gown: fade out.

On the face of it, *The Graduate* is a revolutionary, enthusiastic fable about the revolt from convention and the necessity of ignoring the rules of the game whenever those rules come into conflict with human passion and the need to love and be loved. But it is subtler than that. Ben and Elaine escape, indeed, from the restrictions and hypocrisies of the class to which they belong and from a world of soulless, life-denying "plastic" (to use the term immortalized in *The Graduate* when a noisy, drunken guest at Ben's graduation party tells him where to get a job): but to what? Mike Nichols has said that, after the end of the film when Ben and Elaine have made their daring escape by bus (that most officially regimented, ineluctably scheduled of vehicles) her first words to him, sitting as she is in full bridal regalia, should be "I don't have a thing to wear." The class to which Ben and Elaine belong, that great middle class which includes everyone, promises everything, and reimburses nobody for the cost of membership (at least in the bitter vision of this film), can absorb an infinite number of antiestablishment gestures, since with the serenity of its own affluence it absorbs any degree of revolutionary "heroism" into itself, trivializing it in the process. An essential part of *The Graduate*'s power is the score by Simon and Garfunkel; and, in what virtually became the theme song of the year of its release, "Mrs. Robinson," the lyrics underscore what is really Mrs. Robinson's (and Ben's an Elaine's and their world's) problem in the most explicitly mock-heroic of ways:

> Where have you gone, Joe DiMaggio?
> A nation turns its lonely eyes to you.
> (Ooo Ooo Ooo)
> What's that you say, Mrs. Robinson?
> Joltin' Joe has left and gone away—
> (Hey, hey, hey. Hey, hey, hey).

It is the only time Joe DiMaggio is mentioned in the film: and what he has to do with *The Graduate* is, simply, everything. The most heroic and perhaps the most beautiful of baseball players, the public hero *precisely* of Mrs. Robinson's generation, he represents all those lost, submerged values which in Ben Braddock's world have been commercialized, transformed symbolically into 'plastic": all those chances which for the young graduate (most hopeful of words and states) are inevitably perverted into stale miniatures of real passion, absurd masques of revolt. The film, finally, is a wry and bitter satire not only of the world of its hero, but of its own ironically, desperately hinted vision of salvation. You may, in a grand moment of revolt, defy the conventions, invade the bourgeois sanctity of the church, even—sacriligeously and "heroically"—fight off your enemies with an aluminum cross for a sword. But after the final battle the world is still there; the battle is not final, after all. And you run away, and you board a bus whose destination you do not know, enduring the puzzled, mildly frightened stares of the other passengers. And you have, really, no place to go.

Land's End, Land's Beginning

Where do you go after a vision of the end; after an understanding of the inevitable, universal entropy of civilization so complete and so unrelentingly intelligent that it understands and mocks even its own intelligence, even its own most carefully articulated hopes for survival and continuity? In one of two directions, each of which dangerously resembles the other and both of which represent the end of storytelling, and its beginning again on a new basis, in a new world. For the sake of convenience we can call these alternatives madness and sainthood, although the names mask their similarity and, perhaps, their interrelationship. The literary terms most appropriate to their respective forms of expression, likewise—fantasy and apocalypse—are useful only as long as they do not conceal the ways these two alternatives can merge, unite, and even reinforce one another.

I have been tracing throughout this chapter a parallel between the satirist's methods and the paradox of the myth of the Incarnation. And this final, most extreme phase of satiric narrative also has a parallel there; not so much in the figure of the Christ of the Gospels but in the Christology of the Epistles of St. Paul and the Book of Revelations. The

Jews look for a sign, Paul writes in his first letter to the Corinthians (one of the earliest of Christian documents, predat-
ing the earliest Gospel), and the Greeks seek after Wisdom
(literally *Sophia,* a quasi-goddess of late Hellenistic rationalism); but we preach Christ, and Christ crucified. The
spectacle of the reviled victim, broken and disgraced, who is
also the Son of the Most High, exalted beyond the greatest
of kings and a king himself of a world-renewing order: this
is what is preached in all scandalousness against the official
and abstract sanities of law, theology, and codified morality.
And it *is* a scandal, an afront to the orderly arrangement of
things and a stumbling-block for the merely wise: the transformation—again paraphrasing Paul in First Corinthians—of the foolishness of this world into the wisdom of
the next. But this transformation, in the Book of Revelations, is shown to be a truly apocalyptic fiction, one that
does not simply annihilate the sordid reality of this world,
but substitutes for it a new city, a new world:

> And there came unto me one of the seven angels which
> had the seven vials full of the seven last plagues. . . .
> And he carried me away in spirit to a great and high
> mountain, and showed me that great city, the holy Jeru-
> salem, descending out of heaven from God, having the
> glory of God: and her light was like unto a stone most
> precious, even like a jasper stone, clear as crystal. . . .

This magnificent passage from Revelations (21:9–11)
catches perfectly the transition, from the last plagues to the
shining city of the just, from the lowlands to the high mountain, all of it organized around the central, heroic figure of
the reviled fool of God who is soon to return as the Son in
glory. "And I saw no temple therein; for the Lord God Al-
mighty and the Lamb are the temple of it" (21:22). The
image is a crucial one for the history of Western thought,
not only in itself, but as the evident source of what may well

be the single most influential book in the formation of Europe and of European attitudes toward society, Augustine's *City of God*. Beginning with a satirical polemic against the pagans who charge Christianity with weakening Rome for the onslaught of the barbarians from the north, Augustine proceeds to develop an intricate, radiant vision of the true City, as opposed to the City of the damned of this world—a City which is both of this world and of the next, both a political entity and an eschatological reality. And from Augustine through the Middle Ages, through the revolutionary thought of the eighteenth and nineteenth centuries and into today, the best and most creative of our political theories, social mythologies, and narratives have all been involved in one way or another with the visionary task of changing the City of man into the City of god; god with a small "g" since the quest survives the doctrine that gave it birth, including Rousseau and Marx among its participants as well as Aquinas or Cardinal Newman.

"Apocalypse," after all (from *apo* and *kalypto,* to take away the covering from something that was previously concealed), means "revelation": though our normal associations with the word are not in terms of the final revelation of the new City, but rather with the blood-and-thunder, end-of-the-world violence that always, in the tradition, precedes that revelation. And though other classic texts in the tradition may not have the ringing self-confidence, the absolute certainty about the deliverance to come that the New Testament texts have, we can nevertheless say that past a certain point of hopelessness satire inevitably tends toward either the deliverance-through-madness of fantasy or the deliverance-through-sainthood of apocalypse.

The *Satyricon* of Petronius is, in its way, the most completely self-conscious and deliberately outrageous mock-epic work of the classical period, written well before the Book of Revelations. It is also the most truly apocalyptic. It is the narrative of a first-century A.D. rhetorician named Encolpius (the name itself is an obscene pun, suggesting Roman slang for "fucker") who is driven through the towns and slums of Nero's world by his unrequitted passion for the beautiful boy Giton. In the course of this homosexual Odeyssey (and the parallelism is quite carefully worked out) Encolpius meets an assortment of hustlers, windy and second-rate epic poets, and wealthy middle-class vulgarians who are the true monsters of his world. Things go from bad to intolerable as the book progresses. At the end (the end of the fragmentary text that we have) Encolpius' friend Eumolpus freeloads off the inheritance-seekers of a small town. He pretends to be a dying, rich old man who will include them all in his will if they will agree to eat his body after he dies: surely a terminal stage of barbarism. But the *Satyricon* is not just a screed against the growing bestiality of Nero's Rome; in its own way, and without benefit of an eschatological idea of salvation, it articulates a way beyond the mess of things, a way out. And that is the way of an intensely private purity of intelligence, coupled with an intensely sophisticated, elegant style. Petronius, who was the official arbiter of taste in Nero's court, shows us horror after horror, vulgarity after vulgarity—but described in the purest, most civilized Latin prose of the late classical period. It is not "salvation" as the author of the Book of Revelations or St. Paul imagined it, but it is perhaps all the more heroic for its last-ditch, defiantly intelligent hopelessness, taking us beyond irony to a level of vision few other writers have achieved.

Federico Fellini, in his film of Petronius, *Fellini-Satyricon*, takes a number of liberties with the plot of the original, but all of them quite in the spirit of the author. Indeed his most brilliant touch in a quite successful way "completes" the incomplete text of the *Satyricon*. At the end of Fellini's film a rich old man (not Eumolpus) does in fact die with that bizare codicil to his will. And in a darkening landscape we see the inheritors of this rotten world grouped along the shore, complacently munching the corpse, while Encolpius,

Eumolpus, and Giton slowly sail away: but to where? The answer is given in terms one feels Petronius would have approved, but which could not be realized outside of film. As Encolpius and his friends sail away, in disgust at the depths to which their world has fallen, their faces are caught first in a freeze-frame which is then gradually, in a bath of golden light, transformed into a Roman wall painting, at once elegant and eloquent in its disengagement. It is the homage film pays to that kind of realistic painting which can be described as pre-filmic. But it is also (and here Fellini is not far from the assertions of *La Dolce Vita*, *8½*, or *Amarcord*) an assertion of the capability of art and intelligence to redeem even the most pathetic, the most abject of human situations.

Salvation through the second coming and salvation through the purity of style: these are the alternatives of satire when its vision of the world has passed the point of hopelessness, and they tend oddly to combine and reinforce each other after the classical age which produces both the *Satyricon* and the *City of God*. T.S. Eliot's *The Waste Land* is perhaps the most influential and widely read poem of the twentieth century, and it successfully—cinematically, one is tempted to say—combines and unites both possibilities in its attack upon the spiritual desert of modern life.

The Waste Land was published in 1922, and was almost immediately accepted and celebrated as the poem of its generation, the great statement of the early century about the breakdown of Western culture and its sterile, longing expectation of deliverance from without. In fact, as we now know, the poem as it was originally conceived and written had little if anything to do with the state of "Western culture," being simply the hallucinatory, free-associative record of Eliot's experience of a mental breakdown following the disastrous failure of his first marriage. But that after all makes no difference. Eliot's imagination of his own possible deliverance from impotence, and his imagination of his culture's deliverance from a deeper, spiritual as well as physical impotence, are both part of the same crisis. And if the solution to this problem, the climax of this great poem, is in terms of an escape to the certainties of religious belief and religious renewal, the epigraph—significantly and splendidly—is from the *Satyricon* of Petronius: "For I myself, with these very eyes, once saw the Cumaean Sibyl hanging in a jar; and when the little boys would ask her, 'Sibyl, what would you like,' she would answer, 'I would like to die.' " *

The Cumaean Sibyl is in many ways the great prophetess of classical antiquity, the god-possessed woman who forecast for Aeneas his ultimate founding of the new Troy, Rome. But, according to some legends, she did not die but simply grew steadily older and more withered. The speaker of this passage from the *Satyricon* is Trimalchio, an incredibly ostentatious, vulgar merchant who has risen to a richly undeserved eminence and who recites his tale of the Sibyl at a banquet of unparalleled profligacy and gracelessness. It is, then, the perfect epigraph for Eliot's *Waste Land*, since it captures not only the hopeless image of a mercantile, capitalist middle class taking over the world and turning it into the replica of its own crudity, but also the image of the rich, religious and cultural heritage which is being debased. In one of his all-but-uninformative notes to *The Waste Land*, Eliot discusses the figure of the prophet Tiresias, another of the great seers of classical antiquity, who appears in the third section of the poem, "The Fire Sermon":

> Tiresias, although a mere spectator and not indeed a "character," is yet the most important personage in the poem, uniting all the rest. . . . What Tiresias *sees*, in fact, is the substance of the poem.

* My translation.

An epigraph and a footnote are, usually, not very substantial things upon which to build an interpretation of a poem. But in *The Waste Land* they are crucial, and make great good sense, indeed, of what goes on in the body of the text. This complex poem, which has become almost a byword for modernist obscurity, makes simple and radiant sense once one realizes that it is written under the sign of the shriveled prophet, the once-epic bard, the once-creative storyteller whose stories have dried up because his culture no longer will accept them as basic equipment for living. What can the aged, shriveled prophet—which is to say, the poet at the fag-end of the world—write? Only a collection of mock-heroic citations from the noble past, each of which painfully indicates the distance we have fallen from the great ages in which their utterance was possible. "These fragments I have shored against my ruins," says the speaker (Eliot, Tiresias, the Sibyl, our world) near the end of the poem. And the "fragments" shored against ruin are, in fact, the whole texture of the pastiche which is *The Waste Land*. Almost everything of importance in this great and original poem is a quotation from a prior text. And just as the plot of the poem is a parody, and something more than a parody, of the Grail Knight's quest for the sacred cup that will bring fertility back to the land, so the technique of the poem is a frantic searching, a rummaging about among the monuments of culture for a saying, a line, a text that will open the sterility of the shriveled prophet to the rain, that will re-create the life of culture by returning the archaic and magical figure of the storyteller to his original primacy as a lawgiver. Like the *Satyricon,* though perhaps with more difficulty, it is a parody beyond the point of parody, a satire that finally tries to transcend its own mockery.

The idea of the "waste land," to be sure, has become a fairly current metaphor for the state of contemporary society. It is invoked by people who have never understood its origin, even by people who have never read or tried to read

Eliot. But, in its way, that is all to the good. "You don't need a weatherman to know which way the wind blows," said Bob Dylan in one of his late-romantic songs; and you don't need to have read *The Waste Land* to know that it is, for better and worse, where you live. The theologian Hans Urs von Balthasar suggests, in his essay "Christianity and Anthropology," that the supposed "secularization" of society since the Protestant Reformation has been, in fact, not a secularization at all, but rather a progressive refinement of our ideas of where the divinity resides and what its relation to us might be. This may or may not be good theology, but it is excellent literary and film history. It helps define the simultaneous abstraction and intensification of the heroic idea which accompanies satire as it makes the transition into fantasy or apocalypse, into the madman's or the saint's legend.

Cool Hand Luke is an especially interesting case of this transition, a film which—like *One Flew Over the Cuckoo's Nest*—is patterned on the story of Christ, though more explicitly, ostentatiously, and, oddly enough, just as satisfyingly. Luke (Paul Newman) is sent to a southern chain gang after having been arrested, one drunken evening, for beheading parking meters with a large wrench—a pointless and noble revolt against the pettiness of "the law" if there ever was one. As in *Cuckoo's Nest,* the place he is imprisoned is an unmistakable parallel to the society we inhabit: enclosed, regimented, brooded over by authority figures whose habit of command masks a deep hypocrisy and corruption. But there is an important difference. In *Cuckoo's Nest* the heroic, delightfully blustering McMurphy comes into a society of voluntarily committed, self-loathing failures and teaches them to trust themselves, to rediscover and honor their own humanity. But Luke comes into a society of the truly condemned, men who have no option to leave when they want to. And what he has to teach them is not so much how to trust themselves or regain control of their own lives—that control is irrevocably lost for the term of their imprisonment—but rather how to escape inward, toward a freedom that demolishes external controls precisely because it establishes the identity of the self on another plane entirely. All of this sounds rather mushy. And I think a good socialist would be entirely justified in preferring the vision of *Cuckoo's Nest* to that of *Cool Hand Luke*—or the revolutionary Christ of the Gospels to the mystical one of Revelations. But the point is that satire, past a certain point of self-consciousness, inevitably becomes so self-conscious that it distrusts even its own distrust of things as they are, and begins to establish an idea of personality, of the community, on a different plane altogether. Luke is a "cool hand" precisely because he does *not* assert himself outrageously. He is drawn inexorably into a life-and-death struggle with the captain of the chain gang (Strother Martin playing God the Father as a nasty old man) much against his will; he is not noisily self-assertive but, in Newman's excellent performance, the inhabitant of a silent, ironic, personal space whose existence authority cannot tolerate precisely because of its privacy. His passive resistance is not to the orders of the authorities, but more radically to the *authority* of the authorities. And at the end of his second escape, holed up in an abandoned church surrounded by the cars of state troopers, he ironically accepts his own death by repeating to the captain the captain's own favorite, fake-liberal condescending phrase: "What we have here is a failure to communicate." After Luke is killed, though, his legend only grows among the chain gang. His amiable, apelike friend and disciple Dragline (George Kennedy)—the Peter, Matthew, Mark, Luke and John of the fable—reports the tale of his death and his calm disengagement from the world of the bosses to the other prisoners. And, in the stunning last shot of the film, while Dragline and the others are still working at the chain gang's backbreaking, senseless task of clearing an endless road, they are smiling.

That smile, that special inner distance from a world gone sour, is—at least potentially—the beginning of a new world, a new community founded by an exile, a madman, a saint who replicates the activity of the hero of epic. It is a smile that has been recorded in apocalyptic stories almost since stories were first told; for, as I have suggested throughout this book, the "cycle" of storytelling is a cycle that is altogether present at any of its phases—not a graph of real history, but a real graph of the ways we like to think about history. Steven Spielberg's film *Close Encounters of the Third Kind* is another such apocalyptic tale, and an appropriate one to conclude with, since it could not be told outside the medium of film itself. It is a "science-fiction" film, if that designation has any meaning (by the same method of classification, *Anna Karenina* is a "love story"). But it is a science-fiction film which both satirizes the tradition of science-fiction films and goes beyond that satire to discover something ennobling, something profoundly humanizing, in even the most sensationalist and (runs the cliche) most "escapist" of film genres.

Close encounters of the third kind (the phrase is from Dr. J. Allen Hynek's book *The U.F.O. Experience*) are defined as actual, physical meetings between earthlings and visitors from another world. But Hynek (who makes a brief appearance in Spielberg's film) is careful to specify that "another world" may signify outer space, another psychic or spiritual level of reality, or even another as yet unmapped depth of that massive continent, the subconscious, we all carry within us and all share. This is an important distinction, not only for Hynek's book but also for *Close Encounters* the film. For while, at the simplest level of narrative, it is indeed about the first recorded contact between extraterrestrial aliens and human beings, there are a number of other levels of meaning—insisted upon throughout the film—at which it is not so much "about" aliens as about our imagination of aliens, or, rather, about the myths of film culture itself and their power to energize and ennoble our lives beyond the point of irony and dissatisfaction. The film is a joke shared between filmmaker and audience, and like all good jokes a very serious one. The film is *play*. Pauline Kael called it the most intelligent naive film ever made, but even that does not quite catch its special quality. It is filled with vehicles, modes of transportation, and toys, all of which are established, by a kind of visual punning, as being as much "UFOs" as the gorgeous spaceships that appear in the finale. And the film is quite earnest about insisting that we learn—or re-learn—to trust toys, to trust those early impulses toward play and wonder which are, after all, the first civilizing and artistic impulses of the race, and which our society keeps insisting are there only to be transcended for a putative, fictive, cynical "maturity."

George Lucas' *Star Wars,* released before *Close Encounters,* goes very far toward this kind of wisdom, one is tempted to say, of romantic poetry at its best. As I have already said, *Star Wars* is by no means a simpleminded exercise in comic-book fantasy or a cynical throwback to "escapist" filmmaking; it is in the nature of an experiment to see how far the mythologies of heroism, love, and honor, for all their devaluation by a century of analysis and, in America, ten years of Vietnam and Richard Nixon, can retain their power to move us. It is an "epic," to be sure, but an *internalized* epic, which takes place within the experience of the viewer who—if he is past the age of ten—*knows* that all this derring-do, all this heroism, all these dazzling special effects are cliche, but who as he watches them rehearsed again recognizes that they are still things that can lead us to civilization, to good humor, to a recognition of our own capability for decency.

But *Close Encounters* is, if anything, more self-conscious and more moving. Roy Neary (Richard Dreyfuss), the Indiana electrical worker who sees a UFO and is thereafter

driven, compelled, to go to the site where the extraterres-
trials will establish first contact, is a contemporary everyman, one of us in his boredom and confusion, in his imprisonment in a world of jobs and failures. But he has become
possessed by a vision of transcendence, of something more:
a terrible thing to experience, as St. Paul told us long before
Spielberg got around to it. Neary is an everyman whose
vision is both nourished and shaped by the popular mythologies of transcendence with which we are surrounded.

When we first see him, in this film whose special effects
are its main selling point, he is watching television with his
children. He is watching the parting of the Red Sea in De-
Mille's *The Ten Commandments,* that wonderful translation
of biblical miracle into special effects, of transcendence into
kitsch. Later, when he finally understands the message im-
planted in his mind by the UFO, his daughter is watching a
Bugs Bunny cartoon about invaders from Mars. And in the
climactic sequence, when the UFOs land and speak to us,
they speak through a lovely, funny jazz fugue, transforming
the giant ship into a cosmic synthesizer, playing the Muzak
of the spheres.

The point is not that *Close Encounters* is a "religious"
film, as some of its admirers and many of its critics have
taken it, a pop gospel of transfiguration. It is something
much better, an examination of our lives as already tran-
scending their own limitation, if we can listen to our day-
dreams. "We are not alone," to borrow the film's advertising copy, because we speak to one *another*—and nowhere at
a deeper level than the mythology of the popular film.

Spielberg's original plan (would he had kept to it) was
that, as the mother ship leaves at the end—transporting
Neary into a new world, where no man has ever gone before—the sound track would carry not the massive orches-
tral theme we now hear, but the original voice of Jiminy
Cricket from Disney's *Pinocchio,* singing "When You Wish

upon a Star." The effect is not to trivialize the myth of the film, but precisely to ground it firmly in a sense of its own fictitiousness and of the necessity of that fiction of deliverance. Neary voyages not so much to outer space as into the inner space of all our stories; so that the stories can begin again.

VI

Images and Archetypes

Six Heroes
(Stills 1–6)

In this series we can see the phases of storytelling caught in a particularly graphic way, in terms both of costume and of gesture. Still 1, from the end of *Ivan the Terrible, Part One,* shows the moment when Ivan sees the masses who have come through the snow from Moscow to recall him to his kingly duties. But the epic correspondence of king to people, founder to civilization, is not just narrated here, it is visually represented, articulated. The procession of citizens beseeching Ivan forms a random angle as they trek toward his retreat, an angle that is doubled and abstracted by the line of the aperture through which Ivan sees them. But it is Ivan's own figure, a massive foreground against that background mass, that gives sense and shape to the procession. The angle between his arm and staff exactly duplicates the angle of the pilgrims' progress, just as his solemn presence is the very reason for their being there in the first place. Perhaps nowhere in film has the idea of the epic founder, the primor-

1. Ivan the Terrible

dial king whose presence gives life to his people, been more fully or more elegantly realized.

In Still 2 we see a roughly equivalent situation, but with a vast difference in both visual and narrative effect. It is from *Lawrence of Arabia,* at the moment of Lawrence's early, splendid successes against the Turks. But there are strains implicit in his career, as a man trying to lead an epic existence is a less-than-epic world, and they are implicit in this shot. Note that his foregrounded figure—unlike Ivan in still 1—does not organize and incarnate the masses whom he salutes, but rather echoes them: whereas Ivan's giant shape balances the crowd, left to right, Lawrence is placed in the center of the shot. The movement of the shot is all vertical, except for the shape of Lawrence's robe which balloons out behind him—an accident, perhaps, but one that emphasizes how "flowing," how vulnerable to more elemental forces, is the temporary nobility of this romantic but flawed leader. As vulnerable, indeed, as the battered luggage his followers have absurdly strewn about the desert landscape.

Lawrence is a man who tries to be king and finds that his world no longer allows that kind of purity or primacy. But *Patton* (still 3) is a film about a man who tries to be a good knight only to find that knighthood is considered inefficient and undesirable by his society. This shot is from the opening

2. **Lawrence of Arabia**

3. Patton

of the film, just before Patton delivers his famous address to his troops. And here, if nowhere else, he is allowed to be the perfect knight. He is in full battle array: but of course no one would or could ever wear into a real battle the complex, stylized uniform he has on. It is not a warrior's armor but the dazzling symbolic expression of a warrior's *function*.

And—most importantly—the salute he gives is, as befits a hero of romance, a salute to an abstraction. He is saluting the flag while the national anthem plays. But the flag is behind him. His eyes are focused, as should be those of a good soldier at attention, on infinity. He does not so much organize a multitude as represent one—the multitude of those who believe in, accept, and are willing to die for the values of the nation-state whose icon he stands before, stands for, and takes his stand upon.

Still 4 was made a half-century before *Patton,* but is nevertheless an ironic, latter-day commentary upon *Patton*'s mythology. The face of George C. Scott as General Patton displays no weakness, no flabbiness; that of Emil Jannings as the Doorman in *The Last Laugh* shows little else. We began, in *Ivan,* with the sight of the ritual robes of the king; and in *Patton* saw the evolution of those hierarchical garments into the symbolic structure of the uniform. But here the uniform itself has become trivialized. Patton could not wear his full costume into any real battle, but Jannings could not wear this uniform anywhere but at the hotel that employs him. It is a parody of military order, just as Jannings' sloppy salute (note the umbrella—unfurled—held in place of a sword) is a parody of heroic bearing. The visual counterpoint between his uniform and his umbrella, indeed, is truly and essentially melodramatic: locating a world where people try to behave as if they were knights when they are only, terrifyingly, men upon whom the rain can fall. And just as Patton seems to draw his strength and purpose from the giant flag behind him, Jannings here is a particularly poignant expression, the living symbol, of the full implications of the tenement staircase in front of which he stands.

A final salute: still 5, from *Duck Soup,* shows us madness triumphant in a world grown too rotten for the structures of sanity. At the end of the film Groucho, Chico, Zeppo, and Harpo have managed to destroy the fantastic and very real kingdom they inhabit, and this is their final victorious pose

4. The Last Laugh

after everything around them has been blown to hell.
Harpo, always the most beautiful of the Brothers Marx,
echoes the poses of Patton and the Doorman. But his eyes
are not focused on infinity, nor are they complacent mirrors
of his world. They have a lunatic gleam, just as his absurdly
overdecorated uniform, complete with feathered hat, has a

goofy, negative nobility Jannings' costume never approaches. At the other end of the scale from the epic founder, the madman and satirist may not be able to organize his people into a coherent civilization, but he is at least the perfect, and perfectly outfitted, man to preside over his world's demise.

But if the world is really mad, and really presided over by madmen, then there is the chance, at least, for another kind of order, another kind of civilization, and that is the civilization of those who have accepted their own madness—the civilization of those who are not proud.

But it is more than that; it is an assertion that something meaningful and heroic might be made from even such a cor-

5. **Duck Soup**

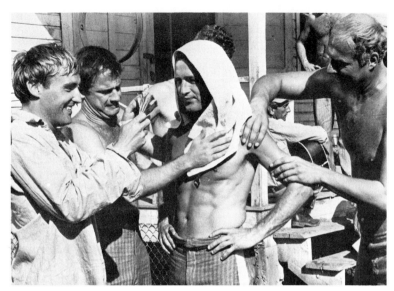

6. Cool Hand Luke

rupt world. In still 6, Luke (Paul Newman) is being pre-
pared by his fellow inmates for an absurd contest, a contest
to see if he can eat, as he has claimed, fifty hard-boiled eggs.
But the silliness of the occasion does not detract from the
solemnity of the scene. All the men save one are stripped to
the waist as becomes the naked victims of an impersonal
and abstract justice. But Luke, in the center of the group, is
cowled in a bath towel that not only shields him from the
sun, but establishes his archaic predominance. It is not quite
a crown—nor is the hat Ivan wears in still 1—but it is a
badge of difference, and therefore of symbolic preeminence,
granted him by the group at whose center he stands. Luke is
the king of this tiny, put-upon society; but a king whose
royalty is conditional upon their tolerance, and who does
not abstract and transform their mass but rises from and
completes it.

Kings and Fools
(Stills 7–8)

Still 7, from *Ivan the Terrible,* is as graphic a representation as one could hope for of the superhuman, epic nature of kingship. Ivan, seated, is instructing his retainer to send certain messages to his relative and ally Queen Elizabeth of England. But note that while the retainer stares at Ivan and does not see the gigantic shadow his king casts upon the wall behind him, he nevertheless falls within that shadow—as does the model of the globe which stands between the two men. Neither does Ivan himself see the shadow he casts—and this is an important part of the content of the scene: his greatness, which soon after this episode will cost him his beloved wife, has grown beyond his own control.

7. Ivan the Terrible

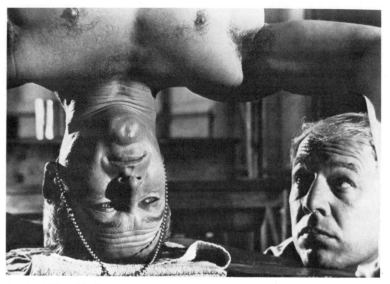

8. Cool Hand Luke

Still 8, from *Cool Hand Luke,* inverts still 7. Luke is in the midst of his heroic—and absurd—feat of eating fifty hard-boiled eggs, and is here being stood on his head by his supporters/retainers/backers simply to make more room in his stomach. But the proper role of the fool anyhow is to invert, subvert, and literally turn on its head our conventional idea of the normal and the ordinary: it is just by doing this that the fool reminds us what is really normal, what is really ordinary and human. Luke's retainer (George Kennedy) gazes at him with the same stare Ivan's retainer maintains in still 7, and Luke, like Ivan, stares into infinity. It is only his upside-downness that makes him appear the fool rather than the monarch of this scene; and the one role, of course, imperceptibly blends into the other.

When Worlds Collide
(Still 9)

This is the climactic face-off in *Red River* between Matt Garth (Montgomery Clift) and Tom Dunson (John Wayne). It is also the collision between two worlds, two dispensations of order: the archaic, epic, harsh rule represented by Dunson and the gentler, more fully "civilized"—but also thereby softer—order represented by Garth. The confrontation is an elemental one, upon which the direction of culture turns—a detail underscored here by the crowd of townspeople who await the outcome of the struggle.

9. Red River

Three Levels of Romance
(Stills 10–12)

These three stills, all from *My Darling Clementine,* indicate three aspects of the complex relations that romance narrative establishes among the ideas of nature, culture, and individuality. In still 10, Henry Fonda as Marshal Wyatt Earp strikes an archetypal heroic pose upon a rooftop, against the big sky, balanced at the left by gigantic cactuses. The elements of nature and culture—the monstrous plants on the one hand and the rough-hewn building upon which he stands on the other—are poised in as graphic a counterpoint as one could wish. Indeed, throughout *Clementine* John Ford's camerawork emphasizes that the town Earp fights to civilize is still in process of being built: it is already founded, that is, but founded at the very edge of the inhospitable wilderness. And this makes his civilizing action as marshal, i.e. as knight of a rich civilization concerned to wrest that wilderness to its own ends, all the more urgent.

Still 11 catches this urgency in an almost ritual moment. It is the dance at the church-raising, and one of the most expressive scenes in *Clementine.* Marshal Earp has escorted Clementine (Cathy Downes), the visitor from the civilized East, to the party, and agrees to lead off the dancing with her. This still can be usefully compared to the one from *Red River.* Here as there a crowd of townspeople watches the enacting of a ceremony that reflects a crucial stage in their own evolution. But this time the ceremony is one of culture triumphant. At least three levels of ritual order—which is to say, human order—are superimposed upon one another. The church is the ritual center of the community's life, and the dance is performed upon the platform that will be its floor when it is finished. But the dance itself is a ritual both older and fresher than the wooden structures of formal religion, a choreography of courtship and civility that organizes the community in the happy self-consciousness of its

10. My Darling Clementine

11. My Darling Clementine

12. My Darling Clementine

own fecundity. And, of course, the central participants in
the dance are themselves ritually invested characters: the
marshal and the lady from the East, living twin icons of the
civility whose measures they tread. But the scene would not
be nearly as powerful or as poignant if it were not for the
infinite horizon of yet-untamed land and the stark, monumental cliff towering in the background over this joyful liturgy. It is, indeed, a scene of culture triumphant: but the
triumph is both qualified and underscored by the context of
massively impersonal nature, the big sky under which it occurs.

Still 12, is, in its way, the bitter end of romance. Doc
Holliday, played by Victor Mature, is the spoiled knight in
Clementine, the man from the cultured East whose civilization has somehow turned decadent and murderous in opposition to the sustained decency of Earp. And though Holliday—Clementine's original lover—aids the Earp brothers

in their epochal fight with the Clantons at the O.K. Corral, it is appropriate that he should die there, since he is tainted with the same barbarity as the Clantons themselves. (Details such as Doc's death at the O.K. Corral and the personalities of the Earp brothers are of course mythic, John Ford's fantasia upon historical fact.) Here he has just been shot. And while his left hand still holds the gun which has been the violent instrument of his wasted life, his right hand holds a handkerchief—because he is in the last stages of tuberculosis, to be sure, but also because it is an odd, graceful, almost dandified accouterment for a gunfighter, and as such the perfect visual expression of Doc's refined, cynical, and somehow diseased culture. Unlike Wyatt in still 10 he does not stand upon but takes (inefficient) shelter behind a wooden structure of the town. And he does not face, in profile, the potential encroachments of nature into culture; rather he stares straight ahead, into infinity or into the heart of our own darkness.

Knights in Check
(Stills 13–15)

Each of these three stills introduces us to the problematic, dangerous world of melodrama—where our pretensions to nobility, to being the heroes of our own life stories, are threatened by the very complexity of the world we live and strive in. They can also be taken as grim "After" counterparts to their "Before" opposite numbers in the first series of stills.

Still 13, from *The Last Laugh,* incarnates the tragic, foolish implications of Emil Jannings' initial pompous attitude (still 4). Here the Doorman has been told that he is too old for his job and that he has been demoted to washroom attendant. Jannings' stooped pose and weary, emptied-out face create what well may be the most shattering mask of

13. The Last Laugh

total defeat in the history of film acting. And it is worth noting that his cap, held limply as a beggar would hold it,
emphasizes the clumsiness and encumbrance of the absurd
uniform which he, too, has now learned is a sham. What he
has thought of as the insignia of a *role*, a lordly function
which he could take pride in incarnating, has been reduced
to the paraphernalia of a *job*, a simple and minimal economic activity from which he can be fired. And the knowledge, like the uniform itself, seems literally to weigh upon
him.

Still 14, from *Patton*, represents a more complex, and a
more bitter, moment. Patton, after all, is in reality what the
Doorman of *The Last Laugh* is only in his own fantasies: a
knight, a warrior, the chosen and publicly designated carrier

and defender of his culture's values. But the mechanisms
themselves through which those values are to be defended
have developed beyond—or, indeed, beneath—Patton's own
imagination. His tragedy is not to discover that he has been
holding down a job instead of fulfilling a role; it is, rather,
to learn that the role he has devoted his life to fulfilling is

14. Patton

rendered supremely irrelevant by the very society he defends. In this scene Patton maintains the hierarchical authority he enjoyed in still 3; he is a massively self-assured
figure, and the three stars on his helmet obviously belong to
such a man. But his face expresses a profound weariness—
not the despair of Jannings in the previous still, but something perhaps darker. He has successfully led his army of
tanks, of steel and machine guns, into Italy. But that success
itself is less personal, less heroic, than the life he would have
wished: it is the warfare of a mechanized world, not of a
knightly one. And this shot particularly establishes a kind of
visual counterpoint that is central to the meaning of *Patton:*
in the foreground, suspended from the general's waist, is
one of his famous pearl-handled revolvers, a weapon of individual conflict and individual value which is rendered absurdly ornamental, cosmically and sadly trivial by the gigantic tank gun that looms in the background. It is the latter
weapon that will win, that matters, in this kind of war. But
it is the former one, small and ceremonial as it is, that symbolizes the sort of warfare this tired soldier really loves.

Still 15, from *Lawrence of Arabia,* is a further complication of the elements in the scene from *Patton.* Lawrence has
just returned from his first, brilliant success, the leading of
Arab troops to take the Turkish stronghold of Aquaba. He
is still in the Arab dress which is the symbol both of the
heroic life he would like to realize for himself and of the impossibility of that realization (for what tall, fair, blond Englishman does not look absurdly out of place in Arab dress?).
General Allenby (Jack Hawkins, with moustache) and diplo-
mat Dryden (Claude Rains, in mufti) have nevertheless
talked Lawrence, against his better judgment, into returning
to Arabia and continuing the war in the desert. It will be the
springboard to international fame, to possible historical
greatness, to a truly mythic identity, and also to a gigantic
despair for Lawrence. And here, as he discusses his plans for
the "Arab revolt" with his British superiors, we see not only

how "out of place" in the usual sense of the word are Lawrence's garb and idealism, but also how truly, finally out of place they are in a world dominated by the (literal) uniformity of big politics, international diplomacy, and sociopolitical ordinariness. Doc Holliday, the Doorman, and Patton directed their weary stares into the camera, into us: but this shot shows us something worse. Lawrence stares ahead, lost in his own dreams of heroism, while everyone else in the frame stares at *him,* at this noble and pathetic figure who is the unwilling instrument of policies he chooses not to understand. It makes him immensely vulnerable in his last-ditch espousal of the romance myth of quest and accomplishment his world has outlived.

15. Lawrence of Arabia

Looking and Being Looked At
(Stills 16–18)

In the world of melodrama the pressure of *other people* upon the individual begins to be more and more strongly felt. In these three stills, that pressure is variously expressed—and in each case, with a special importance for the idea of melodrama itself. Still 16 is from *North by Northwest*. Roger Thornhill (Cary Grant) has accidentally, absurdly fallen into the midst of a spy ring and been accused of murder. Here he is in Chicago's Union Station, about to embark on his voyage of escape from his pursuers (a voyage that will take him north by northwest across the United States), reading a newspaper whose first page advertises his name, description, and crime. But the brilliant thing about this scene is that you don't need to know the story of the film—you don't even need to know what Cary Grant looks like—to get its point. In still 15 Lawrence is unaware that he is being looked at by everyone else; here Cary Grant only *thinks* he is being looked at. And with the transition to that special kind of panic, the panic of the man lost in the crowd, we cross over to true melodramatic narrative—the perfect form to incarnate our urban paranoia.

Still 17, from *Murder, My Sweet*, made a decade before *North by Northwest*, is actually a complication and a richer version of the dialectics of being looked at. Roger Thornhill is an ordinary private citizen caught up against his will in a net of intrigue and murder. But Philip Marlowe (here played by Dick Powell, at right) is a private detective: that is, a private citizen who for his livelihood—and perhaps out of a sense of justice—*chooses* to enter the dark mazes of crime and passion that underlie the lives of men and women in cities. This is Marlowe's first meeting with the family—aged husband, beautiful and unfaithful young wife,. and "nice" daughter—who have hired him. And the shot is a criss-cross

16. North by Northwest

17. Murder, My Sweet

of gazes, implications, relationships, and interrogations. But the obvious center of this structure of gazes is Marlowe himself, who also subtly but surely distances himself from the other three by the sardonic quality of his expression, as well as by his pose. Reading the frame from left to right in terms of "body language," we can see a progression from blatant sexual challenge, to diffident and insecure questioning, to nervous, frightened appraisal (note especially the half-clenched hands of the daughter), to Marlowe's own self-assured and ironic overview of the whole scene. Indeed, one of the most brilliant things about this fine still is its use of *hands:* every other character signals as much with his or her hands as with expression and glance. But Marlowe's hands are hidden in his pockets. And the effect of that minimal detail is overwhelming, since it turns him into *pure* gaze, into a man who looks but does not signal, as he looks, what he himself is thinking: into a private eye, in short. When *Murder, My Sweet* was made it was something of a risk for the producers and for Powell himself, who had previously appeared only as a romantic singer/dancer type in light comedies. But he is one of the best, one of the rightest, private eyes in film, and not least so for the kind of underplayed but firm intelligence he brings to the part in a scene like this one.

Still 18 is also from *Murder, My Sweet.* The story of the film is told in extended flashback, beginning and ending with Marlowe, blinded, being questioned in a police station. The archetypal hero of melodrama, as I have been saying, is the man who looks—at other people, at his own life—and who fears being looked at by the crowd that constitutes the city. This figure achieves a kind of mythic status in the idea of the private eye, the looker *par excellence,* who is protected from the prying gaze of others mainly by the power and penetration of his own intelligence. But what more grimly appropriate fate for the private eye than blindness— blindness not through a deficiency, but through an overload of light, through too much information? There is another implication of this still. One of the few truly iconic figures available to modern culture, one of the few symbols still immediately recognizable and understandable by most citizens, is that of blind justice. And Marlowe's bandage—not dark glasses, not a black mask—is surely also a deliberate invocation of that figure. But an ironic one. The private eye has solved the case, but has become too involved in the fates of the people whose crimes and failures he tracks down and sorts out. He has been blinded, that is, by an overplus of information and has also become a figure of "justice," precisely by discovering to his cost that justice makes no sense, doesn't work, without an understanding of the vulnerability, the tears of human things. The detail of Marlowe's bandage, by the way, is probably the source of a detail in Roman Polanski's 1974 film *Chinatown*. In that very Marloweesque, thirties era story, private eye J. J. Gitties (Jack Nicholson) has his nose sliced early on by a mobster, and spends most of the remainder of the film with an absurd bandage across the middle of his face. The private eye, that is, is also a "snooper"—and in the later film is punished not for his excess of vision, but for smelling out the wrong things in a corrupt, smelly world.

18. Murder, My Sweet

Ordinary Life
(Stills 19–20)

These two stills, from *The Big Heat,* are a good example of the way melodramatic narrative regards the proportions of "normal" and "abnormal" experience in ordinary life.

In still 19, from early in the film, Detective O'Bannon (Glenn Ford) is having a peaceful dinner at home with his wife. The decor of the home is suburban-pastoral-tacky, from the cute clutter of the dinner table to the phony paneling on the wall behind the detective. He is dressed in a homey sweater, she in that polka-dot-plus-apron outfit that, in American film at least, is an almost permanent symbol of the values of home, fidelity, and middle-class solidarity. But as she serves the meal and he reads his evening paper, they do not look at each other. It is the perfectly comfortable, at-home scene, with husband and wife so assured of their mutual security that they do not even need to assert it; except for the fact, not evident from the still itself, that he is a police detective and that he is involved in a dangerous, potentially explosive investigation of organized crime. The security of this scene, in fact, is established only to be violently and suddenly destroyed a few moments later, when O'Bannon's wife will be killed in a mined automobile meant for him.

In still 20, from later in the film, O'Bannon has been relieved of his police duties. But he continues his investigation of the mob and his attempt to avenge the murder of his wife, and in that investigation is aided by the ex-mistress of a mobster, played by Gloria Grahame, who has been brutally scalded by her former lover. Here she visits O'Bannon in the seedy hotel where he has taken up residence. The spare details of the hotel room, highlighted by the regulations and check-out time on the door, are themselves a grim counterpoint to the smarmy (perhaps too smarmy) atmosphere of the home scene in still 19. And her mink coat, a

19. The Big Heat

20. The Big Heat

symbol of ill-gotten gains as surely as polka dots and aprons symbolize propriety, makes her as surely as her half-scarred face a marked woman. But she is the woman upon whom O'Bannon's fate depends; the world of seedy hotels and scarred, half-respectable humans is somehow more real, more truly alive than that of the secure, semiconscious respectability it underlies and supports. There is little doubt that Detective O'Bannon, at whatever cost, is more conscious in the second still from *The Big Heat* than in the first. And part of that increased consciousness is learning that he himself lives in the society of outsiders, indeed that the security of the "insiders" rests upon a shaky foundation beneath which lies the abyss of human fallibility, passion, vengeance, and pathos.

Outsiders
(Stills 21–22)

The intelligence, irony, and distance of the melodramatic hero finally can lead him to a position so pure that he cannot reenter the society he seeks to understand: that is the implication of the previous two sets of stills. In the two scenes that follow, we see outsiders whose distance from their world has become so great that they in fact become judges, living and absurdist criticisms of that world's pretensions.

Still 21, from *City Lights,* shows us Charlie Chaplin and the wealthy drunkard he has saved from suicide. The drunkard only recognizes the Little Tramp when he is intoxicated—Chaplin's parable, perhaps, of the irrational and arbitrary quality of class brotherhood under capitalism. But more important than possible socialist allegories is the fact that there are actually three characters in this shot: the Tramp, the Millionaire, and the sheaf of bills the Millionaire waves between them. Money matters. And it matters not least because it is a boundary between classes, a way people differentiate themselves from one another. The drunken Millionaire stares at the Tramp, but the Tramp stares at the money he holds. And while in their clothes and even their moustaches the two men are mirror images of one another, it is obviously a Jekyll-Hyde twinship. The Tramp's wide eyes and frightened pose are a sign of his discomfort in this opulent world, but also of how much he understands its absurd chanciness, how much his vulnerability to it is an extension and projection of our vulnerability, only here rendered lyrical. It is useful to compare this shot with still 17. The sardonic gaze of the private detective has been replaced by the clownish, befuddled stare of the fool. But, if anything, the fool's stare tells us more rather than less about the

21. City Lights

22. Duck Soup

world he inhabits and witnesses—and reflects an intelligence fuller, if also more easily wounded, than that of the private investigator.

The fool in still 21 is passive, vulnerable, an outsider who does not know how to get back inside. The fool in still 22— Groucho Marx, of course, in *Duck Soup*—does not care about getting back inside; indeed, all by himself he defines an "outside" that is fully adequate to any challenges that might arise from the kingdom of the drab, the sane, or the normal. Here Groucho, as President Rufus T. Firefly of Fredonia, is about to precipitate war with a neighboring Prime Minister's country at a garden party. But what appears in this shot, and what is made resplendently obvious in the rest of the film, is that Firefly/Groucho in his chaotic, absurdist violence is saner, more human that the overcivilized pseudo-rational diplomats and politicians who surround him. I noted that the umbrella Emil Jannings holds in his salute in still 4 is a deliberately ridiculous detail undercutting his self-inflated, paramilitary stance. But here the parasol Groucho holds—an even more ridiculous, less useful accouterment than a forthright umbrella—has quite the opposite effect. Jannings' umbrella is a negative detail because he obviously wishes it were a real sword. But Groucho's brandished parsol claims, as it were, to be nothing but itself, undercutting at once the heroic militarism of warfare, the stylized warfare of garden-party diplomacy, and the wooden, dehumanized diplomacy of "high society" stereotypes. The figure of the hero, in other words, has reemerged. And though now he waves an umbrella instead of a staff of office or a sword, his function remains the same: to be more conscious than the rest of us, and to reestablish in his sanity ways we can live together in truly civilized fashion.

Bibliography

Andrew, J. Dudley. *The Major Film Theories: An Introduction.* New York: Oxford University Press, 1975.

Appel, Alfred. *Nabokov's Dark Cinema.* New York: Oxford University Press, 1974.

Ardrey, Robert. *African Genesis.* New York: Dell, 1961.

Auerbach, Erich. *Mimesis: The Representation of Reality in Western Literature.* Trans. by Willard R. Trask. Garden City, N.Y.: Doubleday, 1957.

Barsam, Richard Meran. *In the Dark: A Primer to the Movies.* New York: Viking Press, 1977.

Barthes, Roland. *Image, Music, Text.* Trans. by Stephen Heath. New York: Hill and Wang, 1977.

———. *Writing Degree Zero and Elements of Semiology.* Trans. by Annette Lavers and Colin Smith. Boston: Beacon Press, 1970.

Bawden, Liz-Anne, ed. *The Oxford Companion to Film.* New York: Oxford University Press, 1976.

Bazin, André. *What Is Cinema?* Trans. by Hugh Gray. Vol. 1. Berkeley: University of California Press, 1967.

Bloom, Harold. *The Anxiety of Influence.* New York: Oxford University Press, 1973.

———. *A Map of Misreading.* New York: Oxford University Press, 1975.

Bobker, Lee. *Elements of Film.* New York: Harcourt, Brace and World, 1969.

Booth, Wayne. *The Rhetoric of Fiction.* Chicago: University of Chicago Press, 1961.

Braudy, Leo. *The World in a Frame*. Garden City, N.Y.: Doubleday, 1976.

————, and Morris Dickstein, eds. *Great Film Directors*. New York: Oxford University Press, 1978.

Brownlow, Kevin. *The Parade's Gone By*. New York: Bonanza Press, 1968.

Bultmann, Rudolf. *Kerygma and Myth*. New York: Harper and Row, 1961.

Burke, Kenneth. *A Grammar of Motives and A Rhetoric of Motives*. New York: World, 1962.

————. *The Philosophy of Literary Form*. 3d ed. Berkeley: University of California Press, 1973.

Campbell, Joseph. *The Hero with a Thousand Faces*. New York: World, 1965.

————. *Primitive Mythology*. Vol. 1 of *The Masks of God*. New York: Viking, 1959.

Cavell, Stanley. *The World Viewed*. New York: Viking, 1971.

Cawelti, John G. *Adventure, Mystery and Romance*. Chicago: University of Chicago Press, 1976.

————. *The Six-Gun Mystique*. Bowling Green, Ohio: Bowling Green University Press, 1971.

Childe, V. Gordon. *Man Makes Himself*. New York: New American Library, 1951.

Cook, Albert. *The Dark Voyage and the Golden Mean: A Philosophy of Comedy*. New York: W. W. Norton, 1966.

Corliss, Richard. *The Hollywood Screenwriters*. New York: Discus Books, 1972.

Davis, Walter R. *Idea and Act in Elizabethan Fiction*. Princeton, N.J.: Princeton University Press, 1969.

Derrida, Jacques. *Of Grammatology*. Trans. by Gayati Spivak. Baltimore: Johns Hopkins University Press, 1976.

Dewey, Edward R., and Og Mandino. *Cycles: The Mysterious Forces That Trigger Events*. New York: Hawthorn Books, 1971.

Dodds, E. R. *The Greeks and the Irrational*. Berkeley: University of California Press, 1966.

Dunne, John S. *Time and Myth*. Notre Dame, Ind.: University of Notre Dame Press, 1973.

Durgnat, Raymond. *Films and Feelings*. Cambridge, Mass.: M.I.T. Press, 1967.

Eisenstein, Sergei. *Film Essays*. Ed. and trans. by Jay Leyda. New York: Praeger, 1970.

————. *Film Form*. Ed. and trans. by Jay Leyda. New York: Harcourt Brace, 1949.

Eliade, Mircea. *Cosmos and History*. Trans. by Willard R. Trask. New York: Harper and Row, 1959.

———. *Occultism, Witchcraft, and Cultural Fashions*. Chicago: University of Chicago Press, 1976.

———. *Patterns in Comparative Religion*. Trans. by Rosemary Shield. New York: New American Library, 1963.

———. *Rites and Symbols of Initiation*. Trans. by Willard R. Trask. New York: Harper and Row, 1965.

———. *The Sacred and the Profane*. Trans. by Willard R. Trask. New York: Harper and Row, 1962.

Fell, John. *Film: An Introduction*. New York: Praeger, 1975.

———. *Film and the Narrative Tradition*. Norman: University of Oklahoma Press, 1974.

Foucault, Michel. *Discipline and Punish: The Birth of the Prison*. Trans. by Alan Sheridan. New York: Pantheon, 1977.

———. *Madness and Civilization*. Trans. by Richard Howard. New York: Pantheon, 1965.

———. *The Order of Things*. New York: Pantheon, 1970.

Freud, Sigmund. *Civilization and Its Discontents*. Trans. by James Strachey. New York: W. W. Norton, 1962.

———. *The Interpretation of Dreams*. Trans. by James Strachey. New York: Basic Books, 1958.

———. *Moses and Monotheism*. Trans. by Katherine Jones. New York: Alfred A. Knopf, 1939.

———. *Totem and Taboo*. Trans. by James Strachey. New York: W. W. Norton, 1950.

Frye, Northrop. *Anatomy of Criticism*. Princeton, N.J.: Princeton University Press, 1957.

———. *Fables of Identity*. New York: Harcourt, Brace and World, 1963.

Gombrich, E. H. *Art and Illusion*. New York: Pantheon, 1960.

Greene, Graham. *Graham Greene on Film*. New York: Simon and Schuster, 1972.

Hartman, Geoffrey. *Beyond Formalism*. New Haven, Conn.: Yale University Press, 1970.

———. *The Fate of Reading*. Chicago: University of Chicago Press, 1975.

Hawkes, Jacquetta, and Sir Leonard Woolley. *Prehistory*. New York: Harper and Row, 1963.

Houston, Penelope. *The Contemporary Cinema*. Baltimore and Middlesex, Eng.: Penguin Books, 1963.

Hynes, Samuel L. *The Auden Generation*. London: The Bodley Head, 1976.

———. *The Edwardian Turn of Mind*. Princeton, N.J.: Princeton University Press, 1968.

The Interpreter's Bible. New York: Abingdon Press, 1952.

Jacobs, Lewis, comp. *The Movies as Medium.* New York: Farrar, Straus and Giroux, 1970.

Jung, C. G. *Psyche and Symbol.* New York: Doubleday, 1958.

————. *Symbols of Transformation.* Trans. by R. F. C. Hull. New York: Pantheon, 1956.

————, et al. *Man and His Symbols.* New York: Doubleday, 1964.

Kaminsky, Stuart M. *American Film Genres.* Dayton, Ohio: Pflaum, 1974.

Kawin, Bruce F. *Mindscreen.* Princeton, N.J.: Princeton University Press, 1978.

————. *Telling It Again and Again.* Ithaca, N.Y.: Cornell University Press, 1972.

Koszarski, Richard, comp. *Hollywood Directors, 1914–1940.* New York: Oxford University Press, 1977.

Kracauer, Siegfried. *Theory of Film.* New York: Oxford University Press, 1965.

Larsen, Stephen. *The Shaman's Doorway.* New York: Harper and Row, 1976.

Lévi-Strauss, Claude. *From Honey to Ashes.* Trans. by John and Doreen Weightman. New York: Harper and Row, 1973.

————. *The Raw and the Cooked.* Trans. by John and Doreen Weightman. New York: Harper and Row, 1969.

————. *Structural Anthropology.* Trans. by Claire Jacobson and Brooke Grundfest Schoepf. New York: Basic Books, 1963–76.

Lewis, C. S. *The Allegory of Love: A Study in Medieval Tradition.* London: Oxford University Press, 1936.

Long, Norton. *The Unwalled City.* New York: Basic Books, 1972.

Loomis, Roger Sherman. *The Development of Arthurian Romance.* New York: Harper and Row, 1963.

Lord, Albert B. *The Singer of Tales.* New York: Atheneum, 1968.

Lyons, John. *An Introduction to Theoretical Linguistics.* Cambridge: Cambridge University Press, 1969.

Macksey, Richard, comp. *Velocities of Change.* Baltimore: Johns Hopkins University Press, 1974.

McLuhan, Marshall. *Understanding Media.* New York: McGraw-Hill, 1964.

————, and Quentin Fiore. *The Medium Is the Massage.* New York: Random House, 1967.

Malinowski, Bronislaw. *Magic, Science, and Religion.* New York: Doubleday, 1954.

Mast, Gerald, and Marshall Cohen, comps. *Film Theory.* New York: Oxford University Press, 1974.

Metz, Christian. *Film Language*. Trans. by Michael Taylor. New York: Oxford University Press, 1974.

Monaco, James. *How To Read a Film*. New York: Oxford University Press, 1977.

————. *The New Wave*. New York: Oxford University Press, 1976.

Nicholson, Lewis, ed. *An Anthology of Beowulf Criticism*. Notre Dame, Ind.: University of Notre Dame Press, 1963.

Otto, Rudolf. *The Idea of the Holy*. 2d ed. Trans. by John W. Harvey. New York: Oxford University Press, 1967.

Panofsky, Erwin. *Studies in Iconology*. New York: Harper and Row, 1962.

Perkins, V. F. *Film as Film*. Baltimore and Middlesex, Eng.: Penguin Books, 1972.

Piaget, Jean. *The Construction of Reality in the Child*. Trans. by Margaret Cook. New York: Basic Books, 1954.

————. *The Language and Thought of the Child*. 3d ed. Trans. by Marjorie Galvain. New York: Humanities Press, 1959.

————. *Play, Dreams, and Imitation in Childhood*. Trans. by G. Gattegne and F. M. Hodgson. New York: W. W. Norton, 1962.

Ramsaye, Terry. *A Million and One Nights*. New York: Simon and Schuster, 1964.

Róheim, Géza. *The Origin and Function of Culture*. Garden City, N.Y.: Doubleday, 1971.

Rotha, Paul. *The Film Till Now*. London: Spring Books, 1967.

Sarris, Andrew. *The American Cinema*. New York: Dutton, 1968.

Schwartz, Richard B. *Boswell's Johnson*. Madison: University of Wisconsin Press, 1978.

Solomon, Stanley. *The Film Idea*. New York: Harcourt Brace Jovanovich, 1972.

————, ed. *The Classic Cinema*. New York: Harcourt Brace Jovanovich, 1973.

Talbot, Daniel, ed. *Film: An Anthology*. Berkeley: University of California Press, 1972.

Teilhard de Chardin, Pierre. *The Phenomenon of Man*. Trans. by Bernard Wall. Rev. English ed. New York: Harper and Row, 1965.

Tudor, Andrew. *Theories of Film*. New York: Viking, 1973.

Turner, G. W. *Stylistics*. Middlesex, Eng., and Baltimore: Penguin Books, 1973.

Tyler, Parker. *The Hollywood Hallucination*. New York: Simon and Schuster, 1970.

————. *Sex Psyche Etcetera in the Film*. New York: Horizon, 1969.

————. *The Shadow of an Airplane Crosses the Empire State Building*. Garden City, N.Y.: Doubleday, 1972.

Weiner, J. S. *The Natural History of Man*. New York: Doubleday,
    1973.
Wittgenstein, Ludwig. *Philosophical Investigations*. Trans. by G. E. M.
    Anscombe. New York: Macmillan, 1968.

Index

DATE DUE